POPULAR FLY PATTERNS

POPULAR FLY PATTERNS

Terry Hellekson

With Illustrations by Scott Geary

Peregrine Smith, Inc.

SALT LAKE CITY
1977

Library of Congress Cataloguing in Publication Data:

Hellekson, Terry, 1938-
   Popular fly patterns.

   1. Flies, Artificial.   2. Fly tying.   I. Title.
SH451.H34   688.7'9   76-49452
ISBN   0-87905-066-7
ISBN   0-87905-065-9 pbk.

Designed by Richard A. Firmage

Manufactured in the United States of America

PREFACE

Ours is an age of contradiction. In some respects the finest moments of fly fishing are behind us, memories only to the oldest among us, and yet the eve of each new season brings with it a renewed enthusiasm which seems to exceed that of seasons past. The first fish of the season is always something special. That first encounter has a rare harmony associated with it which is hypnotizing to all of us. Attempting to beach that fighting giant "eleven incher" you hear a familiar murmuring behind you. It is your partner with those often asked questions: What pattern are you using? Is it a wet or a dry fly? Is it a dark or a bright pattern? A benumbness falls over his face when you relate that it is tied dry but you have been fishing it wet, it is neither a bright nor a dark pattern and you have no idea as to what it might be called. With the variety of patterns offered to the fly fisherman one would think that most of us are ready for just about any situation on any given lake or stream. Unfortunately, that is rarely the case. As a rule, you can obtain a particular pattern from ten different fly tyers and receive ten different variations of that pattern. We of the fly-tying fraternity choose to pass this inconsistency off as improvement or creativity and thus leave many fly fishermen in a constant state of bewilderment.

As a professional fly-tyer, I have found it necessary to try to overcome the confusion which is associated with many of our fly patterns. During the late 1950s I started collecting information on patterns and their variations so that the flies I tied would be as authentic as possible. Even in those early days I found the subject of fly patterns to be in a total state of confusion. When fly-tying and fly fishing is both your avocation and vocation one has the tendency to take the subject much more seriously. Possibly too seriously. Even though I was purchasing every title on fly fishing that the publishers could crank out, I was still missing the necessary information contained in titles which were out of print. In those days I was totally obsessed with authenticity and patterns "by the book." Later I started asking myself the question, whose book?

My fly-tying abilities progressed through the years and I had tied most of the more common patterns which were offered commercially when a whole new awareness came to me. The unfamiliar patterns that were being brought to me for custom work were actually some super-effective flies and they were not being offered commercially. I now realize that because they were either difficult to tie or their materials were unusual or hard to find resulted in a whole arsenal of good fly patterns which were known to only a few. I believe that far too many of us have become overly obsessed with respect to some of our patterns. The day I came to the realization that I did not have to stop tying a particular pattern because a dictated material was no longer available to me opened up many new avenues. This was the day that "suitable substitute" was added to my vocabulary. Defining suitable substitute in fly-tying can in itself often bring further confusion to many. I define it as substituting a material for another material which was originally called for in a specific pattern without altering the effect or appearance of the finished fly. It does not include the changing of the color or design of the original pattern. That falls into the area of variation and often results in another pattern entirely. This is why I have always attempted to seek out the original pattern whenever possible and then take it from there. In most cases every good pattern was created for a purpose. The originator will create his pattern to fill the needs of the waters he fishes. I have found that when any pattern proves to be successful even its originator will be found carrying several variations of the original. From this, over a period of months and years, is generated a single pattern which is used more than any of the other variations. But what often results is that the title is attached to the original pattern rather than the best of the variations. Would it violate something in our fly fishing heritage to tell it the way it really is?

One can collect many pounds of paper when delving into fly patterns. After several years of correspondence and the purchasing of others' flies to obtain more correct patterns, it became evident that a very useful reference work could be published from all that had been gathered if I could only get the good material sorted out and organized. Noticing that numerous areas were still lacking in many respects, I attempted to further plug the holes with additional correspondence and telephone calls with fly shops and amateur and professional fly-tyers throughout the west. This only opened up new holes to be plugged, and in some cases giant craters were created which never could be filled. What a subject for one to pursue. A fly pattern reference encompassing all areas of the west was indeed needed. I realized that I could never hope to compile a reference which would be inclusive of every useful pattern. Many of our great fly-tyers have taken much valuable information with them in their passing. But my efforts have been sincere and hopefully they will add to the lot of the flyfisher, however insignificant they may ultimately prove to be in the future. The object of this book is to provide the angler with a reference to western fly patterns, acquaint fly-tyers and fly fishermen everywhere with some very new tying techniques and deadly patterns, and include many of the eastern patterns which have proven to be useful in the west. It all should prove meaningful to both the neophyte and the expert. Knowing that some controversy will be aroused, hopefully and understandably so, I believe it can only bring improvement and further understanding and standardization of our patterns without destroying the initiative of the fly-tyer in continuing to experiment and substitute until he discovers something more useful for all of us. As a group, fly fishermen are among the most technically minded of all sportsmen. Often even to the point of being rather ridiculous. But it is seldom ridiculous to strive for greater accuracy and completeness. I welcome all criticism, thoughts, ideas, new patterns and new or unusual methods so that future editions of this book can be made even more meaningful. I am the first to admit that my efforts are not complete; however, by your sharing with me I will be able to share with others. Direct any correspondence to: Terry Hellekson, P.O. Drawer 489, Clearfield, Utah 84015.

ACKNOWLEDGMENT

I would like to express my thanks to the many leading fly-tyers who have given of their time and talents to help make this book more meaningful. Their unselfish interests in sharing their patterns with their fellow tyers and anglers attests to the true fellowship of our fraternity.

I would especially like to express my thanks to Frank Johnson for sharing with all of us his Waterwalker style of hackling the May Fly imitations and then working closely with me in developing some splendid patterns.

Also, to E. H. "Polly" Rosborough, whose friendship I regard with the highest respect, for sharing his lifetime of creative patterns with us. Now they are recorded under one cover. Last but not least, I would like to express a special thank you to Scott Geary, friend, artist, and fly-tyer, for working with me very closely in illustrating this book so that the reader can effectively grasp some of the complexities of fly tying. None of this could have been possible were it not for Scott's dual talents with pen and vise.

TABLE OF CONTENTS

POPULAR FLY PATTERNS

INTRODUCTION

Many of the patterns which appear in this book represent flies which are generally used in fly fishing on the waters of the western United States and Canada. Materials have been listed with the description of each fly pattern in the order in which they are generally applied to the hook. Often applying materials in any other sequence will only make a complete "bumble" of the fly. The mechanics involved in constructing a good quality fly must be followed in a step by step process, each step a preparation for your next. This is especially true in the tying of some of the more complex nymphs and dry flies. Many of the patterns included have fragile quill or peacock bodies. I have suggested the use of fine wire to reinforce the bodies of these flies and extend their usefulness. Fish don't care one way or the other about the wire; but I have always felt that if a fly is worth tying it is worth tying well and in the most realistic manner possible. If it is necessary for me to take an additional five or ten minutes on a fly to make it appear more like a natural then I take it. However unimportant it may be to the fish, it is very important to me and my confidence in the fly. I believe it actually makes me fish harder and more effectively when I know that my offering is as good as I can possibly make it.

With our ever increasing interest in fly tying we have been assisting in expanding the drain on many species of our wild birds and fur bearing animals. The exotica of Macaw Quills, Polar Bear Hair, Albino Beaver, eye brows from the Great Horned Owl, and three day old baby seal fur are behind us. The staunch purists among us, whether they like it or not, must forget "the days of the Jungle Cock" and start taking into consideration the reality of synthetics. If we do not like what is available, we should work towards finding something better. The endangered species list published and enforced by the U.S. Fish and Wildlife Service is a reality and it continues to grow each year. If we want to continue to enjoy our fly tying we must look more seriously into synthetics for many of our needs. The use of synthetics in the tying of our flies opens up a whole new era in fly tying. With very little imagination any tyer can adapt to the usage of these materials. The synthetic dubbing furs that we now have are certainly a step forward. There is a wide range of basic colors and blends available to the tyer today.

My first thoughts with respect to synthetics as substitutes for the real thing were completely negative. Later, I started to have a change of heart when I found it was getting harder and harder to obtain certain materials. I started looking for some suitable synthetic substitutes. A good friend, Bob Brewer, was a plastics engineer so I went to him in my quest for something that was really usable. My bad experiences with poly materials as a dubbing material had driven me to abandon them. All of them. Good as a winging material substitute, but that was all. They were all just too brittle and hard to work with. Bob sent me a variety of samples over a long period of time, some good and some not so good. All overly expensive. Then one day there it was. Something not just good, it was really good and it carried a moderate price tag also. A synthetic dubbing fur that was waterproof so it was most suitable for either wet or dry flies. It blended superbly with both itself and natural furs. It had a very desirable sparkling sheen. Because of this sheen it was possible to develop a full spectrum of colors. The light reflected off the fibers in such a manner that they appeared to melt the colors together. Whenever I needed a new color I would just dig out my blender and it was a simple task to obtain any color or shade I desired. Just like mixing water colors. Later I found that due to the fiber length I had better success if I cut this material a bit finer for dubbing midge bodies but this only required running the scissors through it a couple of times. After I got to using this material on a regular basis I found that I could spin it right on my tying thread. By building my bodies extra large, almost one third larger than I really wanted, and dubbing rather loosely, allowing the thread to pull into the material, I could form excellent uniform tapered bodies every time by simply clipping them to the desired shape and size with my tying scissors. Just like clipping deer hair, only easier. I could construct bodies much faster than I could previously with yarn. It even made the larger streamer and steelhead flies much simpler for me. Due to the versatility of the new material and its wide range of colors it ended up being called DUB-ALL.

I am a sincere believer in the proper size, coloration and silhouette of my flies. There are a number of schools of thought about this subject, however, I find I have the greatest success when I try to simulate and duplicate the naturals. By just tipping over a few rocks and collecting specimens from every stream bed I visit I know reasonably well what I need to carry with me on any trip that might follow. You do not have to be a schooled entomologist to collect and try simulating insects. If you are anything like I am and your inquisitiveness leads you to want to know even more, most colleges and universities are more than happy to assist you in identification. Even though this book is intended as a ready reference to fly patterns you will most want to tie, it is hoped that it will give you enough of a background so that you can start tipping some rocks over on your own. I know I get a lot of attention from passers-by when they see me out in the middle of a stream struggling with rocks or running up and down the bank swinging a net in the air. I bet that only a handful ever figure out what I am doing. Get some of your own local specimens and take them home and try to duplicate them on a hook. Through a little creative tying and innovation in the selection of your materials you should be able to come up with patterns far more valuable to you than those contained in any book. Do not let your search for materials stop with the mail-order catalogues you collect either. Some of our more used materials today were only available on the notions counters of the local variety stores yesterday.

Today we are fortunate to have organizations like the Sierra Club, Trout Unlimited, Federation of Fly Fishermen, National Wildlife Federation, Wilderness Society, and many more all working to give us pollution free waters and undammed streams. They all need your strong support so that your sons and daughters and others to follow may have Nature at its best. Some of these organizations conduct fly casting and fly tying courses which are very helpful. Also, due to popular demand many high schools and colleges throughout the country are conducting fly tying classes in conjunction with their adult education classes. To associate and share with others adds a further value and richness to the wonderful world of the fisherman. Part of the true pleasure of fly fishing and fly tying is experimentation. The angler who ties his own flies is unquestionably the most successful. He has the opportunity to alter his patterns to meet his own conditions or whims. The tying techniques that we will be dealing with in this book are what I have found through the years to be the most flexible for me to create my own innovations and carry on my own experiments.

The purchase of a fly-tying kit at any price is dollars unwisely spent. You can soon enough find yourself with stuff you will never be able to totally use, so why start out with a box of feathers which are better suited for making artificial flowers? With respect to the purchasing of materials, you must first decide what you want to tie. If your fishing is confined to just one area your needs will more than likely be surrounding not more than a dozen patterns. A five dollar investment in materials will tie a very large number of flies. More flies than the average fly fisherman can use and lose in any given season. If one uses a bit of reason, fly fishing can be the least expensive of any of the categories of sport fishing. Flies are without a doubt the most expensive part of the total overall investment. The law of supply and demand controls the price you must pay for your flies and when you consider that 90% of what you are paying for is labor and not the cost of the materials, you just simply cannot keep from asking yourself, why not tie my own?

The tools needed for tying flies need not make you consider taking out a loan to finance their purchase. If you were to purchase all of the gadgets that are available and that you think you might need your bill would easily exceed $150.00. Your first thought should be the purchase of a vise to hold your hooks. In my opinion one cannot spend too much for a vise. This is the one tool that must function properly. Unfortunately, most vises are of rather poor quality when you look at the vast technical know-how available to the manufacturing industry. If all things were equal, there would be at least a 90% recall of all vises. Fly tying is expanding so rapidly that even more inferior vises are now being imported and placed on the market. For your money, the Thompson Model A, the Orvis or Leonard vises give you the best value. There are a limited few exceptionally good vises now becoming available which are worth looking into. If the maker will stand behind his vise—which few of them can or will—then that is the one to buy.

A bobbin is also needed to hold your spool of thread. After the creation of the bobbin it took many decades to convince the fly-tyers, myself included, that it was an essential tool of the trade. Traditionally, all flies have been tied with a strand of silk thread using a series of half hitches. The late Wayne "Buz" Buszek converted me and my thinking to using bobbins around 1959. It was felt by many at that time that good durable flies could not be constructed with a bobbin and that the bulky half hitches were necessary to hold the fly together. Besides this , a good pair of scissors, either curved or straight point, a pair of hackle pliers and a bodkin (dubbing needle) are all you really need in the way of tools to get you started tying flies.

No, I did not forget to mention a whip finish tool. An essential in tying a good fly of any kind is to produce one that will not fall apart while you are fishing. Often this is the reason many of us tie our own flies today. All too often the store bought variety just do not meet even the lowest standards. If the head of the fly is not tied off properly or securely a rapidly disintegrating fly will result. Tools are available to aid the tyer in this regard but they often prove to be very difficult to master. With more than 25 years of tying experience behind me, I have not yet found it necessary to master the fundamentals of using the whip finish tools. I hand whip all of my heads and have done so from the very start. I find it is much easier and also saves having one more piece of equipment on my tying bench. Should you attempt to tie any of the wire body steelhead flies or streamer flies using mylar piping for the bodies, this same old hand whip is used. No tool can assist you in completing these ties due to their location on the fly. Whip finish tools are solely designed to complete the head. If you insist on spending your money on a whip finish tool, I recommend you obtain a ''Charlie's Whipper'' which is available from most fly shops for $1.95. It works well, possibly even better than those offered for $5.95. Because of its simplified construction it should last you a lifetime and it can be used by either the left or right hander. The following instructions are provided for those who want to practice my own preferred alternative.

Instructions for completing the hand whip:

STEP 1: Cross your tying thread over.

STEP 2: Slide the thread up firmly against the hook.

STEP 3: Wrap over the crossed thread.

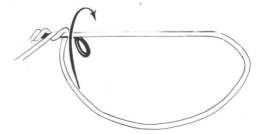

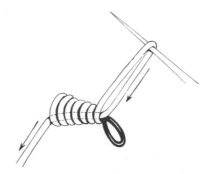

STEP 4: You should have a minimum of four wraps over your thread. Using a dubbing needle or the point of your scissors catch hold of the loop of thread and pull it tightly. I use my scissors because I always hold them in my hand all of the time that I am tying. In fact, my tying scissors have almost become a part of my right hand.

All too often when we pick up a book or article on a fly pattern we become confused by the descriptive nomenclature of the fly because the parts of the fly are not always named in one part of the country as they are in another. For the purposes of this book the fly parts identified below relate to the patterns contained herein:

1. Tip.
2. Tag.
3. Tail.
4. Butt.
5. Body.
6. Ribbing.
7. Shoulder.
8. Wings.
9. Hackle.
10. Cheek.
11. Topping.
12. Thorax.
13. Shellback.
14. Wingcase.
15. Feelers/Antenna.
16. Legs.
17. Head.
18. Hook point.
19. Hook bend.

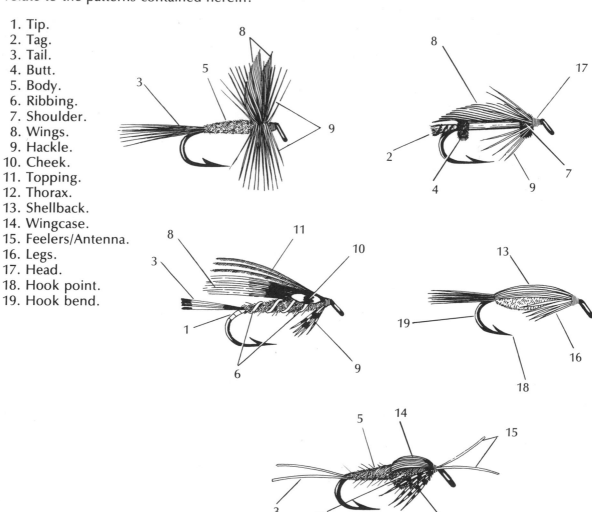

DRY FLIES

The dry flies are essentially what the name implies. They are flies which are designed to float on the surface of the water and simulate May Flies, Caddis Flies, Stone Flies, and the list goes on through the insect world. The insects we try to duplicate come to the stream and land on the surface voluntarily or they emerge from the stream bed itself. In tying dry flies one must strive to obtain some likeness to that of the natural floating insect. Dry flies should only be tied on hooks which are designed for that purpose. There is often not enough emphasis placed on the importance of correct proportions in dry fly design. When any single part of the fly is not in correct proportion to that of the other parts then you have an unbalanced fly. If the hackle is too long your fly will often fall forward on its face. If the wings are too long and wide they will twist your leader tippet when casting. It takes some practice on the part of the tyer, but the results are rewarding when you can consistently produce dry flies with good proportions and balance. The following step by step instructions are provided to give you a better general idea of how materials are applied to the hook in order to help you better understand the fly patterns which follow.

STEP 1: Attach tying thread to the hook shank and tie in wings. Wing length should be equal to the length of the hook shank. Wings should be tied far enough back on the hook shank, about ⅓, to allow space for hackling of the fly and the tying of a nice clean tapered head. Wings should be tied in with butts towards the rear of the hook.

STEP 2: Pull wings upward and wrap tying thread in front of them.

7

STEP 3: Wrap tying thread to the rear of the hook and tie in tailing material. Tailing material should be stiff enough to keep the weight of the fly from bending it and allowing the back of the fly to sink. Tail should be equal to the length of the shank and bend of the hook.

STEP 4: Tie in body material. In this example peacock. Also, tie in fine wire ribbing.

STEP 5: Wrap peacock herl forward and tie off just behind the head. Then reverse wrap the fine wire ribbing through the peacock. This strengthens the body.

STEP 6: Select hackles and tie in. The barbles on the hackle you select should be equal to the length of your wings. An average dry fly will normally

have at least two good hackles tied in. In our western fishing we often find it necessary to use as many as six hackles to obtain a heavily dressed dry fly which will float well on rough water. This must be judged by the tyer. The size of the fly being tied and the quality of the hackle being used all play an important part in this judgement.

STEP 7: Wrap two turns of hackle behind the wings and three in front with each hackle. With practice you will be able to position your wings better at this time.

STEP 8: Tie off your head with a good clean taper and apply cement. I prefer to use a cement which is rather well thinned down so it will penetrate into the base of the wings and hackle. I find this gives me a much more durable fly. After the first coat of cement has dried I apply a second thicker coat of cement to give the head a good protective shield.

Your finished dry fly, when set upon a flat surface, should have the bottom of the hackle, the tail and the bend of the hook all touching the surface equally. This is what is referred to as a "perfect float line."

Tying a trude or hair wing style dry fly is much like the conventional dry flies except the steps are somewhat reversed.

BASIC DRY FLY DESIGNS

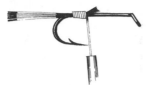

STEP 1: Attach tying thread to the hook shank and tie in tailing material.

Divided Quill Wing

STEP 2: Tie in body material at rear of hook shank and wrap tying thread to the front.

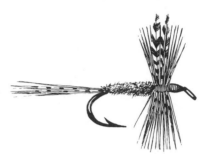

Divided Hackle Tip Wing

STEP 3: Wrap the body material forward and tie off.

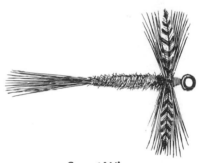

Spent Wing

STEP 4: Tie in the hair wing over the body.

Divided Hair Wing

STEP 5: Next tie in hackles in front of the wing. When possible I prefer to use Indian Saddle hackle on these types of flies.

STEP 6: Wrap hackles and tie off the head.

Fan Wing

Tent Style

Plain Hackle

Palmered Hackle

Parachute Style

Spider

Variant

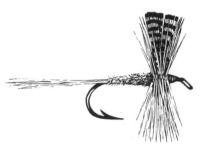

Rolled Divided Wing

Trude Style (Hair Wing or Bucktail)

ADAMS

HOOK:	Mustad 94840, sizes 10-20.
THREAD:	Gray.
WINGS:	Grizzly hackle tips tied upright and divided.
TAIL:	Grizzly and brown hackle fibers mixed.
BODY:	Dubbed muskrat fur with guard hairs removed.
HACKLE:	Brown and grizzly mixed.

ADAMS, BLUE WING

Tied the same as the Adams except blue dun hackle tips are substituted for the grizzly hackle tips. Many feel this is a much more effective pattern because of the more definite outline given by the darker wings.

ADAMS, FEMALE

Tied the same as the Adams except a dubbed yellow fur egg sac is tied in at the rear of the body. Most popular sizes are 12-16.

ADAMS, FEMALE SPENT WING

Tied the same as the Adams Female except the wings are tied spent. By substituting hackle tip wings almost any dry fly pattern can be successfully tied in the spent wing fashion. Spent wing dry flies are designed to simulate delicate imitations of dead May Fly drakes and spinners. They light on the water's surface with their wings outstretched. This type of fly is most effective during the evening hours. These are not rough water flies and they perform best on pools and slicks of a quiet character.

ADAMS, YELLOW BODY

Tied the same as the Adams except dubbed yellow fur is substituted for muskrat fur. This variation is considered very productive in the High Sierra Country of California. It saved the day for us on Wyoming's Flat Creek on a dull fall rainy afternoon.

The Adams was first tied by Leonard Halladay of Mayfield, Michigan. This fly is used in all parts of the United States and Canada with many variations being generated for each area. The tailing material is sometimes substituted with either dark moose or elk hair. Some years back I came by a Cree neck from Korea which was useless to me for tying anything, I thought, until some days later I was tying some Adams. That big old neck with its big shining feathers with barbles an inch long had the perfect markings for tailing the Adams. The neck lasted me for several seasons. Keep your eyes open for odd feathers. On many of the different variant necks they often have spade hackles on the sides that are ideal for tailing material on the Adams. Saves mixing brown and grizzly.

ASH DUN

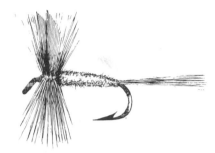

HOOK:	Mustad 94840, sizes 12-18.
THREAD:	Gray.
WINGS:	Natural light gray duck quill sections tied upright and divided.
TAIL:	Dyed gray hackle fibers.
BODY:	Dubbed gray fox fur with guard hairs removed.
HACKLE:	Dyed gray.

The Ash Dun has proven to be a good pattern anywhere it is used from May until the end of the season.

AUGUST DUN

HOOK:	Mustad 94840, sizes 10-14.
THREAD:	Brown.
WINGS:	Dyed brown duck quill sections tied upright and divided.
TAIL:	Dark ginger hackle fibers.
RIBBING:	Orange thread.
BODY:	Brown floss.
HACKLE:	Dark ginger.

AUTUMN ANT

HOOK:	Mustad 94840, sizes 14-16.
THREAD:	Black.
TAIL:	Black hackle fibers.

BODY: Dubbed black rabbit or synthetic fur. Body should be tied in two distinctive lumps to simulate the shape of an ant's body.

WINGS: Cree hackle tips tied flat back over the body. Select dark cast cree hackle with good markings.

HACKLE: Black.

This is a good dressing for any area. It is my favorite ant pattern for fast water conditions. I sometimes substitute dark moose or porcupine bristles for the tailing material. It was originated by Lloyd Byerly of Oregon.

BADGER HACKLE PEACOCK

HOOK: Mustad 94838, sizes 10-18.

THREAD: Black.

TAIL: Lady Amherst pheasant tippet fibers.

BODY: Peacock herl tied fat and full. Reverse wrap the body with fine silver wire.

HACKLE: Badger.

NOTES: It is helpful to wrap an underbody of yarn or floss to obtain the desired fullness on sizes 10 and 12. This also applies anytime a nice full body is needed and the quality of your peacock just is not up to snuff.

BADGER QUILL

HOOK: Mustad 94840, sizes 12-18.

THREAD: Black.

WINGS: Barred lemon wood duck tied upright and divided.

TAIL: Badger hackle fibers.

BODY: Moose mane. Select one light and two dark pieces of hair and wrap together. Construct an underbody of black floss to give the body a good natural taper. Reverse wrap the body with fine silver wire.

HACKLE: Badger.

BEAVERKILL

HOOK: Mustad 94840, sizes 10-16.

THREAD: Brown.

WINGS: Natural gray duck quill sections tied upright and divided.

TAIL: Brown hackle fibers.

RIBBING: Brown hackle tied Palmer over body.

BODY: White floss.

HACKLE: Brown. This hackle is in addition to Palmered hackle.

BEAVERKILL, FEMALE

HOOK: Mustad 94840, sizes 12-14.

THREAD: Brown.

WINGS: Natural gray duck quill sections tied upright and divided.

TAIL: Brown hackle fibers.

BUTT: Dubbed yellow rabbit fur tied in as egg sac.

BODY: Dubbed muskrat fur.

HACKLE: Brown.

BETTY McNALL

HOOK: Mustad 7957B, sizes 8-14.

THREAD: Brown.

TAIL: Scarlet red hackle fibers.

BODY: Red floss with peacock herl tied in at the butt.

WING: White calf tail tied over body and extending to length of body and tail.

HACKLE: Brown.

Originated by fly-tyer Betty McNall of Denver, Colorado. A variation of the Royal Coachman Trude which is desirable when a little more red is wanted.

BIG TROUT

HOOK: Mustad 94840, sizes 8-12.

THREAD: Black.

WINGS: Dyed brown barred mallard tied upright and divided.

TAIL: Dyed brown grizzly hackle fibers.

BODY: Dyed yellow and natural brown neck hackle stems wrapped together. Wrap so stems do not cross each other and you get alternating color bands of brown and yellow.

HACKLE: Brown and dyed gray dark ginger variant mixed.

The Big Trout pattern was developed by Bob Teig of Vernal, Utah, for fishing Northern Utah and Western Colorado. It has been in use for many years and has accounted for many pounds of fish.

BI-VISIBLE, BADGER

HOOK: Mustad 94840, sizes 10-18.
THREAD: White.
TAIL: Badger hackle fibers.
BODY: Flat silver tinsel.
HACKLE: Badger tied Palmer over the body with two or three turns of white hackle tied in at front.

BI-VISIBLE, BLACK

HOOK: Mustad 94840, sizes 10-18.
THREAD: White.
TAIL: Black hackle fibers.
BODY: Flat silver tinsel.
HACKLE: Black tied Palmer over the body, two or three turns of white hackle tied in at front.

BI-VISIBLE, BLUE DUN

HOOK: Mustad 94840, sizes 10-18.
THREAD: White.
TAIL: Blue dun hackle fibers.
BODY: Flat silver tinsel.
HACKLE: Blue dun tied Palmer over the body with two or three turns of white hackle tied in at front.

BI-VISIBLE, BROWN

HOOK: Mustad 94840, sizes 10-18.
THREAD: White.
TAIL: Brown hackle fibers.
BODY: Flat gold tinsel.
HACKLE: Brown tied Palmer over the body with two or three turns of white hackle tied in at front.

BI-VISIBLE, FURNACE

HOOK: Mustad 94840, sizes 10-18.
THREAD: White.
TAIL: Furnace hackle fibers.
BODY: Flat silver tinsel.
HACKLE: Furnace tied Palmer over the body with two or three turns of white hackle tied at the front.

BI-VISIBLE, GINGER

HOOK: Mustad 94840, sizes 10-18.
THREAD: White.
TAIL: Light ginger hackle fibers.
BODY: Flat gold tinsel.
HACKLE: Light ginger tied Palmer over the body with two or three turns of white hackle tied in at front.

BI-VISIBLE, GRIZZLY

HOOK: Mustad 94840, sizes 10-18.
THREAD: White.
TAIL: Grizzly hackle fibers.
BODY: Flat silver tinsel.
HACKLE: Grizzly tied Palmer over the body with two or three turns of white hackle tied in at front.

BI-VISIBLE, OLIVE

HOOK: Mustad 94840, sizes 10-18.
THREAD: White.
TAIL: Olive hackle fibers.
BODY: Flat gold tinsel.
HACKLE: Olive tied Palmer over the body with two or three turns of white hackle tied in at front.

BI-VISIBLE, PINK LADY

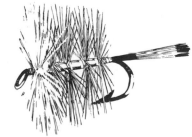

HOOK: Mustad 94840, sizes 10-18.
THREAD: White.
TAIL: Lady Amherst pheasant tippet fibers.
RIBBING: Flat gold tinsel.

BODY: Pink floss tied thin.

HACKLE: Light ginger tied Palmer over the body with two or three turn of white hackle tied in at front.

NOTES: Except for the Pink Lady Bi-Visible, these flies are often tied with embossed tinsel bodies to give them a bit more flash. Some tyers prefer to tie them without tinsel bodies. They feel that the unnatural flash only puts the fish down. When trying any of the Bi-Visibles, tie the hackle in **by the tip** rather than the butt. This puts the shorter **hackle** barbles to the rear of the fly and gives it a better float line. Some commercial dressings of the Bi-Visibles have oversized hackles which only destroys the float line and makes the fly float in a unnatural manner.

The Bi-Visibles were among the many creations left us by Edward Hewitt. Because of their wide range of colors and sizes any fly fisherman can meet a good many varied fishing conditions and be successful. Their Palmered hackles give them good floating qualities and it is not so necessary to change flies. These flies were designed to serve a dual purpose. They provide visibility to both the fish and the fisherman but under exactly opposite conditions. They are very easy to see during the period of varying light conditions.

BLACK ANT

HOOK: Mustad 94840, sizes 10-16.

THREAD: Black.

WINGS: Black crow quill or dyed black quill sections tied upright and divided.

TAIL: Black hackle fibers.

BODY: Black floss with black ostrich herl tied in at butt.

HACKLE: Black.

BLACK BEETLE

HOOK: Mustad 94838, sizes 14-18

THREAD: Black.

BODY: Dubbed black synthetic fur.

HACKLE: Black saddle. Select hackle which has fine textured barbles. Wrap about six turns over body and pull down all barbles and clip off even with point of hook.

BACK: Dyed black goose quill section tied in at rear and pulled over back and tied in at front. Quill section should be tied in so shiny side of quill is showing after it is tied in.

Terrestrial insects should not be over looked by the fly-tyer when he is looking for something useful to tie. Over the years I have discovered that during the warm summer fish seem to develop a taste and a degee of selectivity for many of the terrestrials.

BLACK GNAT

HOOK: Mustad 94840, sizes 12-20.

THREAD: Black.

WINGS: Natural gray duck quill sections tied upright and divided.

TAIL: Black hackle fibers.

BODY: Dubbed black rabbit or synthetic fur. Body should have a good plump taper.

HACKLE: Black.

NOTE: The tailing material on the Black Gnat is often substituted with crimson red hackle fibers.

BLACK GNAT SPECIAL

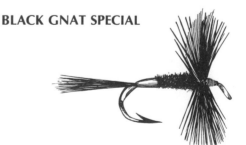

HOOK: Mustad 94840, sizes 12-16.

THREAD: Black.

WINGS: Natural gray duck quill sections tied
            upright and divided.

TIP: Red floss.

TAIL: Scarlet red hackle fibers.

BODY: Rear ⅓ red floss and front ⅔
            black synthetic fur.

HACKLE: Black.

This is a good early morning and evening, from
dusk to dark, pattern. Also, a good fly on dark and
cloudy days.

BLACK GNAT TRUDE

HOOK: Mustad 7957B, sizes 8-14.

THREAD: Black.

TAIL: Golden pheasant tippet fibers.

BODY: Dubbed black synthetic fur. Body
            should have a good plump taper.

WING: Dark coastal blacktail deer body hair,
            tied over the body and extending the
            length of body only.

HACKLE: Black.

The Black Gnat is a universal fly and can be found
anywhere there are fly fishermen. It rates with the
Royal Coachman and the Adams when reference is
made to the top ten flies. The Black Gnat Special and
the Black Gnat Trude are western variations of the
pattern.

BLACK PRINCE

HOOK: Mustad 94840, sizes 10-16.

THREAD: Black.

WINGS: Natural gray duck quill sections tied
            upright and divided.

TAIL: Golden pheasant tippet fibers.

RIBBING: Flat gold tinsel.

BODY: Black floss.

HACKLE: Black.

BLACK QUILL

HOOK: Mustad 94840, sizes 12-18.

THREAD: Black.

WINGS: Natural gray duck quill sections
            tied upright and divided.

TAIL: Black hackle fibers.

BODY: Dark peacock quill. Underbody of
            dark gray floss should first be
            wrapped to give good taper to
            finished body. Reverse wrap the
            body with fine silver wire.

HACKLE: Black.

NOTES. Dark peacock quill refers to an un-
bleached quill. For dark quills the herl must be
removed with the thumb nail or some other
process. Light peacock quills are obtained by a
bleaching method. This is accomplished by dipping
an entire eyed peacock feather in a solution of
household bleach until the herl is burned off. Then
the feather is immediately placed in a solution of
baking soda and water to neutralize the chemical
action of the bleach. Bleached quills are brittle
after the process. Whether you are bleaching your
own or buying them already bleached (trade name
is stripped peacock quill) it is best to soak them in
a jar with a solution of glycerin and water until they
are ready for use.

BLACK TRUDE

HOOK: Mustad 7957B, sizes 8-14.

THREAD: Black.

TAIL: Black hackle fibers.

RIBBING: Embossed silver tinsel.

BODY: Black wool yarn.

WING: Black calf tail tied over the body and extending to middle of tail.

HACKLE: Black.

BLACKFOOT DREAM

HOOK: Mustad 7957B, sizes 6-14.

THREAD: Gray.

TAIL: Brown elk hair.

BODY: Dubbed with one part muskrat and one part woodchuck fur. Remove guard hairs from both furs.

WING: Woodchuck tail hair tied over the body and extending to the middle of tail.

HACKLE: Dark ginger.

The Blackfoot Dream was created for fishing the upper portions of the Blackfoot River. It is also good on the Snake River. I have only had the opportunity to use it on Northern California's Salmon Rivers where a size 14 did a fine job during a caddis hatch. Originated by Robert Elsworth of Salt Lake City, Utah.

BLUE DAMSEL

HOOK: Mustad 79580, sizes 14-16.

THREAD: Gray.

TAIL: Light blue elk hair.

REAR HACKLE: Light blue. Hackle should only extend just past point of hook.

RIBBING: Fine silver wire.

BODY: Light blue floss tied thin.

WINGS: Two light grizzly hackle tips tied together on edge over the body.

FRONT HACKLE: Light blue.

NOTES: If light grizzly hackle tips are not available dyed light gray hackle tips can be substituted. In either case they should be as narrow as possible and extend full length of body and rear hackle with tips just touching top of rear hackle.

This is a very good lake fly to use during those hot summer afternoons when nothing is moving. Cast it out on the still water and wait for the action. Keep your eye on the fly, however, for it can be sucked under and spit right back out before you are aware of what is happening.

BLUE DUN

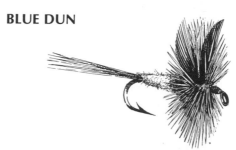

HOOK: Mustad 94840, sizes 10-20.

THREAD: Gray.

WINGS: Natural light gray duck quill sections tied upright and divided.

TAIL: Blue dun hackle fibers.

BODY: Dubbed muskrat fur with guard hairs removed.

HACKLE: Blue dun.

BLUE FOX

HOOK: Mustad 94840, sizes 12-18.

THREAD: Gray.

WINGS: Grizzly hackle tips tied upright and divided.

TAIL: Grizzly hackle fibers.

BODY: Dark blue dun fox fur. This should be taken from the back of the gray fox. Guard hairs should be removed and the tannish top of fur clipped off.

HACKLE: Grizzly.

NOTES: Cottontail rabbit fur may be substituted

for body material. It is darker in color and considered to be much better for the pattern. All grizzly hackle used in this pattern should be dark cast.

BLUE QUILL

HOOK: Mustad 94840, sizes 12-18.

THREAD: Gray.

WINGS: Dark blue dun hackle tips tied upright and divided.

TAIL: Blue dun hackle fibers.

BODY: Blue dun saddle hackle stem. Reverse wrap the body with fine silver wire.

HACKLE: Blue dun.

BLUE UPRIGHT

HOOK: Mustad 94840, sizes 12-20.

THREAD: Gray.

WINGS: Natural gray duck quill sections tied upright and divided.

TAIL: Blue dun hackle fibers.

BODY: Light peacock quill. Reverse wrap the body with fine silver wire.

HACKLE: Blue dun.

Both the Blue Quill and the Blue Upright are good patterns and worth tying. Due to the multiple variations of the two patterns they often become confused with each other.

BOB SLEE SPECIAL

HOOK: Mustad 94840, sizes 10-14.

THREAD: Orange.

WINGS: Natural gray duck quill sections tied upright and divided.

TAIL: Orange hackle fibers.

BODY: Light peacock quill. Reverse wrap the body with fine gold wire.

HACKLE: Orange.

Many people shy away from this pattern feeling it is too bright. It is an old pattern which has been around at least since the 1940s. I have used it successfully on the low land lakes of Western Washington and Oregon and in the Yellowstone area. I find it works best during the early morning and evening fishing.

BRADLEY M.

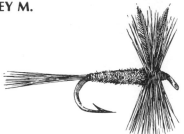

HOOK: Mustad 94840, sizes 8-14.

THREAD: Brown.

WINGS: Brown hackle tips tied upright and divided.

TAIL: Brown hackle fibers.

BODY: Dubbed woodchuck fur with guard hairs removed.

HACKLE: Grizzly dyed light blue and furnace mixed.

This pattern was orginated by Don Martinez to represent the May Fly, *Ephemera simulans*. This May Fly is common throughout North America. This is an improved pattern from the original dressings. The original pattern had a body constructed of red macaw wing quill fibers. Later it was improved by using fibers from the argus pheasant tail. Due to the lack of the two previous materials evolution has carried this pattern even further to make it resemble the natural even more closely.

BROWN DRAKE

HOOK: Mustad 94840, sizes 10-14.

THREAD: Brown.

WINGS: Light ginger variant hackle tips tied upright and divided.

TAIL: Woodchuck tail hair.

BODY: Dubbed dark brown synthetic fur.

HACKLE: Dark brown.

BROWN HACKLE BROWN

HOOK: Mustad 94838, sizes 10-18.

THREAD: Brown.

TAIL: Scarlet red hackle fibers.

RIBBING: Flat gold tinsel.

BODY: Brown floss.

HACKLE: Brown.

There is an endless number of Brown Hackles one can tie. The basic Brown is one of the least used and yet it is one of the better producers.

BROWN HACKLE PEACOCK

HOOK: Mustad 94838, sizes 10-18.

THREAD: Brown.

TAIL: Scarlet red hackle fibers.

BODY: Peacock herl. Reverse wrap the body with fine gold wire.

HACKLE: Brown.

I had the opportunity to fish Washington's Lewis lake with some friends about 10 years ago. We had tossed almost everything we had at the raising and rolling fish for over an hour. It had started to get rather flustering and I changed to the common old Brown Hackle Peacock. I had been fishing it for several minutes with little success when it finally soaked up and sank. It had not been a second and I had a fish on. For the next two hours up until it turned so dark we could not see our lines the three of us hooked and released well over 100 fish, some

going over 3 pounds. I have since had a high respect for a sunken dry fly, as unorthodox as it is, and especially the Brown Hackle Peacock which has saved the day for me many times since.

BROWN HACKLE YELLOW

HOOK: Mustad 94838, sizes 10-18.

THREAD: Brown.

TAIL: Scarlet red hackle fibers.

RIBBING: Flat gold tinsel.

BODY: Yellow floss.

HACKLE: Brown.

BUZZ HACKLE

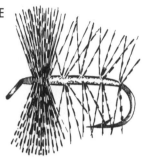

HOOK: Mustad 94840, sizes 10-16.

THREAD: Gray.

BODY: Rear half gold embossed tinsel and front half silver embossed tinsel. Body is Palmered with grizzly hackle. The barbles on one side of the hackle stem are stripped off before winding.

HACKLE: Grizzly. This is in addition to the Palmered hackle.

This fly is very popular in Northern California. E. C. "Pop" Powell of Marysville, California, is responsible for popularizing this pattern. It is a good pattern and has yielded fish everywhere it has been used.

CADDIS

HOOK: Mustad 7957B, sizes 8-12.

THREAD: Orange.

TAIL: Cock ringneck pheasant center tail feather fibers.

BODY: Orange wool yarn or dubbed
              synthetic fur.
HACKLE: Brown tied Palmer over body.
WING: Grayish brown deer body hair tied
              over the body and extending
              to middle of tail.

CADDIS, BUCKTAIL

HOOK: Mustad 7957B, sizes 6-14.
THREAD: Brown.
TAIL: Dark ginger hackle fibers.
BODY   Light yellow wool yarn or dubbed
              synthetic fur.
HACKLE: Dark ginger tied Palmer over body.
WING: Natural brown bucktail taken from
              back of tail. Tie over body with
              hair extending slightly past end of
              body.

CADDIS, DARK

HOOK: Mustad 7957B, sizes 8-14.
THREAD: Yellow.
TAIL: Yellow hackle fibers.
BODY: Yellow wool yarn or dubbed
              synthetic fur.
HACKLE: Yellow tied Palmer over body.
WING: Dark coastal blacktail deer body hair
              tied over the body and extending
              length of body only.

NOTES: Yellow hackle for the Dark Caddis should
be a deep golden yellow.

CADDIS, LIGHT

HOOK: Mustad 7957B, sizes 8-14.
THREAD: Tan.
TAIL: Light tan elk hair.
BODY: Light yellow wool yarn or dubbed
              synthetic fur.
HACKLE: Light ginger tied Palmer over body.
WING: Light tan elk hair over the body
              and extending slightly past end of
              body.

All of the above Caddis patterns, Bucktail Caddis
Flies, have been proven on our western rivers for
many years. They enjoy their greatest popularity in
the Northwest. Their Palmered hackled bodies and
hollow hair wings float them like corks, and they
are very easy to fish on heavy water.

CAHILL

HOOK: Mustad 94840, sizes 12-18.
THREAD: Brown.
WINGS: Barred lemon wood duck tied
              upright and divided.
TAIL: Dark ginger hackle fibers.
BODY: Dubbed cottontail rabbit fur.
HACKLE: Dark ginger.

NOTES: Original pattern called for a barred lemon
wood duck tail. Sometime later cock hackle fibers
were adopted due to their superior stiffness. A
variation of this pattern includes a gold tinsel tip.
Another has a flat gold tinsel body.

CAHILL, DARK

HOOK: Mustad 94840, sizes 12-18.
THREAD: Brown.
WINGS: Barred lemon wood duck tied
              upright and divided.
TAIL: Brown hackle fibers.
BODY: Dubbed muskrat fur.
HACKLE: Brown.

CAHILL, LIGHT

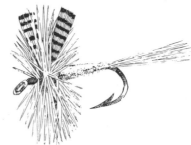

HOOK: Mustad 94840, sizes 10-20.
THREAD: Tan.
WINGS: Barred lemon wood duck tied
              upright and divided.
TAIL: Light ginger hackle fibers.
BODY: Dubbed creamy badger underfur or
              synthetic fur.
HACKLE: Light ginger.

CAHILL QUILL, DARK

HOOK: Mustad 94840, sizes 12-18.
THREAD: Brown.
WINGS: Barred lemon wood duck tied
              upright and divided.
TAIL: Brown hackle fibers.

BODY: Dark peacock quill. Wrap gray floss underbody before wrapping quill to give good natural taper. Reverse wrap the body with fine gold wire.

HACKLE: Brown.

CAHILL QUILL, LIGHT

HOOK: Mustad 94840, sizes 12-18.

THREAD: Tan.

WINGS: Barred lemon wood duck tied upright and divided.

TAIL: Light ginger hackle fibers.

BODY: Light peacock quill. Wrap tan floss underbody before wrapping quill to give good natural taper. Reverse wrap the body with fine gold wire.

HACKLE: Light ginger.

Daniel Cahill of New York created these flies. A very good example of some eastern patterns which have made it good in the west. The Light Cahill is probably the most popular of the lot. I find it is the best fly in my box when it comes to matching some of the Wyoming mosquitoes.

CARMICHAEL

HOOK: Mustad 94840, sizes 12-16.

THREAD: Brown.

WINGS: Grizzly hackle tips tied upright and divided.

TAIL: Cree hackle fibers.

BODY: Dubbed pink rabbit or synthetic fur.

HACKLE: Cree.

CHAUNCEY

HOOK: Mustad 94838, sizes 6-14.

THREAD: Brown.

BODY: Brown hackle tied Palmer over thread base. Grizzly hackle is tied in at front of fly. All hackles should be wrapped very close together.

CHOCOLATE DUN

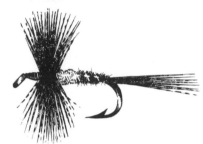

HOOK: Mustad 94840, sizes 10-16.

THREAD: Brown.

TAIL: Dyed brown grizzly hackle fibers.

RIBBING: Fine gold wire.

BODY: Rear ⅔ dubbed dark brown rabbit fur and front ⅓ yellow chenille tied in behind hackle. Chenille should be fine and not too bulky.

HACKLE: Light blue and dark ginger mixed.

This is another one of the Don Martinez patterns. I understand that he tied this as a variation of the Bradley M. and at times it worked much better.

CLARET GNAT

HOOK: Mustad 94840, sizes 12-16.

THREAD: Black.

WINGS:	Natural gray duck quill sections tied upright and divided.
TAIL:	Claret and blue dun hackle fibers mixed.
RIBBING:	Gray thread.
BODY:	Dubbed claret rabbit or synthetic fur.
HACKLE:	Claret and blue dun hackle fibers.

This pattern was originated by California fly-tyer Carl Glisson. It has been a good fly for coastal hatches.

COACHMAN

HOOK:	Mustad 94840, sizes 10-18.
THREAD:	Brown.
WINGS:	White duck quill sections tied upright and divided.
TIP:	Flat gold tinsel.
TAIL:	Golden pheasant tippet fibers.
BODY:	Peacock herl. Reverse wrap the body with fine gold wire.
HACKLE:	Dark brown.

Fly-tyers since the days of Issak Walton have evidently not been content to leave established standard fly patterns unaltered and in their original forms. If you want to start a heated argument, start talking about the origins of the Coachman family of flies that we have today. The best I can tell from looking into the matter is that the Coachman came to us from England, as so many other patterns did, in the form of a wet fly. Theodore Gordon took the pattern and started dressing it in the form of a dry fly. Later, John Haily, in his little shop on Henry Street in New York City, tied the Coachman with a red silk center band to suit the whim of a customer. Around 1878 he sent one to Charles F. Orvis in Manchester, Vermont, who liked it and named it the Royal Coachman. From then on the variations that followed appear to be without end. It would appear that every time someone came up with a new pattern it would be dubbed Coachman something or another. Possibly the word "Coachman" was a status symbol of some sort which signified acceptance by the flyfishers of yesterday.

COACHMAN, LEADWING

HOOK:	Mustad 94840, sizes 10-18.
THREAD:	Brown.
WINGS:	Natural dark gray duck quill sections tied upright and divided.
TIP:	Flat gold tinsel.
TAIL:	Golden pheasant tippet fibers.
BODY:	Peacock herl. Reverse wrap the body with fine gold wire.
HACKLE:	Dark brown.

COACHMAN, ROYAL

HOOK:	Mustad 94840, sizes 10-18.
THREAD:	Brown.
WINGS:	White duck quill sections tied upright and divided.
TAIL:	Golden pheasant tippet fibers.
BODY:	Peacock herl with a red floss center band. Reverse wrap the body with fine gold wire.
HACKLE:	Brown.

COACHMAN, ROYAL FAN WING

Tied the same as the Royal Coachman except the wings are white wood duck breast feathers rather than duck quill. Popular sizes are 8-14. Tie the fan wing on 7957B hooks as regular fine wire hooks are too light to stabilize the fly in the air when it is being cast and the fly will spin because of its larger wind resistant wings and twist leader tippets. This fly I feel catches more fishermen than it does fish. It is sure pretty.

COACHMAN, ROYAL SPENT WING

Tied the same as the Royal Coachman except the wings are tied spent using white hackle tips rather than duck quill. Popular sizes are 14-16, tied on Mustad 94840 hooks. I prefer my Royal Coachmans tied with the hackle tip wings tied upright and divided. They resist the wind better when casting and are more durable than duck quill sections.

COACHMAN, ROYAL TRUDE

HOOK:	Mustad 7957B, sizes 8-14.
THREAD:	Brown.
TAIL:	Golden pheasant tippet fibers.
BODY:	Peacock herl with red floss center band. Reverse wrap the body with fine gold wire.
WING:	White calf tail tied over the body and extending to middle of tail.
HACKLE:	Brown.

COACHMAN, SURESTRIKE

HOOK:	Mustad 7957B, sizes 8-14.
THREAD:	Brown.
TAIL:	Crimson red hackle fibers.
RIBBING:	Oval gold tinsel.
BODY:	Peacock herl.
WING:	White calf tail tied over the body and extending to middle of tail.
HACKLE:	Dark brown.

COACHMAN TRUDE

HOOK:	Mustad 7957B, sizes 8-14.
THREAD:	Brown.
TIP:	Flat gold tinsel.
TAIL:	Golden pheasant tippet fibers.
BODY:	Peacock herl. Reverse wrap the body with fine gold wire.
WING:	White deer body hair tied over length of body only.

HACKLE:	Dark brown.

This pattern is also known as the Western Coachman. A more durable wing of white calf tail is also used for this fly.

COLORADO KING, BROWN

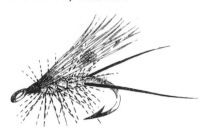

HOOK:	Mustad 94840, sizes 6-18.
THREAD:	Brown.
TAILS:	Two fibers of peccary or moose body hair tied in at each side, tied long and widespread.
BODY:	Dubbed brown hare's mask fur.
HACKLE:	Brown tied Palmer over body.
WING:	Dark deer body hair tied over body and extending slightly past hook bend.

COLORADO KING, DARK

HOOK:	Mustad 94840, sizes 6-18.
THREAD:	Black.
TAILS:	Two fibers of peccary or moose body hair tied in at each side, tied long and widespread.
BODY:	Dubbed muskrat fur.
HACKLE:	Grizzly tied Palmer over body.
WING:	Dark deer body hair tied over body extending slightly past hook bend.

COLORADO KING, DARK FEMALE

Tied the same as the Dark Colorado King except a dubbed yellow rabbit fur egg sac is tied in at rear of the body.

COLORADO KING, LIGHT

HOOK:	Mustad 94840, sizes 6-18.
THREAD:	Black.
TAILS:	Two fibers of peccary or moose body hair tied in at each side, tied long and widespread.
BODY:	Dubbed yellow rabbit fur.
HACKLE:	Grizzly tied Palmer over body.

WING: Light deer body hair tied over body extending slightly past hook bend.

NOTES: A small ball of body material is dubbed in at rear of the hook shank before tying on tails. In the case of the Dark Colorado King Female this would be the yellow rabbit fur egg sac. When tails are tied in at each side the ball of dubbed fur assists in giving the desired spread of the tails. This spread is essential in tying the Colorado Kings as it helps stabilize the fly on the water.

The Colorado King flies were developed in 1971 by George Bodmer of Colorado Springs, Colorado. They have become a universally effective dry fly. George reports that they sold over 6,000 of them during the 1975 season and he keeps getting glowing reports on them from all over the country and abroad. They have the ability to bring up lots of fish. They are not the final solution, no fly is, but they are suggestive enough of a variety of trout foods to be successful over a broad range of fishing conditions. Though developed primarily as attractor type patterns, these flies have an excellent caddis and stone fly silhouette, are close enough for many may fly hatches and, as a bonus, the light pattern is readily taken as a grasshopper. They are excellent floaters. Their open construction permits good drying on false casts and prevents waterlogging. George now ties these flies with elk hair rather than deer hair. This produces a more durable fly.

DARK RED QUILL

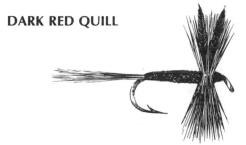

HOOK: Mustad 94840, sizes 14-18.

THREAD: Black.

WINGS: Black hackle tips tied upright and divided.

TAIL: Dark blue dun hackle fibers.

BODY: Dark brown neck hackle stem.

HACKLE: Dark blue dun.

Dark Red Quills hatch sporadically during May and June. This pattern does an excellent job during these hatches.

DAVE'S HOPPER

HOOK: Mustad 9671, sizes 6-14.

THREAD: Brown.

TAIL: Natural tannish gray deer body hair dyed red.

RIBBING: Brown hackle tied Palmer over body.

BODY: Yellow yarn. After yarn is tied in make a small loop with the yarn extending it half way over the tail.

UNDERWING: Yellow deer hair.

OVERWING: Brown mottled turkey wing quill sections tied tent style over body and covering underwing.

HEAD: Spun deer body hair trimmed to shape. Leave a few natural tips extending out on both sides. Heads should be wide and flat on top and bottom.

NOTES: After fly is completed trim down brown hackle so barbles only stick out just past body. Ringneck pheasant quill sections can be substituted for turkey. Wing quills should be treated with a thin solution of cement and trimmed to shape before they are tied in.

This hopper pattern was originated by Dave Whitlock. Dave applies varnish to his wings to give them even more durability. This is not a new idea in tying variations of the Joe's Hopper. A pattern called the Muddled Hopper, one almost like Dave's except for the tail, appeared on the West Coast during the 1957 season.

DEER FLY

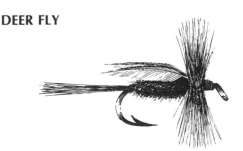

HOOK: Mustad 94840, sizes 12-14.

THREAD: Gray.

TAIL: Dark ginger hackle fibers.

BODY: Dubbed light gray fox or synthetic fur.

WINGS: Dyed gray hackle tips tied in a V back over the body.

HACKLE: Dark ginger.

DEER HAIR HOPPER

HOOK: Mustad 9672, sizes 6-14.

THREAD: Brown.

TAIL: Dyed crimson red deer body hair. Tail should be half the length of the body.

BODY: Yellow deer body hair spun on and clipped to shape. Body should have a good full taper and be trimmed rather flat on the bottom.

FIRST WING: Yellow bucktail tied over the body and extending to middle of tail.

SECOND WING: Mottled hen ringneck pheasant quill sections tied tent style over body and extending to end of hook bend. Quill tips should point upwards.

THIRD WING: Dyed yellow bucktail taken from the back of the tail. This is the natural brown hair dyed yellow. Tie over body and extend to end of tail.

HACKLE: Brown and grizzly mixed.

NOTES: Hair for first and third wings of this pattern should be rather sparse. Quill sections for second wing are treated with a thin solution of cement and trimmed to shape before they are tied in.

The Deer Hair Hopper is much like the Joe's Hopper but it has far better floating qualities because of the deer body hair incorporated in the pattern. For this reason it is preferred by many.

DESCHUTES CADDIS

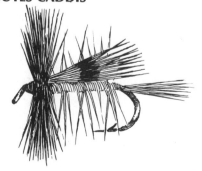

HOOK: Mustad 7957B, sizes 8-14.

THREAD: Brown.

TAIL: Dark ginger hackle fibers.

BODY: Yellow raffia wrapped thin. Dark ginger hackle tied Palmer over body. Hackle should be tied in by its tip and barbles should only extend just past hook point.

WING: Medium brown elk hair tied sparse over the body and extending to the end of body.

HACKLE: Dark brown.

DR. GRANT

HOOK: Mustad 94840, sizes 10-14.

THREAD: Black.

WINGS: Natural dark gray duck quill sections tied upright and divided.

TAIL: Black hackle fibers.

BODY: Tan floss.

HACKLE: Black.

DUNHAM

HOOK: Mustad 94838, sizes 10-16.

THREAD: Gray.

TAIL: Red fibers from golden pheasant breast feather.

BODY: Yellow and blue saddle hackle stems wrapped together. Reverse wrap the body with fine silver wire.

HACKLE: Furnace with a few turns of dyed light blue grizzly tied in at front.

NOTES: Crimson red hackle fibers may be substituted for tailing material.

This is another of the many good fly patterns of Don Martinez. The original pattern used yellow and blue macaw quill fibers.

DUSTY MILLER

HOOK: Mustad 94840, sizes 10-14.

THREAD: Gray.

WINGS:	Natural gray duck quill sections tied upright and divided.
TAIL:	Dyed gray hackle fibers.
BODY:	Dubbed one part muskrat and one part hare's mask fur mixed.
HACKLE:	Dyed gray and dark ginger mixed.

ELK HAIR CADDIS

HOOK:	Mustad 94840, sizes 10-18.
THREAD:	Tan.
RIBBING:	Gold wire.
BODY:	Dubbed hare's ear fur.
HACKLE:	Furnace.
WING:	Tannish cream elk hair.

Instructions for tying the Elk Hair Caddis:

STEP 1: Tie in gold wire ribbing at rear of hook. Spin hare's ear dubbing fur on the tying thread.

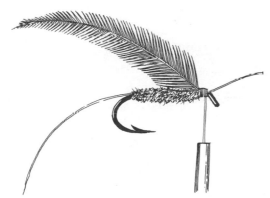

STEP 2: Wrap dubbing material forward and tie in furnace hackle.

STEP 3: Wrap hackle to the rear of the hook using about five turns. Tie hackle down with gold wire using three or four turns.

STEP 4: Wrap wire forward through the hackle and tie off at head.

STEP 5: Tie in elk hair winging material.

STEP 6: Clip off hair butts. You should press your thumbnail into the base of the wing to give the finished wing a triangular shape. Insure head cement is applied to the base of the wings so they hold their shape.

This is one of the good Al Troth patterns. This fly is one of the more productive hair wing style dry flies.

EXOTIC GNAT

HOOK:	Mustad 94840, sizes 12-16.
THREAD:	Brown.
WINGS:	Dyed brown barred mallard tied upright and divided.
TAIL:	Dark ginger hackle fibers.
RIBBING:	Orange thread.
BODY:	Dubbed woodchuck fur with guard hairs removed.
HACKLE:	Dark ginger.

FALL RIVER

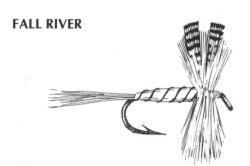

HOOK:	Mustad 94840, sizes 12-18.
THREAD:	Light yellow.
WINGS:	Barred lemon wood duck tied upright and divided.
TAIL:	Light tan elk hair.
BODY:	Light yellow tying thread or floss with yellow thread ribbing.
HACKLE:	Light ginger.

This is a Northern California pattern which has gained a lot of attention in recent years. It was originated by Patrick Butler of Redding, California, and named after the river of the same name. Pat fishes this fly exclusively in Fall River, Hat Creek and McCloud with very good success. Personally, I like this fly much better than either the Light Cahill or Meloche. Often a slightly darker body is needed to interest the fish.

FALLING MAY

HOOK:	Mustad 94840, sizes 12-16.
THREAD:	Tan.
WINGS:	Dyed light yellow barred mallard tied upright and divided.
TAIL:	Light ginger variant hackle fibers.
BODY:	Light green wool yarn or dubbed synthetic fur.
HACKLE:	Light ginger variant.

This pattern was originated by Wes Hartman of Idaho Falls, Idaho. Wes tied some of these up on the spot to match a May Fly hatch on the Beaverhead River in Montana. He admitted that the winging material that he had was an "accident." He had tried to dye some barred mallard into imitation lemon wood duck using Veniard Summer Duck dye. It turned out too yellow for anything close to an imitation wood duck. He now uses no. 1 yellow Rit dye and just tints the feathers to get his light yellow for the Falling May. For imitation lemon wood duck he uses no. 1 yellow, no. 16 and no. 23 gold Rit dye mixed in equal parts and gets an imitation that cannot be detected from the real thing. I am surprised at the number of fly-tyers who do not really know what the true lemon wood duck color is and who believe those yellow feathers they are receiving from the supply houses are a good imitation because they are told so. Maybe yellowish ginger would be a better way to indicate the color rather than "lemon."

FFF MAY FLY

HOOK:	Mustad 94840, sizes 10-18.
THREAD:	Brown.
WINGS:	Grizzly hackle tips tied upright and divided.
TAIL:	Black and brown hackle fibers mixed.
RIBBING:	Tan thread.
BODY:	Dubbed dark brown fur.
HACKLE:	Black and brown mixed.

Fenton Roskelley originated this fly to simulate the large range of dark hatches which occur in the west and named it in honor of the Federation of Fly Fishermen.

FIRE COACHMAN

HOOK:	Mustad 94840, sizes 10-16.
THREAD:	Black.
WINGS:	Natural dark gray duck quill sections tied upright and divided.
TAIL:	Hot orange hackle fibers.
BODY:	Black ostrich with dark orange floss center band. Reverse wrap the body with fine gold wire.
HACKLE:	Black.

FIRE COACHMAN TRUDE

HOOK: Mustad 7957B, sizes 8-14.

THREAD: Black.

TAIL: Hot orange hackle fibers.

BODY: Black ostrich with dark orange floss
           center band. Reverse wrap
           the body with fine gold wire.

WING: Dark coastal blacktail deer body hair
           tied over body and extending
           to the end of body.

HACKLE: Black.

These two Fire Coachman patterns are considered
to be the only tool by many fly fishermen. They
were originated in the Roseburg, Oregon area.

FLYING BLACK ANT

HOOK: Mustad 94840, sizes 12-16.

THREAD: Black.

WINGS: Badger hackle tips tied upright
           and divided.

TAIL: Black moose hair.

BODY: Dubbed black fur. Body should
           be tied in two distinctive
           lumps to simulate the shape of
           an ant's body.

HACKLE: Black.

NOTES: Wings of the Flying Black Ant should be
tied widespread and pointing towards the rear at
about a 70 degree angle.

FLYING CADDIS

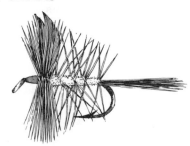

HOOK: Mustad 94840, sizes 8-12.

THREAD: Brown.

WINGS: Natural gray duck quill sections tied
           upright and divided.

TAIL: Brown hackle fibers.

BODY: Dubbed yellow synthetic
           fur. Brown hackle Palmered
           over the body.

HACKLE: Brown. This hackle is in addition
           to that tied over the body.

An Oregon pattern which is very useful most any
place during caddis hatches.

FORKED TAIL

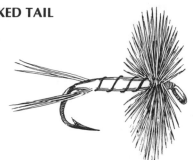

HOOK: Mustad 94840, sizes 10-14.

THREAD: Green.

TAILS: Green elk hair tied in at
           each side and widespread.

RIBBING: Green thread.

BODY: Light green floss.

HACKLE: Dark ginger and light green mixed.

FUR ANT, BLACK

HOOK: Mustad 94840, sizes 14-18.

THREAD: Black.

BODY: Dubbed black synthetic fur tied in
           two distinctive lumps to simulate
           the shape of an ant's body.

HACKLE: Black tied in at center joint of
           body. Use two or three turns of
           hackle only.

FUR ANT, BROWN

Tied the same as the Black Fur Ant except materials
are brown.

These patterns are designed to float the ant in the
surface film where it belongs. Ants cannot walk on
water as do many other insects. When fished right
you will have some unbelievable action. Your
leader tippet and the fly should be treated with a
good floatant before use.

GINGER DAMSEL

HOOK: Mustad 79580, sizes 14-16.

THREAD: Tan.

TAIL: Light tan elk hair.

REAR HACKLE: Light ginger variant. Hackle should only extend just past point of hook.

RIBBING: Fine gold wire.

BODY: Tan floss tied thin.

WINGS: Light ginger variant hackle tips tied together on edge over the body.

FRONT HACKLE: Light ginger variant.

NOTES: Wings should be as narrow as possible and extend the full length of body and rear hackle with tips just touching top of rear hackle.

This is another one of the Damsel Fly imitations which are effective. Although I have seen green and other shades on the water, the blue and ginger seem to dominate the scene in most areas.

GINGER QUILL

HOOK: Mustad 94840, sizes 10-20.

THREAD: Tan.

WINGS: Natural light gray duck quill sections tied upright and divided.

TAIL: Light ginger hackle fibers.

BODY: Light peacock quill. Wrap floss underbody to give body a good natural taper. Reverse wrap the body with fine good wire.

HACKLE: Light ginger.

NOTES: Many fly fishermen, especially in the Rocky Mountain area, prefer a light tan elk hair tail on this fly.

This is one of our older patterns and can be found almost any place a fly is cast. It is one of those flies you should know better than to leave home without at least a few in your fly box.

NOTES: Because of the short supply of light ginger hackle which continues to plague us year in and year out it is often hard to get hackle of the proper shade to tie such patterns as the Ginger Quill, Light Cahill, etc. If you can obtain white or natural white, off white, you are only steps away from the light ginger of the shade you desire. I have been fighting the problem for many years with little success. Now, Frank Johnson of Missoula, Montana, gave me a formula. Use 1 part no. 16 tan and 1 part no. 23 gold Rit dye. Your dye bath should be weak for this color. A pinch of each color can always be added later if the shade you desire is not darkening into the feathers.

For those of you who would like to do more dying but find the dyes offered by the supply houses unsuited or too expensive, look at the Rit dyes more closely. If you cannot find the color you want on the shelf of your local retailer it is a simple matter to write the Rit people and they can provide a formula for any color in the spectrum you might want. Write: Best Foods, 1437 West Morris Street, Indianapolis, Indiana 46206.

GOLDEN BADGER

HOOK: Mustad 94840, sizes 10-16.

THREAD: Black.

WINGS: Golden badger hackle tips tied upright and divided.

TAIL: Golden badger hackle fibers.

BODY: Golden brown synthetic fur.

HACKLE: Golden badger.

GOLDEN BADGER

HOOK: Mustad 7957B, sizes 6-10.

THREAD: Black.

TAILS: Two golden badger hackle tied in a V.

BODY: Golden badger hackle wrapped closely over the hook shank.

GRAYBACK

HOOK: Mustad 94848, sizes 6-14.

THREAD: Black.

TAIL: Deer body hair tied heavy.

BODY: Yellow or orange chenille with deer body hair pulled over the back and tied in at front.

HACKLE: Grizzly.

A very good floater with the yellow body preferred during grasshopper season and the orange during stone fly hatches.

GRAY FOX

HOOK: Mustad 94840, sizes 12-16.

THREAD: Gray.

WINGS: Natural dark gray duck quill sections tied upright and divided.

TAIL: Dark moose hair.

BODY: Dubbed dark gray fox fur.

HACKLE: Grizzly.

GRAY HACKLE PEACOCK

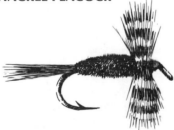

HOOK: Mustad 94838, sizes 10-18.

THREAD: Gray.

TAIL: Scarlet red hackle fibers.

BODY: Peacock herl. Reverse wrap the body with fine gold wire.

HACKLE: Grizzly.

GRAY HACKLE YELLOW

HOOK: Mustad 94838, sizes 10-18.

THREAD: Gray.

TAIL: Scarlet red hackle fibers.

RIBBING: Flat gold tinsel.

BODY: Yellow floss.

HACKLE: Grizzly.

The Gray Hackles can be tied with an assortment of body colors but the two patterns above are probably the most used.

GRAY UGLY

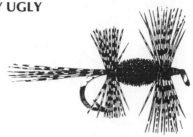

HOOK: Mustad 94838, sizes 8-18.

THREAD: Gray.

TIP: Embossed silver tinsel.

TAIL: Grizzly hackle fibers.

REAR HACKLE: Grizzly. Hackle barbles should only extend to the point of the hook.

BODY: Peacock herl. Reverse wrap the body with fine silver wire.

FRONT HACKLE: Grizzly.

I favor this fly over most other dries. I have taken more fish with it over the past three or four seasons than any other fly. Possibly because I use it so extensively. I picked this pattern up in Denver, Colorado, around 1970. Since then I have had the opportunity to fish it over a variety of waters in many areas. It is certainly one that is worth tying for any area.

GRIZZLY KING TRUDE

HOOK: Mustad 7957B, sizes 8-14.

THREAD: Black.

TIP: Flat gold tinsel.

TAIL: Crimson red hackle fibers.

RIBBING: Flat gold tinsel.

BODY: Green floss.

WING: Coastal blacktail deer body hair tied over the body and extending to middle of tail.

HACKLE: Grizzly.

HATCH MATCHER

HOOK: Mustad 94838, sizes 12-18.

THREAD: Select to match overall coloration of the fly.

TAIL AND BODY: Select a barred mallard flank feather as straight as you can possibly find. Breast feathers are more suitable for the smaller flies. Trim out the center section and strip fibers from butt section, leaving three or four fibers at each side. This must be regulated by the size of fly you are tying. Tie in at winging position to form body and tail.

WINGS: Barred mallard tied upright and divided.

HACKLE: To match overall coloration of fly.

NOTES: This style of fly is tied in a wide range of colors by dying barred mallard into hatch matching colors. Some tyers bring the butt section of the body feather up and use it as wings. I prefer having natural tips on my wings so I tie them in as I would do on any other dry fly. If you have never tried this type of fly it is certainly worth your effort to take some dyed blue dun barred mallard and blue dun hackle and tie some.

Some think this fly was created by Harry Darbee of Livingston Manor, New York, and it may well have been. They first came to my attention in the mid 1950s on the West Coast. There were large boxes of these flies offered for 5¢ each. They were Japanese imports and the style of tying was thought to have been originated by them. I was foolishly turned off by these easy to tie flies and failed to see the importance of their design. Some years later I had my mind changed by a friend when he gave me a few that he had tied to try out. They were just the answer on California's King's River and since then I use them when the fish will not look at a conventionally dressed imitation.

HENDRICKSON, DARK

HOOK: Mustad 94840, sizes 10-16.

THREAD: Gray.

WINGS: Barred lemon wood duck tied upright and divided.

TAIL: Dark blue dun hackle fibers.

BODY: Dubbed muskrat fur.

HACKLE: Dark blue dun.

HENDRICKSON, LIGHT

HOOK: Mustad 94840, sizes 10-16.

THREAD: Gray.

WINGS: Barred lemon wood duck tied upright and divided.

TAIL: Blue dun hackle fibers.

BODY: Dubbed light red fox fur.

HACKLE: Blue dun.

HENRYVILLE SPECIAL

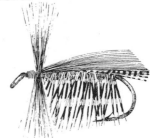

HOOK: Mustad 94840, sizes 14-18.

THREAD: Black.

RIBBING: Two grizzly hackles tied Palmer over the body.

BODY: Olive wool yarn or synthetic dubbing tied thin.

UNDERWING: Barred lemon wood duck fibers. Fibers should just extend very slightly past bend of hook.

WINGS: Natural dark gray duck quill sections tied tent style over the body and extending just past the underwing.

HACKLE: Brown. Wrap two or three turns only.

NOTES: Palmered hackle on top of body should be clipped off before tying in underwing. Palmered hackle should be wrapped so the hackle barbles point towards the front of the fly. Wings should be flared and separated so the fish below will have a good natural-looking silhouette.

The Henryville Special goes back many years and yet only recently started gaining favor here in the west. It was originated by Hiram Brobst of Palmertown, Pennsylvania, to duplicate caddis hatches in the Henryville section of Brodhead Creek. He originally named it "No-Name" but later Al Ziegler got a hold of the fly and renamed it Henryville Special. As with any fly that gets extensive use it has been tied in numerous variations. Some feel it is the best caddis imitation to have ever been created. It has proven to be a deadly fly in the west when it is tied correctly. One of the largest mistakes western tyers are making is overhackling the fly. If the grizzly Palmered hackle is of sufficient dry fly quality as it should be then you will have a good floating fly. Keep the brown hackle to two or three wraps and you will have a productive caddis imitation.

HONEY QUILL

HOOK:	Mustad 94840, sizes 10-18.
THREAD:	Tan
WINGS:	Honey badger hackle tips tied upright and divided.
TAIL:	Light tan elk hair.
BODY:	Light ginger neck hackle stem.
HACKLE:	Honey ginger.

This is a good general purpose pattern useful almost any place from July until late fall.

HORNER'S DEER HAIR

HOOK:	Mustad 94838, sizes 6-14.
THREAD:	Black.
TAIL:	Coastal blacktail deer body hair tied rather heavy.
BODY:	Coastal blacktail deer body hair.
WINGS:	The ends of the body material pulled up and tied upright and divided.
HACKLE:	Grizzly with two turns behind the wings and two turns in front. Keep it sparse.

Jack Horner of San Francisco, California, came up with this pattern many years ago. From it have come such patterns as the Goofus Bug, Humpy, Crazy Goof and others which only attest to the usefulness of this type of fly. It has been copied and the name changed in many areas. It still remains the number one choice of some of our better fly fishermen.

The following step by step instructions should help you better understand how to tie both the Horner's Deer Hair and the Humpies listed below.

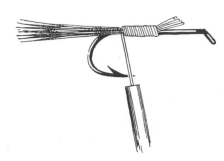

STEP 1: Tie in tail. Select hair which is hard and fine so you will have less flare.

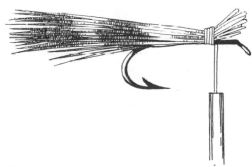

STEP 2: Return thread to the front of the hook shank and tie in another bunch of hair. This bunch of hair should be long enough to form underbody, overbody or back and the wings. Obtaining the correct hair length will take some practice.

STEP 3: Wrap underbody with a criss cross from front to back and return to the front.

STEP 4: Pull hair over the body and tie in. Pull the remaining natural hair tips upright and tie a divided wing.

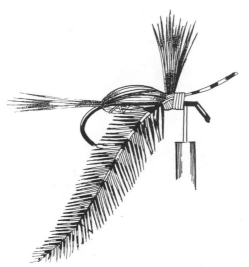

STEP 5: Tie in one grizzly hackle. Hackle need not be of good dry fly quality.

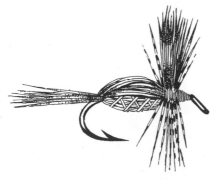

STEP 6: Wrap two turns of hackle in back and two turns in front of wings. The hackle is not intended to support the fly on the water. The deer hair floats the Horner's Deer Hair on the water, not above it.

The same tying procedures apply in tying the Humpies except the underbody is either of tying thread or floss covering the hair, and the hackle is tied heavy enough to support the fly on the water.

HUMPY

HOOK:	Mustad 7957B, sizes 6-14.
THREAD:	Yellow.
TAIL:	Tan elk hair tied rather heavy.
BODY:	Underbody of yellow tying thread or floss with overbody of tan elk hair tied over back.
WINGS:	Tan elk hair tied upright and divided.
HACKLE:	Grizzly and brown mixed.

This pattern is often called the Yellow Humpy. See step by step tying instructions following Horner's Deer Hair. I believe at this time there are about 16 colors of tying thread available to the tyer and each and everyone of these colors have been used at one time or another in tying the Humpy. Deer hair and brown elk hair are also used. Another variation is the Colorado Humpy. In this the wings are left off of the endless color variations.

IDANHA

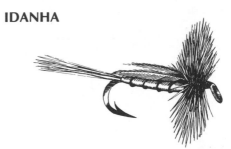

HOOK:	Mustad 94840, sizes 10-14.
THREAD:	Black.
TAIL:	Crimson red hackle fibers.
RIBBING:	Black floss.
BODY:	Yellow floss tied with extra large taper.
WINGS:	Dyed gray hackle tips tied flat in a V over the body.
HACKLE:	Dark ginger.

I have found this pattern very good in areas where Yellow Jackets are present. Northern California has its share and one learns very quickly to wash any fish smell off his hands. They are attracted to the smell and you can suffer some severe bites.

INCH WORM

HOOK:	Mustad 9672, sizes 14-16.
THREAD:	White.

BODY: Dyed chartreuse deer body hair. Select a bunch of hair and tie in at front of hook. Pull hair down and to the rear of the hook and wrap tying thread from front to rear and back to the front and tie off. Clip excess hair from both front and rear and you are ready to go fishing.

NOTES: I find that by using no. 22 chartreuse Rit dye I can get the best color for these little worms. You must leave the hair in the dye bath for about 1 hour and boil for at least 15 minutes of that time to get the richer color desired. Also, use dye powder generously, otherwise the hair will be too yellowish. I find that if I do not try and rinse all of the dye out of the hair after dying that the little that is left will penetrate the white tying thread when head cement is applied and give the worm a more natural appearance.

It takes a bit of practice to tie this simple looking worm. Most tyers have problems in judging just how much hair to use in getting the desired body diameter. Just remember that the hair compacts rather well. I scoffed at the Inch Worm pattern for many years and really did not think it had a place in western angling. A few seasons past I was fishing a large pool in Montana and was having little success. I was surprised to find one of these little green worms inching it's way up my neck. Further inspection revealed that the bushes and trees were just covered with them and they were falling everywhere. I went back to the car and was able to fashion some out of a piece of yarn that I just happened to have and spent a very memorable afternoon.

IRON BLUE DUN

HOOK: Mustad 94840, sizes 12-18.

THREAD: Black.

WINGS: Black hackle tips tied upright and divided.

TAIL: Brown hackle fibers.

RIBBING: Olive thread.

BODY: Dubbed beaver fur with guard hairs removed.

HACKLE: Iron blue dun.

IRRESISTIBLE

HOOK: Mustad 7957B, sizes 6-14.

THREAD: Black.

TAIL: Coastal blacktail deer body hair.

WINGS: Coastal blacktail deer body hair tied upright and divided.

BODY: Gray deer body hair spun on then clipped so it tapers towards the tail.

HACKLE: Dark rusty blue dun.

NOTE: Dark rusty blue dun hackle is obtained by dying dark ginger a blue dun.

IRRESISTIBLE, ADAMS

HOOK: Mustad 7957B, sizes 6-14.

THREAD: Brown.

TAIL: Coastal blacktail deer body hair.

BODY: Gray deer body hair spun on then clipped so it tapers towards the tail.

WINGS: Grizzly hackle tips tied upright and divided.

HACKLE: Grizzly and brown mixed.

IRRESISTIBLE, BLACK

HOOK: Mustad 7957B, sizes 6-14.

THREAD: Black.

TAIL: Dyed black elk hair.

BODY: Dyed black deer body hair spun on then clipped so it tapers towards the tail.

WINGS: Badger hackle tips tied upright and divided.

HACKLE: Black.

IRRESISTIBLE, BROWN

HOOK: Mustad 7957B, sizes 6-14.

THREAD: Brown.

TAIL: Natural brown elk hair.

BODY: Dyed brown deer body hair spun on then clipped so it tapers towards the tail.

WINGS: Honey badger hackle tips tied upright and divided.

HACKLE: Brown.

IRRESISTIBLE, WHITE

HOOK: Mustad 7957B, sizes 6-14.

THREAD: Black.

TAIL: Fine stiff white deer hair taken from either the leg or mask area.

BODY: White deer body hair spun on then clipped so it tapers towards the tail.

WINGS: Badger hackle tips tied upright and divided.

HACKLE: Badger.

IRRESISTIBLE, YELLOW

HOOK: Mustad 7957B, sizes 6-14.

THREAD: Brown.

TAIL: Natural brown elk hair.

BODY: Dyed yellow deer body hair spun on then clipped so it tapers towards the tail.

WINGS: Furnace hackle tips tied upright and divided.

HACKLE: Dark ginger.

Irresistible flies are some of the better floating flies we have. The Irresistible and the Adams Irresistible are often confused with each other due to the popularity of the Adams Irresistible. These flies are not only some fine trout takers, they are preferred by many for bass. Also see Rat Faced McDougal.

JOE'S HOPPER

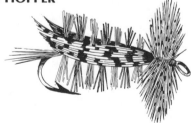

HOOK: Mustad 9672, sizes 6-14.

THREAD: Brown.

TAIL: Crimson red hackle fibers.

RIBBING: Brown saddle hackle. After hackle is wrapped trim off on each side and trim top and bottom into a taper leaving trimmed ends extending to the point of the hook at rear and almost zero at the front.

BODY: Dubbed yellow synthetic fur.

WINGS: Mottled brown turkey wing quill sections tied in at each side with tips curving upward at rear. Wings should extend to almost the end of tail.

HACKLE: Brown and grizzly mixed.

This fly is also referred to as the Michigan Hopper. Joe Brooks popularized it hence the name change. This is one of the best known and most used of all the hopper patterns. After the grasshopper season starts this fly will bring up some very large trout when they are reluctant to take any other fly.

JULY DRAKE

HOOK: Mustad 94840, sizes 10-16.

THREAD: Brown.

WINGS: Light ginger variant hackle tips dyed light gray and tied upright and divided.

TAIL: Ginger hackle fibers.

RIBBING: Fine gold wire wrapped closely.

BODY: Brown floss.

HACKLE: Ginger.

KAHL'S GRAY SEDGE

HOOK: Mustad 94840, sizes 14-20.

THREAD:	Black.
TAIL:	Grizzly hackle fibers.
BODY:	Dark peacock quill. Reverse wrap the body with fine silver wire.
WINGS:	Two sections of barred teal tied tent style over body with ends trimmed to shape.
HACKLE:	Grizzly.

NOTES: Barred mallard may be substituted for teal. Hackle is generally tied sparse but this must be altered to suit the water you might be fishing.

Milt Kahl of Los Angeles, California, created this pattern. It is most effective in the High Sierra County of California and in the Snowy Range area of Wyoming.

KING'S RIVER CADDIS

HOOK:	Mustad 94840, sizes 10-16.
THREAD:	Brown.
BODY:	Dubbed raccoon fur. Body should be rather large and shaggy.
WINGS:	Mottled brown turkey quill sections tied tent style over the body. Wings should be rather long and tied in at tips rather than by their butts.
HACKLE:	Brown.

NOTES: Wings are generally treated with thinned solution of head cement to make them more durable. Ringneck hen pheasant quill sections can be substituted for turkey. This fly is also tied with a black or yellow body.

A superior Caddis Fly pattern developed by Wayne "Buz" Buszek of Visalia, California. This fly provides one of the better silhouettes of the Caddis imitations. It is used throughout North America which may sound odd since Buz tied it originally to match an evening Caddis hatch on the King's River.

LETORT CRICKET

HOOK:	Mustad 9671, sizes 10-14.
THREAD:	Black.
BODY:	Dubbed black rabbit or synthetic fur.
WINGS:	Black goose quill sections tied flat over the body and extending to the end of the body. Black deer hair tied on top and extending just past the bend of the hook.
HEAD:	Trim butts of deer hair leaving about ⅛" for the head.

LETORT HOPPER

HOOK:	Mustad 9671, sizes 10-14.
THREAD:	Yellow.
BODY:	Dubbed yellow, tan and olive rabbit or synthetic fur mixed in equal parts.
WINGS:	Brown mottled turkey wing quill sections tied flat over the body and extending to the end of the body. Tannish gray deer hair tied on top and extending just past the bend of the hook.
HEAD:	Trim butts of deer hair leaving about ⅛" for the head.

These two patterns were developed in the east by Ed Shenk. Since they have come west they have gained wide acceptance.

LOOP WING ADAMS

HOOK:	Mustad 94840, sizes 10-18.
THREAD:	Gray.
WINGS:	Barred mallard fibers.
TAIL:	Brown and grizzly hackle fibers mixed.
BODY:	Dubbed muskrat fur.
HACKLE:	Brown and grizzly mixed.

Instructions for tying the Loop Wing Adams:

STEP 1: Tie in four fibers of barred mallard with underside up. Fibers are tied in by their butts.

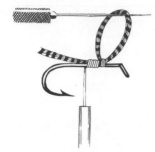

STEP 2: Fold the fibers back and tie in to form the wing. Use your dubbing needle to assist in keeping the fibers from twisting.

STEP 3: Tie in tailing material.

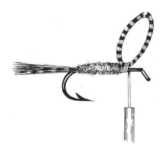

STEP 4: Complete the body.

STEP 5: Tie in hackles.

STEP 6: Separate the wings with your dubbing needle and wrap a figure eight between them to

hold them apart. Apply a drop of head cement between the wings.

STEP 7: Wrap the hackles and tie off the head and the fly is finished.

The Loop Wing idea was originated by Andre' Puyans of Walnut Creek, California. It gives a much more durable wing to your dry flies to say nothing of how much more natural looking it is on May Fly imitations. This tying procedure can be used on most any dry fly pattern with a little innovation on your part. All of the Cahills, the Professor and the Gordon Quill are naturals for this style, and by using white turkey or goose the Royal Coachman and other patterns can also be tied.

MALLARD QUILL

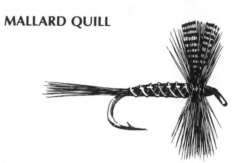

HOOK:	Mustad 94840, sizes 12-18.
THREAD:	Brown.
WINGS:	Bronze barred mallard tied upright and divided.
TAIL:	Dark brown hackle fibers.
BODY:	Dark peacock quill. Reverse wrap the body with fine gold wire.
HACKLE:	Dark brown.

MARCH BROWN, AMERICAN

HOOK:	Mustad 94840, sizes 10-14.
THREAD:	Orange.

WINGS:	Barred lemon wood duck tied upright and divided.
TAIL:	Dark brown hackle fibers.
RIBBING:	Brown thread.
BODY:	Dubbed tannish red fox fur.
HACKLE:	Dark brown and grizzly mixed.

This pattern was developed by Preston Jennings and has been a favorite for many years.

McKENZIE

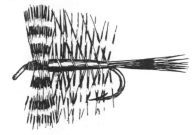

HOOK:	Mustad 94840, sizes 8-12.
THREAD:	Black.
TAIL:	Coastal blacktail deer body hair.
RIBBING:	Grizzly hackle tied Palmer over body.
BODY:	Light green floss.
HACKLE:	Grizzly. This hackle is in addition to Palmered hackle.

This pattern came out of the Eugene, Oregon, area. It works well on the caddis hatches in the Northwest and in Canada.

McKENZIE SPECIAL

HOOK:	Mustad 94840, sizes 10-14.
THREAD:	Black.
WINGS:	Natural gray duck quill sections tied upright and divided.
TIP:	Light green floss.
TAIL:	Golden pheasant tippet fibers.
BODY:	Light green floss.
HACKLE:	Grizzly.

An alternate pattern of the McKenzie. It was some years before I was able to sort out which of the two patterns was the original.

MEADOW HOPPER

HOOK:	Mustad 9672, sizes 8-14.
THREAD:	Green.
TAIL:	Insect green hackle fibers.
RIBBING:	Insect green saddle hackle. After hackle is wrapped, trim off on each side and trim top and bottom into a taper leaving trimmed ends extending to point of hook at rear and almost zero at front.
BODY:	Dubbed pale yellow synthetic fur.
WINGS:	Ringneck cock pheasant wing quill sections dyed insect green. Wings should be tied in at each side with tips curved upwards at rear. Wings should extend to middle of tail.
TOPPING:	Green bucktail tied over back of fly and extending the length of the wings.
HACKLE:	Dark ginger and insect green mixed.

I developed this particular pattern to fill the gap left by our green hoppers. This fly is designed to simulate the green hoppers which are often found along our mountain meadow streams. I have found that this fly will often change my luck when other hopper patterns are not giving me the action they should.

MELOCHE

HOOK:	Mustad 94840, sizes 10-18.
THREAD:	Tan.
WINGS:	Light grizzly hackle tips tied upright and divided.
TAIL:	Light ginger hackle fibers.
BODY:	Dubbed tan fox or synthetic fur.
HACKLE:	Light ginger.

This fly was first tied by Dan Bailey to match the hatch of tiny cream colored naturals that had Gilbert Meloche at his wit's end. He caught one of the naturals and took it to Dan to duplicate. Within an hour Meloche was back with a 4 pound and 6 ounce trout.

MIDGE DRY FLIES

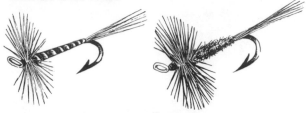

HOOK: Mustad 94842, sizes 18-28.

THREAD: Color to match overall coloration of fly.

TAIL: Hackle fibers to match overall coloration of fly.

BODY: Dubbed fur, floss or quill to match overall coloration of fly.

HACKLE: Same as tailing material.

Midge Dry Flies are most often tied black, brown, blue dun, ginger, olive and cream in color. These flies will often give you good results when no other flies will entice finicky trout. You will see hovering clouds of these tiny insects throughout the season. Rarely have I found a wing to be essential on these flies. True size closely followed by correct coloration is of the utmost importance. While fishing the South Platte River in Colorado during February a few seasons ago this is the only type of fly that would work for us. It started snowing and the fish were going crazy. I put on a Black Midge and soon had a fish. He was bigger and smarter than I gave him credit and took off down stream with my fly and part of my leader tippet. This time I tried a size 18 Black Midge thinking the size 20 that I had started with was just too small for either me or the fish to see in the heavy snow fall or for me to have any chance of holding them due to their unsuspected large size. Not a thing. They would not even look at my second offering. So I changed to a size 20 Brown Midge and once more had a fish on. The fish continued to feed throughout the day and we had some very enjoyable hours of fishing, between trips back to the four-wheel drive to get some feeling back in our frozen bodies. That day color did not mean a thing, size only. Twenty was the magic number for us.

MONTANA BUCKTAIL

HOOK: Mustad 9671, sizes 6-10.

THREAD: Tan.

TAIL: Golden pheasant tippet fibers.

BODY: Orange floss.

HACKLE: Grizzly tied Palmer over body.

WING: Light tan elk hair tied over body and extending to the end of body.

NOTES: Select two grizzly hackles and tie in at rear of hook. Hackles should be placed with their undersides facing each other. Hackles tied in this manner are referred to as being wrapped in the semi-reversed manner or style. I particularly like this style on all of my dry flies, especially the larger ones, since the hackle barbles are curved in towards each other and give better support to each barble.

This fly is a good floater and has been popular in Montana, Idaho and Washington for a number of years. It is most effective during the large hatches of Stone Flies and Salmon Flies which occur on the larger rivers.

MOSQUITO

HOOK: Mustad 94840, sizes 12-18.

THREAD: Black.

WINGS: Grizzly hackle tips tied upright and divided.

TAIL: Grizzly hackle fibers.

BODY: Dark and light moose mane wrapped together.

HACKLE: Grizzly.

MOSQUITO, CALIFORNIA

HOOK: Mustad 94840, sizes 10-18.

THREAD: Black.

WINGS: Grizzly hackle tips tied upright and divided.

TAIL: Grizzly hackle fibers.

RIBBING: Black floss.

BODY: White floss.

HACKLE: Grizzly.

NOTES: If you first run a single strand of black floss through a cake of tying wax you will have better success in wrapping a nice uniform rib. Maybe not as uniform as nature, but close.

Some other variations of the Mosquitoes include bodies of peacock quill and of dark and light peccary.

MUCKLEDUN

HOOK:	Mustad 94840, sizes 6-12.
THREAD:	Black.
BODY:	Gray wool yarn or dubbed fur.
WINGS:	Natural gray goose quill sections. Wings should be tied with concave sides out and back over the body.
HACKLE:	Badger tied on as a collar. Two turns only.

This is one of those odd-ball patterns which is neither wet or dry, fish nor fowl; but it accounts for a great many large fish. From what I can understand it is dressed with a good floatant and fished in the surface film. It was originated by Bob Terrell of Basalt, Colorado.

NER-E-NUFF

HOOK:	Mustad 94840, sizes 8-14.
THREAD:	Gray.
WINGS:	Barred lemon wood duck tied upright and divided.
TAILS:	Two grizzly hackle stems tied in a V. Tails should be twice the length of body.
BODY:	Grizzly hackle stems.
HACKLE:	Grizzly and light ginger mixed.

As the name suggests, this pattern is "near enough" to match a wide range of hatches which occur each season.

OAK FLY

HOOK:	Mustad 94840, sizes 8-14.
THREAD:	Brown.
WINGS:	Mottled brown hen pheasant wing quill sections tied upright and divided.
TAIL:	Brown elk hair.
RIBBING:	Black floss.
BODY:	Orange floss.
HACKLE:	Brown.

OLIVE DUN, DARK

HOOK:	Mustad 94840, sizes 10-18.
THREAD:	Olive.
WINGS:	Dyed gray ginger variant hackle tips tied upright and divided.
TAIL:	Dark olive hackle fibers.
BODY:	Dubbed olive dun rabbit or synthetic fur.
HACKLE:	Dark olive.

OLIVE DUN, LIGHT

HOOK:	Mustad 94840, sizes 10-18.
THREAD:	Olive.
WINGS:	Dyed light gray ginger variant hackle tips tied upright and divided.
TAIL:	Light olive hackle fibers.
BODY:	Dubbed light olive dun rabbit or synthetic fur.
HACKLE:	Light olive.

OLIVE QUILL, DARK

HOOK:	Mustad 94840, sizes 10-18.
THREAD:	Olive.
WINGS:	Dyed gray ginger variant hackle tips tied upright and divided.
TAIL:	Dark olive hackle fibers.
BODY:	Dark peacock quill. Reverse wrap body with fine gold wire.
HACKLE:	Dark olive.

OLIVE QUILL, LIGHT

HOOK:	Mustad 94840, sizes 10-18.
THREAD:	Olive.
WINGS:	Dyed light gray ginger variant hackle tips tied upright and divided.
TAIL:	Light olive hackle fibers.
BODY:	Light peacock quill. Reverse wrap body with fine gold wire.
HACKLE:	Light olive.

The Olive Duns and Olive Quills are found in use almost any place a fly is cast. They are good on all streams and lakes from May through the end of the season.

ORANGE ASHER

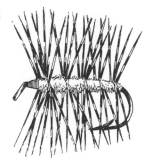

HOOK:	Mustad 94840, sizes 12-16.
THREAD:	Orange.
BODY:	Orange wool yarn or dubbed fur.
HACKLE:	Grizzly tied Palmer over body.

The Orange Asher has been a highly regarded fly in Colorado for many years. It is very effective in Northern Utah's High Uintas area. This fly is generally used wet in Colorado but is considered best tied dry in other parts of the country.

ORANGE SEDGE

HOOK:	Mustad 94840, sizes 8-10.
THREAD:	Orange.
WINGS:	Coastal blacktail deer body hair tied upright and divided.
TAIL:	Dark brown hackle fibers.
BODY:	Select a long brown saddle hackle and strip hackle barbles from one side. Tie in at tip of hackle. Twist hackle around orange tying thread and wrap forward. Trim hackle barbles into a closely tapered body.
HACKLE:	Dark brown.

This pattern originated in the Northwest. It has been used in many areas and is considered to have a lot of merit.

PALE EVENING DUN

HOOK:	Mustad 94840, sizes 12-16.
THREAD:	White.
WINGS:	Natural light gray duck quill sections tied upright and divided.
TIP:	Flat gold tinsel.
TAIL:	Natural white hackle fibers.
BODY:	Dubbed cream fur.
HACKLE:	Natural white.

NOTES: Natural white refers to an off white.

There are probably 30 or 40 alternates to this pattern. They consist of everything from blue floss to yellow dubbed fur bodies with all types of hackle and ribbing variations.

PARACHUTE DRY FLIES

Parachute dry flies generally consist of any of our conventional fly patterns tied parachute style. This is usually accomplished by tying in a single post of hair at the winging position and hackling the fly around the post. The single hair wing, or post, is normally tied using white calf tail to give the fly better visibility on the water. One exception to just tying our conventional patterns in the parachute style is a pattern conceived by Wayne "Buz" Buszek of Visalia, California. He gave us a multi-purpose parachute which he called the Float-N-Fool Multi-Color.

FLOAT-N-FOOL MULTI-COLOR

HOOK: Mustad 94838, sizes 12-16

THREAD: Black.

TAIL: White calf tail. The butts are tied forward to the winging position and are pulled up and tied upright to form a winding post for the hackle. Trim the butts down to a little less than normal wing length.

BODY: Peacock herl. Reverse wrap the body with fine gold wire.

HACKLE: Brown and grizzly wrapped around the post.

As much as I hate trying to cast the parachute type flies I find this pattern worth my time. It does a very good job on almost any water.

PINEDALE FLOATER, DARK

HOOK: Mustad 93838, sizes 6-14.

THREAD: Brown.

TAIL AND BODY: Brown elk hair. Body and tail are fashioned from a single bunch of hair, and body is wrapped in a criss-cross from front to rear and back to the front.

HACKLE: Dark ginger variant.

PINEDALE FLOATER, LIGHT

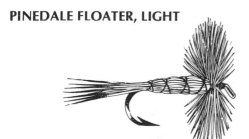

HOOK: Mustad 94838, sizes 6-14.

THREAD: Tan.

TAIL AND BODY: Light tan elk hair. Body and tail are fashioned from a single bunch of hair, and body is wrapped in a criss-cross from front to rear and back to the front.

HACKLE: Light ginger variant.

The Pinedale Floaters were designed for fishing in the Pinedale, Wyoming area. They are most effective on the Green, New Fork and Snake Rivers

during caddis and stone fly hatches. Because of their good floating qualities this style of body and tail could be incorporated into a number of other patterns with success.

PINK LADY

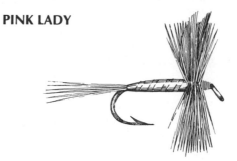

HOOK: Mustad 94840, sizes 10-18.

THREAD: Tan.

WINGS: Natural light gray duck quill sections tied upright and divided.

TAIL: Light ginger hackle fibers.

RIBBING: Flat gold tinsel.

BODY: Pink floss.

HACKLE: Light ginger.

This is a very popular pattern in most areas. It has been effective during hatches of the May Fly, *Epeorus albertae*.

PINK LADY TRUDE

HOOK: Mustad 7957B, sizes 8-14.

THREAD: Tan.

TAIL: Lady Amherst pheasant tippet fibers.

RIBBING: Flat gold tinsel.

BODY: Pink floss.

WING: Dyed light gray elk hair tied over body and extending to the end of body.

HACKLE: Light ginger.

PINK LADY, BLUE WING

Tied the same as the Pink Lady except blue dun hackle tips are used rather than duck quill sections.

PINK LADY, DONNELLY

HOOK: Mustad 94838, sizes 12-16.

THREAD: Gray.

TAG: Yellow floss.

TAIL: Light ginger hackle fibers.

BODY: Dubbed pink rabbit or synthetic fur.

HACKLE: Light ginger with two or three turns of blue dun tied in at front.

POOR WITCH

HOOK:	Mustad 94840, sizes 12-26.
THREAD:	Black.
WINGS:	Two blue dun hackle tips tied spent wing style.
TAILS:	Two dark moose body hairs tied in a V.
BODY:	Dubbed muskrat fur.
HACKLE:	Grizzly and brown mixed.

NOTES: If available, use Mustad 7948A hooks for sizes 12-20. They facilitate a lower floating fly and put it down more into the surface film.

This pattern was sent to me by Jim Poor of Littleton, Colorado. The fly was developed more than 20 years ago by Jack Redhead of Cheyenne, Wyoming. Jack has used the pattern almost everywhere with better than average success. Since Jim started offering this fly commercially he states that it has been one of their best producing flies. Jim operates the Angler's All, Ltd., in Littleton, Colorado. If you are in the Denver area you should pay them a visit.

PROFESSOR

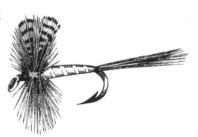

HOOK:	Mustad 94840, sizes 10-18.
THREAD:	Brown.
WINGS:	Barred mallard tied upright and divided.
TAIL:	Scarlet red hackle fibers.
RIBBING:	Flat gold tinsel.
BODY:	Yellow floss.
HACKLE:	Brown.

The Professor is in general use everywhere throughout North America.

QUEEN OF THE WATER

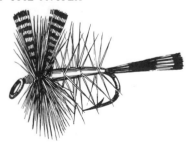

HOOK:	Mustad 94840, sizes 10-16.
THREAD:	Brown.
WINGS:	Barred mallard tied upright and divided.
TIP:	Flat gold tinsel.
TAIL:	Golden pheasant tippet fibers.
RIBBING:	Brown hackle tied Palmer over the body.
BODY:	Orange floss.
HACKLE:	Brown. This hackle is in addition to Palmered hackle.

QUEEN OF THE WATER FAN WING

Tied the same as the Queen of the Water except barred mallard breast feathers are used. This is an effective fly for still water conditions. The silhouette given by the wings sometimes has an unexplainable effect over the fish.

RAT FACED McDOUGAL

HOOK:	Mustad 7957B, sizes 6-14.
THREAD:	Tan.
TAIL:	Light tan elk hair.
BODY:	Light tannish gray deer body hair spun on and then clipped so it tapers towards the tail.
WINGS:	Light grizzly hackle tips tied upright and divided.
HACKLE:	Light ginger.

This is a variation of the Irrestible type flies and a good one. This pattern was originated by Harry Darbee of Livingston Manor, New York.

RED QUILL

HOOK:	Mustad 94840, sizes 12-18.
THREAD:	Brown.
WINGS:	Dyed gray hackle tips tied upright and divided.
TAIL:	Brown hackle fibers.
BODY:	Natural reddish brown neck hackle stem.
HACKLE:	Brown.

RED TRUDE

HOOK: Mustad 7957B, sizes 8-14.

THREAD: Brown.

TAIL: Brown elk hair.

RIBBING: Embossed silver tinsel.

BODY: Red wool yarn or dubbed fur.

WING: Red fox squirrel tail hair tied over body and extending to middle of tail.

HACKLE: Brown.

RED UPRIGHT

HOOK: Mustad 94840, sizes 12-18.

THREAD: Brown.

WINGS: Dyed gray hackle tips tied upright and divided.

TAIL: Brown hackle fibers.

BODY: Light peacock quill. Reverse wrap the body with fine gold wire.

HACKLE: Brown.

RENEGADE

HOOK: Mustad 94840, sizes 6-18.

THREAD: Black.

TIP: Flat gold tinsel.

REAR HACKLE: Brown.

BODY: Peacock herl. Reverse wrap the body with fine gold wire.

FRONT HACKLE: White.

The Renegade is probably used more than any other fly in the Rocky Mountain area. There are more variations (see wet flies) of this pattern than one could ever hope to catch up with.

REVEREND LANGE

HOOK: Mustad 7957B, sizes 8-14.

THREAD: Black.

WINGS: White calf tail tied upright and divided.

TAIL: White calf tail.

BODY: Dubbed black synthetic fur.

HACKLE: Furnace.

RIO GRANDE KING

HOOK: Mustad 94840, sizes 10-18.

THREAD: Brown.

WINGS: White duck quill sections tied upright and divided.

TIP: Flat gold tinsel.

TAIL: Golden pheasant tippet fibers.

BODY: Fine black chenille.

HACKLE: Brown.

RIO GRANDE KING TRUDE

HOOK: Mustad 7957B, sizes 6-14.

THREAD: Black.

TIP: Flat gold tinsel.

TAIL: Golden pheasant tippet fibers.

BODY: Fine black chenille.

WING: White calf tail tied over body and extending to end of tail.

HACKLE: Brown.

The Rio Grande King Trude is a very popular fly

throughout the west. Dan Bailey calls it O'Conner Rio Grande King. Dick O'Conner of Denver, Colorado, fishes this fly almost exclusively and catches more really big Browns in a year than most of us will ever hope to catch. In fact, most of us will never catch anything like he does. The March 1976 issue of *Field and Stream* announced his winning the freshwater fly category for Browns during 1975. He took a 9 pound 11 ounce Brown from Colorado's South Platte River. This is a small fish by the O'Conner standard, however. He has since taken a Brown over 12 pounds. It is thought that he fishes the fly just under the surface. Lots of folks try to duplicate his success with the pattern. Few make it.

ROYAL CUBBAGE

HOOK:	Mustad 94840, sizes 6-12.
THREAD:	Black.
TAILS:	Two fibers of peccary or moose body hair tied in long and widespread at each side.
BODY:	Royal Coachman style but with a new twist. The rear peacock herl is tied in at the rear before the tails. Then the tails are tied in at each side. Red floss is then tied in and wrapped to wing position.
HACKLE:	Brown tied Palmer over red floss only. There should be six or seven turns to give the fly good floating qualities.
WING:	White calf tail tied over the body and extending to the middle of the tail.
HEAD:	Peacock herl.

The Royal Cubbage is named after Tom Cubbage of Amarillo, Texas, who found the Colorado King dressings outfloated the Royal Wulff, but the Montana Browns liked the coloration of the Royal Wulff...hence the pattern.

SALMON FLY

HOOK:	Mustad 79580, sizes 4-8.
THREAD:	Brown.
TAIL:	Brown elk hair.
RIBBING:	Orange thread.
BODY:	Orange bucktail.
WING:	Brown elk hair.
TOPPING:	Fluorescent orange bucktail.
HEAD AND LEGS:	Dark brown elk hair.

Instructions for tying the Salmon Fly:

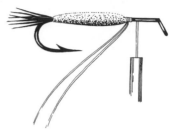

STEP 1: Tie in brown elk hair tail. Wrap an orange yarn underbody and tie in a double strand of orange tying thread.

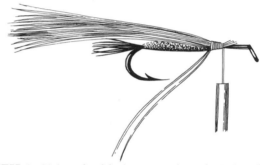

STEP 2: Using doubled orange thread, tie in a large bunch of orange bucktail at front of body.

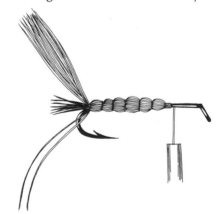

STEP 3: Wrap doubled orange thread to the rear forming a segmented body. Place a half hitch at the rear before completing step 4.

STEP 4: Pull remaining hair back over the body and wrap thread forward, following the same previously formed segments.

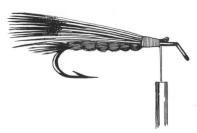

STEP 5: Tie in brown elk hair wing. Be sure to leave enough room for head.

STEP 6: Tie in flourescent orange bucktail topping (over-wing).

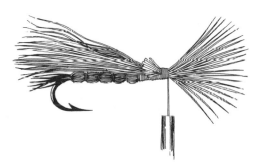

STEP 7: Tie in brown elk hair and clip butts short so they assist in forming base head. Hair should be long enough so that the points almost reach the point of the hook.

STEP 8: Pull hair back forming head and legs (hackle).

This pattern is another one of the Al Troth flies. This fly gives the most realistic silhouette of the large Stone Flies that I have yet encountered.

SIERRA DARK CADDIS

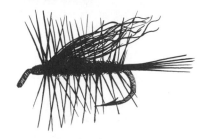

HOOK:	Mustad 94840, sizes 10-14.
THREAD:	Black.
TAIL:	Black hackle fibers.
BODY:	Dark brown wool yarn or dubbed synthetic fur.
HACKLE:	Black tied Palmer over the body.
WING:	Black calf tail tied over the body and extending to the end of the body.

I first became acquainted with this pattern as a boy while fishing the streams of Northern California. It has taken a number of fish for me through the years and I always try to be sure I have a few in one of my fly boxes. For some reason it works great over light colored hatches. The fish must single out the darker imitation in the middle of the lighter naturals because they strike it when nothing else will get their attention.

SOFA PILLOW, BROWN

HOOK:	Mustad 9672, sizes 4-10.
THREAD:	Brown.
TAIL:	Dyed crimson red goose quill section.
BODY:	Red floss tied thin.
WING:	Red fox squirrel tied over body and extending to the end of tail.
HACKLE:	Brown.

SOFA PILLOW, GRAY

HOOK:	Mustad 9672, sizes 4-10.
THREAD:	Gray.
TAIL:	Dyed yellow goose quill section.
BODY:	Yellow floss, tied thin.

WING: Gray squirrel tied over body and
              extending to the end of tail.

HACKLE: Grizzly.

SOFA PILLOW, IMPROVED

HOOK: Mustad 9672, sizes 4-10.

THREAD: Brown.

TAIL: Dyed orange elk hair tied short.

RIBBING: Brown hackle. Hackle should
              be tied in by the tip and
              extend slightly past point of hook.

BODY: Dubbed orange synthetic fur.

WING: Woodchuck tail hair tied over body
              and extending to the end of tail.

HACKLE: Brown.

NOTES: Hackle on all of the Sofa Pillows should be
tied extra thick and heavy.

During Stone Fly hatches in the Rocky Mountain
area these flies are very useful. These flies are far
from being good imitations of the Stone Flies but
when the trout start feeding on the naturals they
do not mind and grab madly at them as they hit the
water.

SPIDER, ADAMS HACKLE

HOOK: Mustad 94838, sizes 14-16.

THREAD: Brown.

TAIL: Grizzly and brown hackle fibers
              mixed and tied long.

BODY: Dubbed muskrat fur.

HACKLE: Brown and grizzly mixed.

SPIDER, BADGER

HOOK: Mustad 94838, sizes 14-16.

THREAD: Black.

TAIL: Badger hackle fibers tied long.

BODY: Black saddle hackle stem.

HACKLE: Badger.

NOTES: Make sure you select a clear silvery badger
hackle when tying this fly. It is intended to give the
impression of a tiny black hovering insect.

SPIDER, BLACK

HOOK: Mustad 94838, sizes 14-16.

THREAD: Black.

TAIL: Black hackle fibers tied long.

BODY: Black saddle hackle stem.

HACKLE: Black.

SPIDER, BLUE DUN

HOOK: Mustad 94838, sizes 14-16.

THREAD: Gray.

TAIL: Blue dun hackle fibers tied long.

BODY: Dubbed muskrat fur.

HACKLE: Blue dun.

SPIDER, BROWN

HOOK: Mustad 94838, sizes 14-16.

THREAD: Brown.

TAIL: Brown hackle fibers tied long.

BODY: Brown saddle hackle stem.

HACKLE: Brown.

SPIDER, DEER HAIR

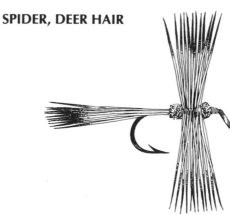

HOOK: Mustad 94838, sizes 12-16.

THREAD: Tan.

TAIL: Light tan elk hair.

HACKLE AND BODY: Deer hair.

NOTES: This unique pattern is very effective if it is
tied properly. The tail should be tied in about the
midsection of the hook. Then a small bunch of
deer hair is spun on the hook and tied in with
butts of hair toward the rear of the hook. An
additional small bunch of deer hair is spun on, just
forward of the first bunch, with butts toward the
front of the fly. Prior to tying in both bunches of
deer hair, the natural tips should be evened. They
should be tied in with the thought in your mind
that the flared tips, once they are tied in, will be
the hackle of the finished fly.

I have seen some feeble attempts to tie these flies for the commercial market. They merely have a bunch of deer hair spun on and clipped, leaving an unnatural hackle tip.

SPIDER, FURNACE

HOOK: Mustad 94838, sizes 14-16.

THREAD: Black.

TAIL: Furnace hackle fibers tied long.

BODY: Dubbed black fur.

HACKLE: Furnace.

SPIDER, GINGER

HOOK: Mustad 94838, sizes 14-16.

THREAD: Tan.

TAIL: Light ginger hackle fibers tied long.

BODY: Dubbed cream fur.

HACKLE: Light ginger.

SPIDER, GRIZZLY

HOOK: Mustad 94838, sizes 14-16.

THREAD: Gray.

TAIL: Grizzly hackle fibers tied long.

BODY: Grizzly saddle hackle stem.

HACKLE: Grizzly.

SPIDER, SKATER

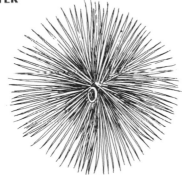

This is a fly design rather than a pattern. Edward Hewitt, one of the most inventive fly fishermen of all time, created this type of fly around 1935. Skater Spiders are tied on regular dry fly hooks in sizes 14 and below. They have no body and tail and have oversized hackles tied over the body. Hackle should be about the size of a silver dollar after it is wrapped. Hewitt's first Skaters were tied with large stiff spade hackles. Now they are generally tied with quality Indian saddle hackles. They can be tied in any color or combination of colors you fancy. They should be dressed heavy with several hackles. With a long rod which will handle a light line and a light breeze to assist you, these flies can be skated across the water surface with ease. Hewitt called this "butterfly fishing," believing that large trout mistake the skated spider for a butterfly.

SPIDER, TROTH HAIR

HOOK: Mustad 94840, sizes 12-14.

THREAD: Yellow.

TAIL: Deer hair tied rather heavy.

BODY: Yellow tying thread.

HACKLE: Deer hair.

NOTES: The hackle on the Troth Hair Spider is tied in with the butts toward the rear of the hook and then pushed upright and tied in place while forming the head.

This is one of the many highly productive flies developed by Al Troth of Dillon, Montana. This style of tying a Spider with deer hair affords the tyer the opportunity to change colors of tying thread to simulate a variety of hatches. Also, the deer hair can be dyed a wide range of colors.

NOTES: Neck hackle stems may be used on the spiders when saddle hackle stems are not available. Saddle hackle stems are recommended because of their finer stem which makes them more desirable on this type of body. The hackle on Spiders should be two times the size as that for the hook being used. That is, a hackle that is right for a size 10 hook is correct for a size 14 spider.

Spiders are tied to produce an illusion of tiny hovering insects. They are superior for hard-fished waters. I have never been able to come up with what could be called a standard Spider pattern. Sometimes they are tied with tinsel bodies. I feel that the "flashy" tinsel bodies are a thing of the past as far as spider bodies are concerned. They destroy the usefulness of the fly and the purpose for which the fly was intended. With less water available to us and more pressure on what we have the Spiders are often the only fly if you want success. After considerable experimentation in several areas with many materials and checking to see what others were doing in tying their Spiders, I was able to single out the best choice of body materials for each pattern. If fished properly, these patterns can really do the trick for you.

SPRUCE FLY

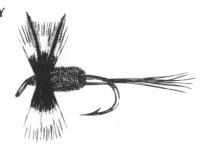

HOOK:	Mustad 94840, sizes 10-14.
THREAD:	Black.
WINGS:	Badger hackle tips tied upright and divided.
TAIL:	Dark moose body hair.
BODY:	Rear 1/3 red floss and front 2/3 peacock herl. Peacock herl portion of body should be reverse wrapped with fine gold wire.
HACKLE:	Badger.

SUNSET

HOOK:	Mustad 7957B, sizes 6-14.
THREAD:	Brown.
TAIL:	Hot orange elk hair.
RIBBING:	Dark ginger hackle tied Palmer over body.
BODY:	Hot orange wool yarn or dubbed synthetic fur.
WING:	Brown elk hair tied over the body and extending to the middle of tail.
HACKLE:	Dark ginger. This hackle is in addition to the Palmered hackle.

This pattern was originated in Oregon. This is the best pattern I have found for large Stone Fly hatches in Idaho and Montana.

SURESHOT

HOOK:	Mustad 7957B, sizes 8-14.
THREAD:	Brown.
WINGS:	White calf tail tied upright and divided.
TAIL:	White calf tail.
RIBBING:	Yellow floss.
BODY:	Peacock herl.

HACKLE:	Brown.

This pattern was developed by Roger Nash of Denver, Colorado. It is patterned after the Wulffs and is fairly popular in some parts of Colorado.

TETON SPECIAL

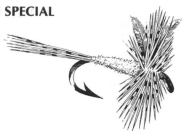

HOOK:	Mustad 94840, sizes 10-16.
THREAD:	Gray.
WINGS:	Ginger hackle tips tied upright and divided.
TAIL:	Ginger hackle fibers.
BODY:	Dubbed cream synthetic fur.
HACKLE:	Ginger and dyed light blue grizzly mixed.

This is another one of the Don Martinez patterns. I have heard some very big "fish stories" about this fly. It has proven to be a very successful pattern in most areas and a particular favorite of mine for Utah's Strawberry River.

TUPS INDISPENSABLE

HOOK:	Mustad 94840, sizes 12-18.
THREAD:	Tan.
TAIL:	Light ginger hackle fibers.
BODY:	Rear 1/3 yellow floss and front 2/3 dubbed red and yellow rabbit or synthetic fur mixed in equal parts.
HACKLE:	Light ginger.

VARIANT, BADGER

HOOK:	Mustad 94840, sizes 14-16.
THREAD:	Black.
WINGS:	Natural gray duck quill sections tied upright and divided.
TAIL:	Badger hackle fibers tied long.

RIBBING: Gray thread.

BODY: Black floss.

HACKLE: Badger.

VARIANT, BLACK

HOOK: Mustad 94840, sizes 14-16.

THREAD: Black.

WINGS: White duck quill sections tied upright and divided.

TAIL: Black hackle fibers tied long.

BODY: Black floss.

HACKLE: Black.

VARIANT, BLUE

HOOK: Mustad 94840, sizes 14-16.

THREAD: Black.

WINGS: Natural light gray duck quill sections tied upright and divided.

TAIL: Dyed light blue grizzly hackle fibers tied long.

BODY: Dark peacock quill. Reverse wrap the body with fine silver wire.

HACKLE: Dyed light blue grizzly.

VARIANT, BROWN

HOOK: Mustad 94840, sizes 14-16.

THREAD: Brown.

WINGS: Furnace hackle tips tied upright and divided.

TAIL: Brown hackle fibers tied long.

RIBBING: Orange thread.

BODY: Brown floss.

HACKLE: Brown.

VARIANT, DONNELLY'S DARK

HOOK: Mustad 94840, sizes 14-16.

THREAD: Black.

WINGS: Furnace hackle tips tied upright and divided.

TAIL: Brown hackle fibers tied long.

BODY: Dubbed muskrat fur.

HACKLE: Grizzly and brown mixed.

VARIANT, DONNELLY'S LIGHT

HOOK: Mustad 94840, sizes 14-16.

THREAD: White.

WINGS: Badger hackle tips tied upright and divided.

TAIL: Light ginger hackle fibers tied long.

BODY: Dubbed cream fur.

HACKLE: Light ginger and white mixed.

VARIANT, FURNACE

HOOK: Mustad 94840, sizes 14-16.

THREAD: Black.

WINGS: Natural dark gray duck quill sections tied upright and divided.

TAIL: Brown hackle fibers tied long.

BODY: Dubbed brown hare's ear fur.

HACKLE: Furnace.

VARIANT, GINGER

HOOK: Mustad 94840, sizes 14-16.

THREAD: Tan.

WINGS: Golden badger hackle tips tied upright and divided.

TAIL: Light ginger hackle fibers tied long.

BODY: Dubbed cream fur.

HACKLE: Light ginger.

VARIANT, HAIR WING

HOOK: Mustad 94840, sizes 12-14.

THREAD: Black.

WINGS: White calf tail tied upright and divided.

TAIL: White calf tail tied long.

BODY: Rear half dark peacock quill and front half peacock herl. Reverse wrap the body with fine gold wire.

HACKLE: Furnace.

This pattern is also known as House and Lot and H. L. Variant.

VARIANT, MULTI-COLOR

HOOK: Mustad 94840, sizes 14-16.

THREAD: Black.

WINGS: Natural gray duck quill sections tied upright and divided.

TAIL: Cree hackle fibers tied long.

RIBBING: Black thread.

BODY: Light orange floss.

HACKLE: Cree, black and white mixed.

VARIANT, RED

HOOK: Mustad 94840, sizes 14-16.

THREAD: Black.

WINGS: Barred lemon wood duck tied upright and divided.

TAIL: Coch-y-bondhu hackle fibers tied long.

BODY: Dark peacock quill. Reverse wrap the body with fine gold wire.

HACKLE: Coch-y-bondhu.

NOTES: Hackle length of the Variants should be the same as with the Spiders, two times the size as that is required for the hook being used. Except for the Hair Wing Variant wing length should only be half the length of the hackle barbles.

The Variants have been with us a good number of years. If tied correctly they are some good high floating flies which respresent tiny hovering insects.

WEST YELLOWSTONE

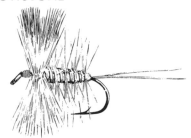

HOOK: Mustad 94840, sizes 6-10.

THREAD: Tan.

WINGS: Light tannish gray deer body hair tied upright and divided.

TAILS: Two ginger hackle stems tied in a V.

RIBBING: Ginger hackle stem. Also, a ginger hackle tied Palmer over the body. The barbles are stripped off from one side of the hackle before it is wrapped. This hackle should be short and wrapped between the first ribbing.

BODY: Dubbed yellow synthetic fur.

HACKLE: Ginger.

This pattern was originated by Letcher Lambuth.

WHIRLING BLUE

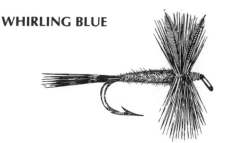

HOOK: Mustad 94840, sizes 10-18.

THREAD: Brown.

WINGS: Blue dun hackle tips tied upright and divided.

TAIL: Dyed brown grizzly hackle fibers.

BODY: Dubbed muskrat fur.

HACKLE: Dark ginger.

A good general purpose fly for many of the darker hatches. This is my favorite for fishing the upper part of the Snake River.

WHITCRAFT

HOOK: Mustad 94840, sizes 12-18.

THREAD: Brown.

WINGS: Grizzly hackle tips tied upright and divided.

TAIL: Brown hackle fibers.

BODY: Two brown and one yellow moose mane fibers wrapped together. Reverse wrap the body with fine gold wire.

HACKLE: Brown and grizzly mixed.

Another Don Martinez pattern.

WHITE MILLER

HOOK:	Mustad 94840, sizes 10-18.
THREAD:	White.
WINGS:	White duck quill sections tied upright and divided.
TAIL:	White hackle fibers.
RIBBING:	Flat silver tinsel.
BODY:	White floss.
HACKLE:	White.

This is an old standby pattern and good during minimal light conditions. It is often tied with a scarlet red hackle fiber tail.

WICKHAM'S FANCY

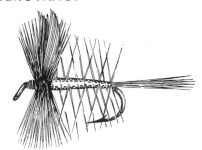

HOOK:	Mustad 94840, sizes 10-16.
THREAD:	Brown.
WINGS:	Natural gray duck quill sections tied upright and divided.
TAIL:	Brown hackle fibers.
RIBBING:	Brown hackle tied over body Palmer style.
BODY:	Embossed gold tinsel.
HACKLE:	Brown.

WILLOW

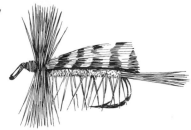

HOOK:	Mustad 9671, sizes 8-12.
THREAD:	Brown.
TAIL:	Dark ginger hackle fibers.
RIBBING:	Dark ginger hackle tied Palmer over body. Hackle should be short and not extend past the point of the hook. Clip off the top after wrapping.
BODY:	Dubbed yellowish olive synthetic fur.

WINGS:	Ringneck hen pheasant wing quill sections dyed ginger and tied tent style over body. Wings should be tied in by their tips, and butts trimmed to shape after fly is completed. Wings should extend to the bend of the hook.
HACKLE:	Dark ginger.

WOODCHUCK CADDIS

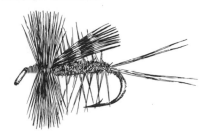

HOOK:	Mustad 9671, sizes 10-16.
THREAD:	Brown.
TAILS:	Brown elk hair tied in at each side and tied long and widespread. Use two or three hairs on each side. This gives the fly good stability on heavy water.
RIBBING:	Dark ginger variant hackle tied in at front of tails and tied Palmer over the body. Palmered hackle should be short and not extend much past point of hook.
BODY:	Dubbed woodchuck fur with guard hairs removed.
WING:	Woodchuck tail hair tied over body and extending to the end of the body.
HACKLE:	Dark ginger variant tied on as a collar in front of wing.

This is an extremely effective fly, and it is one of the better floating caddis imitations available.

WULFF, BLACK

HOOK:	Mustad 7957B, sizes 8-14.
THREAD:	Black.
WINGS:	Black moose hair tied upright and divided.
TAIL:	Black moose hair.
BODY:	Pink floss.
HACKLE:	Furnace.

NOTES: Black calf tail is often substituted for moose hair on this pattern.

WULFF, BLONDE

HOOK:	Mustad 7957B, sizes 8-14.

THREAD: Tan.

WING: Tan elk hair tied upright and divided.

TAIL: Tan elk hair.

BODY: Light tan dubbed fur.

HACKLE: Light ginger.

WULFF, BROWN

HOOK: Mustad 7957B, sizes 8-14.

THREAD: Black.

WINGS: Brown calf tail tied upright and divided.

TAIL: Brown calf tail.

BODY: Cream dubbed fur.

HACKLE: Badger.

WULFF, BROWN

HOOK: Mustad 7957B, sizes 8-14.

THREAD: Brown.

WINGS: Brown calf tail or bear tied upright and divided.

TAIL: Brown calf tail or bear hair.

BODY: Brown wool yarn or dubbed fur.

HACKLE: Brown.

This is an alternate pattern of the Brown Wulff which I find to be more in use than the original.

WULFF, GRAY

HOOK: Mustad 7957B, sizes 8-14.

THREAD: Gray.

WINGS: Natural brown bucktail tied upright and divided.

TAIL: Natural brown bucktail.

BODY: Blue gray wool yarn.

HACKLE: Blue dun.

NOTES: Woodchuck tail hair or bear hair makes a better wing and tail for this pattern.

WULFF, GRIZZLY

HOOK: Mustad 7957B, sizes 8-14.

THREAD: Brown.

WINGS: Natural brown bucktail tied upright and divided.

TAIL: Natural brown bucktail.

BODY: Light yellow floss.

HACKLE: Grizzly and brown mixed.

NOTES: Brown calf tail is preferred over the natural brown bucktail.

WULFF, ROYAL

HOOK: Mustad 7957B, sizes 8-14.

THREAD: Brown.

WINGS: White bucktail tied upright and divided.

TAIL: Deer body hair.

BODY: Royal Coachman style with peacock herl with red floss center band. Reverse wrap the body with fine gold wire.

HACKLE: Brown.

NOTES: White calf tail is generally used for wings on the western dressings of this pattern.

WULFF, WHITE

HOOK: Mustad 7957B, sizes 8-14.

THREAD: Black.

WINGS: White bucktail tied upright and divided.

TAIL: White bucktail.

BODY: Cream dubbed fur.

HACKLE: Badger.

NOTES: White calf tail is considered a better material for the wings and tail on this fly.

These are the original patterns that were created by Lee Wulff and later expanded upon and popularized in the west by Dan Bailey. I have listed what I feel are improvements over the original dressings. These improvements are not necessarily my own ideas since most have been in general use for many years. There are dozens of variations of the Wulff flies.

YELLOW DUN

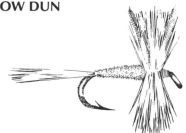

HOOK:	Mustad 94840, sizes 12-14.
THREAD:	Yellow.
WINGS:	Dyed gray hackle tips tied upright and divided.
TAIL:	Ginger hackle fibers.
BODY:	Dubbed pale yellow rabbit or synthetic fur.
HACKLE:	Ginger.

YELLOW FORKED TAIL

HOOK:	Mustad 94840, sizes 10-14.
THREAD:	Gray.
WINGS:	Natural gray duck quill sections tied upright and divided.
TAIL:	Barred mallard fibers. Tail should be twice the length of body and tied in a V. Fibers should be treated with a thin solution of head cement so they will better support the fly.
BODY:	Rear ⅓ light green floss and front ⅔ yellow floss.
HACKLE:	Grizzly.

This fly originated in Northern California and has been in use for a number of years. It is also referred to as California Forked Tail.

YELLOW STONE FLY

HOOK:	Mustad 79580, sizes 6-10.
THREAD:	Brown.
TAIL:	Brown elk hair.
RIBBING:	Yellow thread.
BODY:	Yellow bucktail.
WING:	Brown elk hair.
TOPPING:	Fluorescent yellow bucktail.

HEAD AND LEGS: Dark brown elk hair.

NOTES: See *Salmon Fly* for tying instructions.

This pattern is very useful during hatches of the Yellow Stone Fly. It was also developed by Al Troth.

THE WATERWALKERS

For well over one hundred years the American fly fisherman has been trying to develop the ultimate dry fly. Theodore Gordon and others brought dozens of English patterns on to the scene and many American fly-tyers have borrowed from our European predecessors for several decades. Every now and then I latch on to a fly pattern or tying technique which is professed by its originator to be something entirely new only later to find out that it is only an old idea re-born. I have seen so many variations of the Renegade and Coachman alone that I often wonder in amazement.

When the No-Hackles were first introduced I tried to accept them with an open mind. I was immediately impressed with the extensive aquatic insect research and the importance stressed on proper fly design—a design which would give the correct field of vision to the fish so they would see our imitations on the water as they see the naturals. But when I tied and tried the new No-Hackle style they just would not stay afloat well on our average western streams and rivers.

I still liked the idea though, and decided it was time to take the designs that were offered back to the drawing board. With some adjustments in materials I started dressing the duns in the conventional dry fly style. This proved to be successful to a degree, they floated, but this still did not put the fly in the "trouts window" where it belonged. I tried clipping off the hackle barbles on the bottom of our conventionally hackled dry flies but they only soaked up quickly and I would have been better off if the hackle had been left off entirely. I also tried to trim out a V on the bottom of the fly but this still did not do the trick. It did not get the fly down into the window the way I really wanted it. With this method I also had trouble in obtaining good balance because of the varying textures of the hackle. If we can ever develop a breed of chickens which will grow their hackle barbles at a 90 degree angle to the stem then the V method of trimming may have some application in good fly tying.

I had fairly well given up the whole idea of getting anything close to what one might call a more perfect dry fly design and once more turned my thinking back along the lines of conventional dry fly designs. I simply lack the imagination that many others possess. Then one day a new fly pattern came to me in the mail. It had been sent by my good friend Frank Johnson of Streamside Anglers in Missoula, Montana. It was an extended body Blue Dun tied in what he called the Waterwalker style. I was later to realize that it simply could not have been named anything else. This was without a doubt the finest design for a May Fly imitation I had ever seen. After examining it for some time my only reaction was "I'll be darn, why didn't I think of that?" The same reaction was also expressed by many others when I showed them the new creation. What is that, a double parachute? That it was—and everyone was scampering home to try tying their own Waterwalkers. They had been there before us all of the time yet none of us were creative enough to see something so simple. Old Frank, or Mister Waterwalker as I refer to him now, had been enjoying fishing his little creations for some time and had not given much thought to the fact that he had really created something completely new. Not at least until one day during a winter slack period he received my letter asking, "what's new?" You can be sure I will be asking him that question more often now. He is one who has never been satisfied with the old standards and is continually striving to improve upon every pattern he ties. No one can argue with his high rate of success either. Frank and his partner Rich Anderson probably catch more fish than anyone in the state of Montana. Frank is a very talented fly-tyer who has not let tradition bind his innovative methods. Personally, I feel this is one of the most important contributions to fly-tying to have appeared in my life time. It is not just another re-introduction of an old idea which has been abandoned a century or more before.

There is a considerable amount of mixed emotion over this new design because of the added labor involved in tying dries in this style. This is basically coming from the commercial side, the people who have to tie and market the flies and not from the fishermen who fish them. The No-Hackles are a mere breeze to tie but I have never seen a May Fly, or any other insect for that matter, standing on the water without legs under it for support.

The Waterwalkers style gives our imitations the most realistic silhouette yet to be conceived. Now we at last have imitations which stand on the water, not lay on it, in a natural field of vision. After an additional season of testing and altering materials to suit this new design concept, it was possible to develop some very effective patterns which were suited to conditions in both the east and west. Because of this new method of hackling a dry fly the Mustad 94833, 3X fine wire hooks were essentially out-the-window and no longer required as they were with the No-Hackles. I hate to think of the fish that I have lost because of that hook. Standard fine wire dry fly hooks could now be used. Improved hooking qualities of the fly was now also possible by using one size larger of the Mustad 94838 style hooks. Rather than tying a size 16 on a regular shanked Mustad 94840 hook, it was now possible to use a size 14 Mustad 94838 hook and still duplicate the size of the imitation we were trying to match. Also, it was really unnecessary to tie the extended body style of May Flies since the Mustad 9671, 2X long shanked hooks could be used. During the development of many of the Waterwalker style patterns synthetic dubbing materials were the natural body materials for us to select. The blending of the synthetics allowed us to give these patterns the true colors they demanded to make them appear more natural.

When I was a boy my father demonstrated to me the procedure for testing a quality dry fly. He would drop a fly on the counter top and if it was properly balanced and had good stiff hackle it was supposed to land perfectly upright. Unfortunately this did not always happen even with the best dressed dry flies. Try this little trick with a Waterwalker—they land upright each and every time. Better yet, tie up a selection and use them on your next trip and you will be as hooked on them as I am. This revolutionary new design is excellent any place in the world where dry flies are used and I am sure that we will be using this style for many years to come.

Instructions for tying May Fly imitations using the Waterwalker design:

STEP 1: Select a small bunch of hair and even the tips. Tie in at the winging position, about ⅓ back on the hook shank. Wings should be tied upright and divided. Wrap a good solid figure eight between the wings when dividing them. Wrap slightly up each wing to form a good base, wraping post, for hackles. Wings should be positioned straight up and not slanting slightly forward. Slanting them forward gives one a pigeon-toed Waterwalker. The angle between the wings should be approximately 70 degrees rather than the customary 40 or 50 degrees. This is important because the wings act as the wrapping posts for the hackles / legs. The angle of the wings affects how your fly rests on the water.

STEP 2: Return tying thread to the rear of the hook shank and tie in a small ball of dubbing material.

STEP 3: Tie in tailing material at each side of the hook. Wrap fibers up close to the ball of dubbing material so they are widespread rather than sticking straight back. I prefer this style of tail on many of my dry flies as it assists in stabilizing the fly on the water; however, I revert to conventional tails on many of the smaller sizes.

STEP 4: Return tying thread to the front of the fly and tie in hackles. Insure that the hackles selected have barbles of equal length. This is an important part of constructing a well balanced fly when finished. If the hackle barbles are shorter on one side it is much like having one leg shorter than the other.

STEP 5: Return tying thread to the rear of the hook and complete the dubbing of the body. Dubbing material should be applied over the entire body area to just slightly behind the eye of the hook. Because of the additional build-up of thread at the base of the wings you will find this to be slightly enlarged, thus giving you a more life-like thorax on your Waterwalker. This is another point that really sells me on the design.

STEP 6: Wrap the hackle farthest away from you first. This gives you better vision of what you are doing when the second hackle is wrapped. The hackle farthest from you should be wrapped counter-clockwise and the hackle closest to you should be wrapped clockwise. You should have

both hackle tips coming out from the center of the wings, not from the sides, after hackle is wrapped. At the beginning you will possibly have problems with wrapping down some of the hackle barbles. Do not let this concern you as the hackle can easily be picked out with the bodkin after the fly is completed. Based on the size of the fly you are tying and the area you intend to fish it you will have to make the judgement as to how much hackle you want on your fly. I find that four or five turns of hackle around each wing is just about right for most general conditions. The point to keep utmost in your mind is that each wing should have an equal number of turns of hackle around it to maintain a good balance of the finished fly.

Front view of finished fly.

The following patterns are representative of the major hatches that are found primarily throughout the middle west and western states. Also included are some eastern patterns which have proven to be highly successful most any place they are used. Of course there are several others, but these are the primary hatches which you are most likely to encounter. Emergence dates are approximate. Variances in altitude and climate play an important role in periods of emergence of all insects. It is interesting to discover that a hatch which occurred on a particular stream one week will occur some three or four weeks later five miles up the stream and some 1,500 feet higher. Also, a hatch can be delayed by several weeks on the basis of cool weather and a late spring.

BLACK DRAKE

Epeorus nitidus

Emergence period: June-July.

HOOK:	Mustad 94840, sizes 10-14.
THREAD:	Gray.
WINGS:	Dyed dark gray elk hair tied upright and divided.
TAILS:	Dyed gray elk hair tied in at each side and tied widespread.
BODY:	Dubbed claret synthetic fur.

HACKLE:	Dyed gray tied Waterwalker style.

BLACK QUILL

Leptophlebia cupida

Emergence period: April-August

HOOK:	Mustad 94840, sizes 12-14.
THREAD:	Black.
WINGS:	Dark brown elk hair tied upright and divided.
TAILS:	Dyed dark gray elk hair tied in at each side and tied widespread.
BODY:	Dubbed dark brown synthetic fur.
HACKLE:	Dark blue dun tied Waterwalker style.

BLUE WINGED OLIVE

Baetis (Approximately 20 species)

Emergence period: April-October

HOOK:	Mustad 94838, sizes 12-16.
THREAD:	Brown.
WINGS:	Dyed gray elk hair tied upright and divided.
TAIL:	Dyed light gray hackle fibers.
BODY:	Dubbed brown olive synthetic fur.
HACKLE:	Dyed light gray tied Waterwalker style.

BROWN DRAKE

Ephemera simulans

Emergence period: May-July

HOOK:	Mustad 94840, sizes 10-12.
THREAD:	Brown.

WINGS: Dyed dark gray elk hair tied upright
          and divided.

TAIL: Coastal blacktail deer body hair
          tied in at each side and tied
          widespread.

BODY: Dubbed dark brown, light gray and
          yellow synthetic fur mixed in
          equal parts.

HACKLE: Dyed brown grizzly tied
          Waterwalker style.

BROWN STONE

Taeniopteryx fasciata

Emergence period: June-July

HOOK: Mustad 94840, size 14.

THREAD: Gray.

TAIL: Dyed gray ginger hackle fibers.

BODY: Dubbed light seal brown and
          gold synthetic fur mixed
          in equal parts.

HACKLE: Dyed gray ginger variant tied
          Waterwalker style. Clip off
          hackle barbles on top.

WINGS: Two dyed gray ginger variant hackle
          tips tied flat over the body.

The following instructions will assist you in tying the Brown Stone. They will also assist in tying the Green and Yellow Stones which follow:

STEP 2: Wrap thread to the rear of the body and tie in the tail. Tail should be rather heavy.

STEP 3: Dub the body from the rear to the front, just leaving enough room for the head.

STEP 1: Select two matching hackles and strip off the bottom fluff and softer barbles. Tie the hackle in by the butts. The butts should be wrapped with a figure eight and positioned upright and divided as they will serve as wrapping posts for the hackle.

STEP 4: Wrap hackles around the butts of the protruding hackle stems.

STEP 5: Clip off all hackle barbles on the top of the fly.

STEP 6: Bend the butts forward and tie down. Place a drop of head cement at the base of each hackle stem.

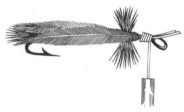

STEP 7: Tie in the wings. Concave side of hackle tips should be down.

STEP 8: Tie off the head and apply head cement.

DARK BLUE QUILL
Paraleptophlebia packi
Emergence period: July-August

HOOK:	Mustad 94838, sizes 12-14.
THREAD:	**Gray.**

WINGS:	Dyed dark gray elk hair tied upright and divided.
TAILS:	Dyed dark gray elk hair tied in at each side and tied widespread.
BODY:	Dubbed olive dun synthetic fur.
HACKLE:	Dyed dark blue dun tied Waterwalker style.

DARK RED QUILL
Cinygmula ramaleyi
Emergence period: May-June

HOOK:	Mustad 94838, sizes 14-16.
THREAD:	Brown.
WINGS:	Dyed dark gray elk hair tied upright and divided.
TAIL:	Brown hackle fibers.
BODY:	Dubbed seal brown synthetic fur.
HACKLE:	Brown tied Waterwalker style.

DARK STONE
Pteronarcys californica
Emergence period: May-June

HOOK:	Mustad 9672, sizes 6-8.
THREAD:	Brown.
TAIL:	Dark brown elk hair tied short.
BODY:	Orange bucktail.
HACKLE:	Dark brown tied Waterwalker style.
WING:	Dark brown bucktail.

The following instructions will assist you in tying the Dark Stone. They will also assist in tying the Golden Stone and Peregrine Hopper:

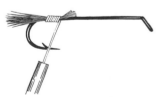

STEP 1: Tie in tailing material. The tail should be rather heavy.

STEP 2: Wrap an underbody of either art foam or poly yarn. Try to use a color which will match the color of the body.

STEP 5: Pull hair forward back over the body and wrap thread following the same segments. FOR THE DARK STONE ONLY: Mark the outer part of segmented body with a waterproof brown marker.

STEP 3: Tie in two matching hackles by the butts. The butts should be wrapped with a figure eight and positioned upright and divided as they will serve as wrapping posts for the hackle. Tie in a loop of thread to match the color of the body material being used. Tie in a large bunch of hair for the body.

STEP 6: Wrap hackles around the butts of the protruding hackle stems.

STEP 7: Clip off hackle barbles on the top of fly.

STEP 4: Pull the hair down around the body and through the wrapping posts and wrap thread to the rear forming a segmented body.

STEP 8: Bend the butts forward and tie down. Place a drop of head cement on the base of each hackle stem.

STEP 9: Select a bunch of hair, even the tips and tie in.

STEP 10: Tie off the head and apply head cement.

GOLDEN STONE

Acroneuria californica

Emergence period: May-June

HOOK:	Mustad 9672, sizes 6-8.
THREAD:	Tan.
TAIL:	Dyed gold elk hair tied short.
BODY:	Dyed gold bucktail.
HACKLE:	Dyed gold grizzly tied Waterwalker style.
WING:	Dyed gold natural brown bucktail.

GORDON QUILL

Epeorus pleuralis

Emergence period: April-May

HOOK:	Mustad 94840, sizes 12-14.
THREAD:	Brown.
WINGS:	Dyed dark gray elk hair tied upright and divided.
TAILS:	Tan elk hair tied in at each side and tied widespread.
BODY:	Dubbed dark brown and pale yellow synthetic fur mixed in equal parts.
HACKLE:	Dyed dark blue dun tied Waterwalker style.

GRAY DRAKE

Siphlonurus columbianus and *occidentalis*

Emergence period: June-October

HOOK:	Mustad 9671, sizes 10-14.
THREAD:	Brown.
WINGS:	Dyed dark gray elk hair tied upright and divided.
TAILS:	Dyed dark gray elk hair tied in at each side and tied widespread.
RIBBING:	Dyed brown round monofilament. Rib body only to the back of wings.
BODY:	Dubbed gray synthetic fur.
HACKLE:	Dyed dark gray tied Waterwalker style.

GREAT RED QUILL

Ephemerella hecuba

Emergence period: July-August

HOOK:	Mustad 94840, sizes 10-12.
THREAD:	Tan.
WINGS:	Dyed gray elk hair tied upright and divided.
TAILS:	Natural light tan elk hair tied in at each side and tied widespread.
RIBBING:	Dyed brown round monofilament. Rib body only to the back of wings.
BODY:	Dubbed tan synthetic fur.
HACKLE:	Light ginger tied Waterwalker style.

GREEN DRAKE

Ephemerella grandis

Emergence period: June-July

HOOK:	Mustad 9671, sizes 10-12.
THREAD:	Brown.

WINGS:	Natural dark brown elk hair tied upright and divided.
TAILS:	Dyed olive elk hair tied in at each side and tied widespread.
RIBBING:	Dyed brown round monofilament. Rib body only to the back of wings.
BODY:	Dubbed green synthetic fur.
HACKLE:	Dyed olive tied Waterwalker style.

GREEN STONE

Alloperla imbecilla

Emergence period: May-July

HOOK:	Mustad 9672, sizes 12-14.
THREAD:	Green.
TAILS:	Dyed green elk hair tied in at each side and tied widespread.
BODY:	Dubbed light green synthetic fur.
HACKLE:	Light green tied Waterwalker style.
WINGS:	Two grizzly hackle tips tied flat over the body.

NOTES: See Brown Stone for tying instructions.

HENDRICKSON

Ephemerella subvaria

Emergence period: April-June

HOOK:	Mustad 94840, sizes 12-14.
THREAD:	Black.
WINGS:	Dyed dark gray elk hair tied upright and divided.
TAILS:	Dyed dark gray elk hair tied in at each side and tied widespread.
BODY:	Dubbed seal brown, olive, tan and yellow synthetic fur mixed in equal parts.
HACKLE:	Dark blue dun tied Waterwalker style.

LEADWING COACHMAN

Isonychia bicolor

Emergence period: May-September

HOOK:	Mustad 94840, sizes 10-12.
THREAD:	Brown.
WINGS:	Dyed dark gray elk hair tied upright and divided.
TAILS:	Brown elk hair tied in at each side and tied widespread.
BODY:	Seal brown synthetic fur.
HACKLE:	Dark blue dun tied Waterwalker style.

LIGHT CAHILL

Stenomena canadense

Emergence period: May-August

HOOK:	Mustad 94840, sizes 12-14.
THREAD:	Tan.
WINGS:	Barred mallard fibers tied upright and divided.
TAIL:	Tan elk hair.
BODY:	Dubbed tan and cream synthetic fur mixed in equal parts.
HACKLE:	Light ginger.

MAHOGANY DUN

Paraleptophlebia adoptiva

Emergence period: April-June

HOOK:	Mustad 94038, sizes 14-16.
THREAD:	Brown.
WINGS:	Dyed dark gray elk hair tied upright and divided.
TAIL:	Brown hackle fibers.
BODY:	Dubbed seal brown and light olive synthetic fur mixed in equal parts.
HACKLE:	Dark blue dun tied Waterwalker style.

MARCH BROWN (AMERICAN)

Stenonema vicarium

Emergence period: May-July

HOOK:	Mustad 94840, sizes 10-14.
THREAD:	Brown.
WINGS:	Dyed light olive elk hair tied upright and divided.
TAILS:	Brown elk hair tied in at each side and tied widespread.
BODY:	Dubbed seal brown and light gold synthetic fur mixed in equal parts.

HACKLE: Light ginger variant tied Waterwalker style.

OLIVE DUN

Rhithrogena hageni

Emergence period: July-August

HOOK: Mustad 94838, sizes 12-14.

THREAD: Olive.

WINGS: Dyed gray elk hair tied upright and divided.

TAILS: Dyed dark olive elk hair tied in at each side and tied widespread.

BODY: Dubbed brown olive synthetic fur.

HACKLE: Dyed dark olive tied Waterwalker style.

PALE EVENING DUN

Ephemerella dorothea

Emergence period: May-July

HOOK: Mustad 94838, sizes 14-16.

THREAD: Tan.

WINGS: Tan elk hair tied upright and divided.

TAIL: Light ginger hackle fibers.

BODY: Yellowish olive synthetic fur.

HACKLE: Light ginger tied Waterwalker style.

PALE MORNING DUN

Ephemerella lacustris

Emergence period: June-July

HOOK: Mustad 94838, sizes 14-16.

THREAD: Olive.

WINGS: Dyed gray elk hair tied upright and divided.

TAIL: Light olive hackle fibers.

BODY: Dubbed yellowish olive synthetic fur.

HACKLE: Dyed light olive tied Waterwalker style.

PEREGRINE HOPPER

HOOK: Mustad 9672, sizes 6-14.

THREAD: Brown.

TAIL: Small bunch of crimson red deer hair over which a large bunch of light yellow deer hair is tied in.

BODY: Light yellow bucktail.

HACKLE: Dark ginger variant tied Waterwalker style.

WINGS: Hen ringneck pheasant quill section tied in at each side with natural brown bucktail tied in over the top.

NOTES: See Dark Stone for tying instructions.

RED DUN

Rhithrogene hageni

Emergence period: July-August

HOOK: Mustad 94838, sizes 12-14.

THREAD: Brown.

WINGS: Dyed gray elk hair upright and divided.

TAILS: Brown elk hair tied in at each side and tied widespread.

BODY: Dubbed with rusty red, seal brown and gold synthetic fur mixed in equal parts.

HACKLE: Dark ginger tied Waterwalker style.

SLATE BROWN DUN

Epeorus longimanus

Emergence period: June-July

HOOK:	Mustad 94840, size 14.
THREAD:	Gray.
WINGS:	Dyed dark gray elk hair tied upright and divided.
TAIL:	Dyed gray hackle fibers.
BODY:	Dubbed blue dun synthetic fur.
HACKLE:	Dyed gray tied Waterwalker style.

SLATE CREAM DUN

Epeorus albertae

Emergence period: July-August

HOOK:	Mustad 94838, sizes 12-14.
THREAD:	Gray.
WINGS:	Dyed gray elk hair tied upright and divided.
TAIL:	Tan elk hair tied in at each side and tied widespread.
BODY:	Dubbed pink and gray synthetic fur mixed in equal parts.
HACKLE:	Dyed gray tied Waterwalker style.

SLATE GRAY DUN

Heptagenia elegantula

Emergence period: August-September

HOOK:	Mustad 94838, sizes 12-14.
THREAD:	Gray.

WINGS:	Dyed dark gray elk hair tied upright and divided.
TAIL:	Dyed gray elk hair tied in at each side and tied widespread.
BODY:	Dubbed olive dun synthetic fur.
HACKLE:	Dyed gray tied Waterwalker style.

SLATE WINGED OLIVE

Ephemerella flavilinea

Emergence period: June-August

HOOK:	Mustad 94838, sizes 12-14.
THREAD:	Gray.
WINGS:	Dyed dark gray elk hair tied upright and divided.
TAIL:	Dyed dark olive elk hair tied in at each side and tied widespread.
BODY:	Dubbed olive synthetic fur.
HACKLE:	Dyed dark olive tied Waterwalker style.

SPECKLED DUN

Callibaetis coloradensis

Emergence period: June-September

HOOK:	Mustad 94838, sizes 12-14.
THREAD:	Brown.
WINGS:	Dyed gray elk hair tied upright and divided.
TAIL:	Tan elk hair tied in at each side and tied widespread.
BODY:	Dubbed brown olive synthetic fur.
HACKLE:	Cream tied Waterwalker style.

YELLOW STONE

Isoperla bilineata and *marmona*

Emergence period: June-August

HOOK:	Mustad 9672, sizes 12-14.

THREAD: Yellow.

TAILS: Dark tan elk hair tied in at
                 each side and tied widespread.

BODY: Dubbed ⅔ yellow rabbit and ⅓
                 insect green synthetic fur mixed.

HACKLE: Lemon yellow tied Waterwalker
                 style.

WINGS: Two deep yellow hackle tips tied
                 flat over the body.

NOTES: See Brown Stone for tying instructions.

NOTES: No. 14 gray Rit dye is ideal for obtaining proper wing color for the patterns listed. Use light tan elk hair to obtain light gray and gray wings. Use brown elk hair for the dark gray wings. Just tint the hair with a pinch of dye in the dye bath to get a good light gray.

Mr. Waterwalker, Frank Johnson, ties some extended body May Fly imitations which work wonders in his area and, because of their natural coloration, they should be good almost anywhere. Frank uses hollow hair for constructing the underbody and tail on his flies. The internal body of hair gives these flies a very desirable floating quality that is not found in most other extended body dry flies.

BROWN WATERWALKER

HOOK: Mustad 94838, sizes 10-14.

THREAD: Brown.

WINGS: Brown elk hair tied upright and
                 divided.

TAIL AND UNDERBODY: Moose hair.

BODY: Dubbed seal brown synthetic fur.

HACKLE: Brown tied Waterwalker style.

CREAM WATERWALKER

HOOK: Mustad 94838, sizes 10-14.

THREAD: Light yellow.

WINGS: Light tan elk hair tied upright
                 and divided.

TAIL AND UNDERBODY: Light tan elk hair.

BODY: Dubbed cream synthetic fur.

HACKLE: Cream tied Waterwalker style.

GRAY WATERWALKER

HOOK: Mustad 94838, sizes 10-14.

THREAD: Gray.

WINGS: Coastal blacktail deer body
                 hair tied upright and divided.

TAIL AND UNDERBODY: Moose hair.

BODY: Dubbed gray synthetic fur.

HACKLE: Grizzly.

OLIVE WATERWALKER

HOOK: Mustad 94838, sizes 10-14.

THREAD: Olive.

WINGS: Brown elk hair tied upright and
                 divided.

TAIL AND UNDERBODY: Moose hair.

BODY: Dubbed olive synthetic fur.

HACKLE: Dyed olive badger.

Frank's feeling, which I wholeheartedly share, is that the use of synthetic dubbing furs and hollow hair, along with the many new types of dry fly floatants has opened up new frontiers for the creative fly-tyer. Elk hair can be substituted with deer hair on any of the Waterwalkers. And you are not confined to just tying the patterns listed. If you will think for a minute, all of the Wulff patterns are easily adapted to this style. Also, by using the tying method for the Dark Stone and using the hackle stem as a wrapping post for your hackle, the adaptations are endless. Any delicate winged dry fly pattern can be tied in the Waterwalker fashion.

NYMPHS, LARVAE AND FRESH WATER SHRIMP

It has been estimated that approximately 85 to 90% of a trout's diet is made up of aquatic insects in their nymphal and larval stage of underwater life. They are available to the fish for months and months before their brief hatching period. Nymph imitations often produce when other types of flies will not. Numerous Stone Fly, Caddis Fly, May Fly, etc., patterns have been created in all parts of the country. As a result of the concentrated interest in the development of new patterns, little has been accomplished with respect to the standardization of the patterns. Due to the different stages of growth and the wide variations in coloration from one area to another it is most doubtful that any true standardization will ever be possible. I am listing some of the more important patterns we have today. Also included are patterns for the aquatic animal, the fresh water shrimp or scud, a crustacean. Many of the nymph patterns do a splendid job of simulating the shrimp; however, if you are fishing in water which you believe harbor the shrimp it is recommended you use patterns which more closely duplicate them. Usually when they are present they are found in large quantity and they rate high on the trout's menu.

When tying the majority of the following patterns you should give serious consideration to the weighting of your flies to assist in sinking them down to a level where the fish are feeding. Naturally this is an individual judgment each tyer must make on his own based on the type of water he fishes and the type of imitation he is presenting. It would be rather fruitless, in most cases, for an angler to cast stone fly nymphs into a large swift river if they were not sweeping the bottom where the naturals are generally found. The following lead wire sizes are recommended as a general guide in selecting weight compatible with hook size:

Hook Sizes	Wire Size
16-28	.011"
12-14	.016"
8-10	.025"
6 and larger	.031"

ALPINE EMERGER

HOOK:	Mustad 3906, sizes 16-18.
THREAD:	Gray.
TAIL:	Dyed blue dun barred mallard fibers tied sparse.
BODY:	Dubbed blue dun synthetic fur.
LEGS:	Dyed blue dun barred mallard fibers tied in at each side and extending half the length of body.

This fly is the most effective I have found for high mountain lakes. I first came in contact with the pattern on Northern Washington's Ross Lake. Since that time I have found it very productive in Wyoming, Utah, Idaho, and California. It is the only fly that I can get the large cutthroat in Wyoming's Snowy Range to take consistently. The Alpine Emerger was originated by Carl Glisson of Pinole, California. Carl is an ardent fly fisherman and fly-tyer who chases trout all over the west. His wife explains that everytime she goes into a department store with him she finds it necessary to take a firm grip on his arm and attempt to keep him out of the fur department. He gets excited over many of the shades of pastel mink. She is afraid he may snip off a sample or two.

ANDRE' PUYANS NYMPHS

Andre Puyans of Walnut Creek, California, has come up with some real winners in his A.P. series nymphs. His nymphs are not only unique in the manner in which they are tied, they are truly good producing flies that have been developed through a considerable amount of trial and error. His series gives you the predominant nymph color categories and all you have to do is select the size to match your own fishing requirements. These patterns are gaining in popularity throughout the country and without a doubt they will be with us for several years to come.

A.P. BEAVER NYMPH

HOOK:	Mustad 3906B.
THREAD:	Black.
TAIL, WINGCASE AND LEGS:	Dark moose hair.
RIBBING:	Copper wire. Rib body only.
BODY AND THORAX:	Dubbed dark beaver fur.
HEAD:	Dubbed dark beaver fur.

A.P. BLACK BEAVER NYMPH

HOOK:	Mustad 3906B.
THREAD:	Black.
TAIL, WINGCASE AND LEGS:	Dark moose hair.
RIBBING:	Copper wire. Rib body only.
BODY AND THORAX:	Dubbed dyed black beaver or synthetic fur.
HEAD:	Dubbed dyed black beaver or synthetic fur.

A.P. CLARET AND BEAVER NYMPH

HOOK:	Mustad 3906B.
THREAD:	Black.
TAIL, WINGCASE AND LEGS:	Dark moose hair.
RIBBING:	Copper wire. Rib body only.
BODY AND THORAX:	Dubbed with a blend of 40% medium color beaver, 20% claret synthetic fur, 20% seal brown synthetic fur and 20% Hare's Ear fur.
HEAD:	Dubbed with body blend.

A.P. HARE'S EAR/BEAVER NYMPH

HOOK:	Mustad 3906B.
THREAD:	Brown.
TAIL, WINGCASE AND LEGS:	Bronze mallard.
RIBBING:	Gold wire. Rib body only.
BODY AND THORAX:	Hare's Ear and beaver fur mixed in equal parts.
HEAD:	Brown thread.

A.P. HENDRICKSON NYMPH

HOOK:	Mustad 3906B.
THREAD:	Brown.
TAIL, WINGCASE AND LEGS:	Bronze mallard.
RIBBING:	Copper wire. Rib body only.
BODY AND THORAX:	Dubbed dyed reddish brown beaver or synthetic fur.
HEAD:	Dubbed with same fur as body.

A.P. MUSKRAT No. 1

HOOK: Mustad 3906B.

THREAD: Gray.

TAIL: Blue dun hackle fibers.

WINGCASE AND LEGS: Bronze mallard (not too dark).

RIBBING: Gold wire. Rib body only.

BODY AND THORAX: Dubbed dark muskrat fur taken from the back of the muskrat.

HEAD: Dubbed with same fur as body.

A.P. MUSKRAT No. 2

HOOK: Mustad 3906B.

THREAD: Gray.

TAIL, WINGCASE AND LEGS: Dark moose hair.

RIBBING: Gold wire. Rib body only.

BODY AND THORAX: Dubbed dark muskrat fur taken from the back of the muskrat.

HEAD: Dubbed with same fur as body.

A.P. OLIVE NYMPH

HOOK: Mustad 3906B.

THREAD: Olive.

TAIL, WINGCASE AND LEGS: Dyed olive barred mallard.

RIBBING: Gold wire. Rib body only.

BODY AND THORAX: Dubbed dyed olive beaver or synthetic fur.

HEAD: Dubbed with same fur as body.

NOTES: Some Olive Nymphs have dark wingcases. This can be darkened with a dark brown or black waterproof felt tip marking pen.

A.P. PEACOCK AND PHEASANT

HOOK: Mustad 9671.

THREAD: Black.

TAIL, WINGCASE AND LEGS: Ringneck pheasant center tail feather fibers. Select so that dark center portion covers wingcase.

RIBBING: Copper wire.

BODY AND THORAX: Bronze peacock herl.

HEAD: Black tying thread.

The following step by step tying procedures will assist you in tying the A.P. series nymphs. The unique manner in which they are easily tied can be incorporated into many other patterns.

STEP 1: Tie in lead wire at the thorax. Enough material for the tail, wingcase and legs is tied in just to the rear of the weight. Amount of material needed is determined by hook size and the amount needed to construct wingcase.

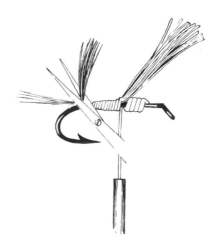

STEP 2: Material is secured and surplus fibers which are not needed to form the tail are trimmed off. Tail is positioned midway between the point and the barb with a couple of thread wraps underneath to lift and spread it.

STEP 3: Ribbing and dubbing for the body is tied in at rear.

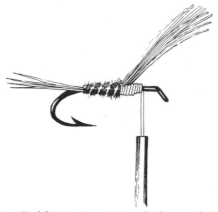

STEP 4: Dubbing is wrapped forward to the wingcase. Ribbing of the body is then completed.

STEP 5: Thorax is dubbed in the same manner as the body but larger.

STEP 6: Wingcase is pulled over the thorax and tied in.

STEP 7: Legs are formed by bringing the tying thread back to a position just in front of the thorax

and separating three fibers on each side and securing with tying thread. Excess material is then clipped off.

STEP 8: Head is then dubbed with a very small amount of dubbing and the legs are clipped off just to the rear of the thorax.

STEP 9: Your fly is finished, so don't just sit there, grab your rod and go try it out.

ATHERTON, DARK

HOOK:	Mustad 3906B, sizes 8-16.
THREAD:	Black.
TAIL:	Furnace hackle fibers.
RIBBING:	Oval gold tinsel.
BODY:	Dubbed muskrat and claret synthetic fur mixed in equal parts.
WINGCASE:	Dyed blue goose quill section or raffia tied in over thorax.
THORAX:	Dubbed muskrat and claret synthetic fur mixed in equal parts.
LEGS:	Furnace hackle tied on as collar and clipped off on both top and bottom.

ATHERTON, LIGHT

HOOK:	Mustad 3906B, sizes 8-16.
THREAD:	Yellow.
TAIL:	Barred lemon wood duck fibers.
RIBBING:	Oval gold tinsel.
BODY:	Dubbed cream synthetic fur.
WINGCASE:	Dyed gold goose quill section or raffia tied in over thorax.
THORAX:	Dubbed cream synthetic fur.
HACKLE:	Gray partridge.

ATHERTON, MEDIUM

HOOK:	Mustad 3906B, sizes 8-16.
THREAD:	Brown.
TAIL:	Brown partridge fibers.
RIBBING:	Oval gold tinsel.
BODY:	Dubbed Hare's Ear fur.
WINGCASE:	Dyed blue goose quill section or raffia tied in over thorax.
THORAX:	Dubbed Hare's Ear fur.
HACKLE:	Brown partridge.

The Atherton patterns are proven winners. By adjusting the size and pattern of these three nymphs you can meet the demands of many areas and conditions.

BABE NYMPH

HOOK:	Mustad 3906B, sizes 10-14.
THREAD:	Black.
TAIL:	Barred teal fibers.
SHELLBACK:	Natural gray goose quill section tied over body and thorax.
RIBBING:	Copper wire. Rib the body and thorax over the goose quill section.
BODY:	Dubbed gray synthetic fur. Body should be tied in a heavy taper. After fly is completed body should be picked out and made shaggy.
LEGS:	Barred teal fibers tied in at each side and extending to the middle of body.

BACKSWIMMER

HOOK:	Mustad 7957BX, sizes 10-14.
THREAD:	Olive.
SHELLBACK:	Brown mottled turkey or substitute.
LEGS:	Dyed olive turkey quill fibers taken from the back of the flight quill and tied in at each side of body.
BODY:	Olive tinsel chenille.

This pattern was originated by the talented Al Troth. Fish this fly with short quick pulls, bring the fly to the surface. Allow the fly to sink and then retrieve in the same manner.

Instructions for tying the Backswimmer:

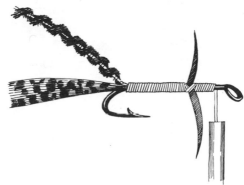

STEP 1: Tie in shellback material at rear of hook and then tie in olive tinsel chenille. Shellback material should be tied in so the underside, shiny side, will be up when it is pulled over the body. Tie in legs at each side of the hook.

STEP 2: Wrap chenille forward and tie off.

STEP 3: Pull shellback over the body and tie in.

STEP 4: Fold shellback material back over the head and tie off at back of head.

BALALOCK

HOOK:	Mustad 9671, sizes 8-12.
THREAD:	Olive.
TAIL:	Dyed olive neck hackle stems tied in a V.
BODY:	Dubbed olive dun synthetic fur.
WINGCASE:	Dyed olive goose quill section tied in over thorax.
THORAX:	Dubbed olive dun synthetic fur.
LEGS:	Dark ginger variant hackle wrapped through thorax.

BEAVER PELT

HOOK:	Mustad 3906, sizes 8-16.
THREAD:	Gray.
TAIL:	Barred mallard fibers.
BODY:	Dubbed beaver fur.
LEGS:	Barred mallard fibers tied in at throat.

This is a simple fly to tie and it simulates many nymph forms.

BEGINNERS

HOOK:	Mustad 3906B, sizes 10-14.
THREAD:	Black.
TAIL:	Ringneck pheasant tail feather fibers.
RIBBING:	Copper wire.
BODY:	Dubbed muskrat and claret synthetic fur mixed in equal parts.
WINGCASE:	Ringneck pheasant tail feather fibers tied in over thorax.
LEGS:	Ringneck pheasant tail feather fibers tied in at throat.

BIG STONE

HOOK:	Mustad 9672, sizes 4-10.
THREAD:	Brown.
TAILS:	Two dark peccary or moose body hairs tied in a V.
BODY:	Brown peccary. An underbody of brown floss should be first wrapped to give a good taper.
WINGCASE:	Brown hen ringneck pheasant quill section tied in over thorax.
THORAX:	Peacock herl.
LEGS:	Dark brown hackle tied on as a collar and clipped on both top and bottom.

This is one of the many Doug Prince creations. Very popular on parts of the West Coast.

BIRD'S STONE FLY NYMPH, BROWN

HOOK:	Mustad 38941, sizes 4-10.
THREAD:	Orange.
TAILS:	Two brown goose quill fibers taken from back of flight quill and tied in a V.
RIBBING:	Orange thread.
BODY:	Dubbed reddish brown fox or synthetic fur.
WINGCASE:	Brown hen ringneck pheasant quill section tied in over thorax.
THORAX:	Peacock herl.
LEGS:	Brown hackle wrapped through thorax.

BIRD'S STONE FLY NYMPH, GRAY

HOOK:	Mustad 38941, sizes 4-10.
THREAD:	Yellow.
TAILS:	Two natural gray goose quill fibers taken from back of flight quill and tied in a V.
RIBBING:	Yellow thread.
BODY:	Dubbed muskrat fur with guard hairs left in. Body should be picked out and made shaggy after fly is completed.
WINGCASE:	Clear plastic tied in over thorax. The 4 mil. zip lock bags found in your kitchen are ideal for this material.

THORAX: Peacock herl.

LEGS: Blue dun hackle wrapped through thorax.

These are some very good old patterns that were created by Cal Bird while he was residing in Sacramento, California. They often get their body materials altered by some tyers but the original materials are still considered the best.

BITCH CREEK

HOOK: Mustad 9672, sizes 4-10.

THREAD: Black.

TAILS: Two white rubber hackles tied in a V.

BODY: Black chenille with orange chenille woven in on belly.

THORAX: Black chenille. Thorax should be tied fuller than the body.

LEGS: Brown hackle wrapped through the thorax.

ANTENNA: Two white rubber hackles tied in a V.

This pattern was originated in Montana and probably accounts for more big trout than any other nymph pattern. It is not a very realistic imitation of anything but no one has told the fish and it is suspected that they accept it as a large stone fly nymph. A variation, the Torpedo, is also used. The orange belly is omitted and black hackle is used rather than brown.

BLACK CREEPER

HOOK: Mustad 3906B, sizes 10-12.

THREAD: Black.

TAIL: Black hackle fibers.

RIBBING: Flat gold tinsel.

BODY: Black floss.

LEGS: Black hackle fibers tied in at each side and clipped short.

NOTES: There is an underbody constructed of lead wire which is flattened. Cement should be applied generously before and while wrapping floss body.

After completion body should be flattened and given another coat of cement.

This is a good dark attractor type nymph which is extremely good during early season high water conditions.

BLACK MAY FLY

HOOK: Mustad 3906B, sizes 10-14.

THREAD: Black.

TAIL: Black hackle fibers.

RIBBING: Gray thread.

BODY: Black floss.

WINGCASE: Black duck quill section tied in over the thorax.

THORAX: Dubbed black synthetic fur.

LEGS: Black hackle wrapped through the thorax.

BLACK MIDGE PUPA

HOOK: Mustad 94838, sizes 12-16.

THREAD: Black.

BODY: Black ostrich tied in at butt and black floss.

FEELERS: Black hackle fibers tied in over eye of hook.

BLACK NYMPH

HOOK: Mustad 3906B, sizes 10-16.

THREAD: Black.

TAIL: Black goose quill fibers taken from back of flight quill and tied in a V.

RIBBING: Silver wire.

BODY: Black synthetic fur. Body should be picked out and made shaggy.

WINGCASE: Black goose quill section tied in at head and extending over thorax. Quill section should be doubled to give wingcase more fullness.

LEGS: Speckled guinea tied in at throat.

This is a good fly to use almost anywhere. This is one of the first nymph patterns I learned to tie and I have used it with success for many years. It is a Jack Horner pattern with an endless list of successes behind it.

BLACK QUILL

HOOK:	Mustad 3906B, sizes 12-16.
THREAD:	Black.
TAIL:	Black hackle fibers.
BODY:	Dark peacock quill. An underbody of black floss should first be wrapped to give good taper. Reverse wrap the body with fine silver wire.
LEGS:	Black hackle fibers tied in at each side and extending back to center of body.

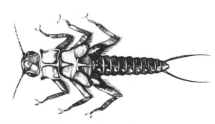

BLACK STONE (Pteronarcys dorsata)

HOOK:	Mustad 79580, sizes 2-8.
THREAD:	Black.
UNDERBODY:	Two pieces of lead wire equal in diameter to hook wire tied in at each side of hook shank.
TAILS:	Dark brown saddle hackle stems tied in at each side. Tails should be equal to length of body only. Exclude thorax and head in this measurement.
RIBBING:	Dyed black flat monofilament.
BODY:	Dubbed black synthetic fur.
WINGCASE:	Natural dark gray goose quill section tied in over thorax.
THORAX:	Dubbed dark brown synthetic fur.

LEGS:	Dark brown hackle wrapped through thorax. Trim hackle barbles from bottom.
HEAD:	Dubbed blackish brown synthetic fur.

BLADES' OLIVE NYMPH

HOOK:	Mustad 3906B, sizes 8-14.
THREAD:	Black.
TAIL:	Blue dun hackle fibers.
RIBBING:	Flat gold tinsel.
BODY:	Dubbed olive rabbit and synthetic fur mixed in equal parts.
WINGCASE:	Orange floss tied in over thorax.
THORAX:	Dubbed olive rabbit and synthetic fur mixed in equal parts.
LEGS:	Honey badger tied on as a collar and tied back.

This fly has been a favorite for many years. The gifted Bill Blades gave us this and many other important patterns.

BOX CANYON STONE

HOOK:	Eagle Claw 1197B, sizes 2-8.
THREAD:	Black.
TAILS:	Dark brown goose quill fibers taken from the back of a flight quill and tied in a V.
BODY:	Black yarn.
WINGCASE:	Brown mottled turkey section tied in over the thorax.
THORAX:	Black yarn.
LEGS:	Furnace hackle wrapped through the thorax.

NOTES: Black yarn for the body should be twisted tightly before wrapping to give good segmentation. A dyed brown goose or duck quill section may be substituted for the wingcase material.

The Box Canyon Stone was developed by Mims Barker of Ogden, Utah. During the 1973 season he fished the Henry's Fork of the Snake River daily for 5 months. He used all of the available imitations, Bitch Creek, Montana, etc., with varying degrees of success and finally started experimenting with some variations of his own. Before the season's end he had perfected a pattern which would take fish on a more regular basis. Since that time this pattern has been used in many other areas with very good reults. Although this pattern fails to resemble the stone fly *Pteronarcys californica* to any exacting degree, it is very effective in rivers where they are present. Use the larger sizes, twos and fours, before and during the hatch and the smaller sizes, sixes and eights, after the hatch. If you fish it on the bottom in a dead drift you will get into some very large fish. It has made a believer out of me as well as many others. If properly presented it will not only increase the number of fish you take, but will also make a significant increase in their size. When fishing the Box Canyon Stone I like to think of it as having ten pounds of horse meat on the end of my line and I set the hook anytime there is even a hint that a fish might be taking a smell.

BRASSIE NYMPH

HOOK: Mustad 3906, sizes 10-20.

THREAD: Black.

BODY: Copper wire. An underbody of floss should be wrapped to give a slight taper.

THORAX: Dubbed muskrat fur.

NOTES: For best results use 26 gauge wire for size 10, 28 gauge wire for size 12, 30 gauge wire for sizes 14 and 16, and 34 gauge wire on sizes 18 and 20.

This pattern was originated by Gene Lynch of Colorado Springs, Colorado. It is a very popular nymph pattern in Colorado. I have used it in many parts of the west with very good success. When I first learned of the pattern I tied the body with brass wire as the name suggests. I still like my version since I carried this fly one step further and developed the Copper Creeper. This fly is tied with copper wire and a thorax of dubbed dyed black muskrat fur. I find that when one uses the two shades it increases the range of nymphal creatures that can be simulated. These flies really get down in the pools and sweep the bottom which I think accounts for their high success. In Colorado you can see many commercial versions of this pattern. Most are just some wire wrapped on a hook. I have tried them many ways and find that the dubbed fur thorax actually makes the fly.

BREADCRUST

HOOK: Mustad 3906, sizes 8-16.

THREAD: Black.

RIBBING: Dark brown neck hackle stem.

BODY: Orange wool yarn or dubbed synthetic fur. Reverse wrap the body with fine gold wire after ribbing has been wrapped.

HACKLE: Soft grizzly. Hen hackle is preferred over that of the cock.

NOTES: Neck hackle stem should be soaked in a solution of water and glycerin at least over night and then flattened with flat-nosed jewelers pliers.

Other variations of this pattern include a body of just the hackle stem or natural tan raffia. This fly was originally classified as a wet fly but because of its usefulness when fished as a nymph the classification was quickly changed.

BRISTLE MIDGE

HOOK: Mustad 3906B, sizes 14-18.

THREAD: Black.

TAIL AND FEELERS: Select two porcupine bristles and tie in at front and rear of hook forming a V tail and feelers at both ends. Trim to about ⅔ body length.

RIBBING: Porcupine bristle.

BODY: Dubbed blackish brown synthetic fur.

This pattern incorporates porcupine bristle which is readily available yet neglected because it does not sound exotic enough to most tyers. It is very good on May Fly tails, nymph feelers and tail, etc.

BROWN BOMBER

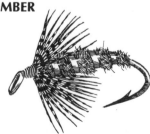

HOOK: Mustad 3906, sizes 10-12.

THREAD: Brown.

RIBBING: Flat gold tinsel.

BODY: Dubbed muskrat fur with guard hairs removed. Use fur from the back of the muskrat.

HACKLE: Brown partridge.

This pattern came from the east and I first started using it in 1970. It has become one of my favorite flies for lake fishing.

BROWN CREEPER

HOOK: Mustad 3906B, sizes 10-12.

THREAD: Brown.

TAIL: Brown hackle fibers.

RIBBING: Flat gold tinsel.

BODY: Brown floss.

LEGS: Brown hackle fibers tied in at each side and clipped short.

NOTES: There is an underbody constructed of lead wire which is flattened. Cement should be applied generously before and while wrapping floss body. After completion body should be flattened and given another coat of cement.

BROWN DRAKE

HOOK: Mustad 9672, sizes 8-12.

THREAD: Yellow.

TAIL: Natural dun gray marabou. Pinch off to obtain correct length.

BODY: Dubbed gold rabbit fur. Strip sides of body with a waterproof black felt tipped marker pen.

GILLS: Natural dun gray marabou. Pinch off to obtain correct length.

WINGCASE: Natural dark gray goose quill section tied in over the thorax.

THORAX: Dubbed gold rabbit fur.

LEGS: Brown partridge. Tie in by the tip and wrap two full turns only. Pull back and down and tie in.

HEAD: Dubbed gold rabbit fur.

NOTES: Tail and gills should be about ¼'' for size 10 and adjusted accordingly for sizes 8 and 12.

This pattern catches the nymph at the pre-emergence stage. I favor it because it is designed closely to the highly effective Marabou Nymphs. This pattern was originated by Al Troth.

BROWN MAY FLY

HOOK: Mustad 3906B, sizes 10-14.

THREAD: Brown.

TAIL: Dark ginger hackle fibers.

RIBBING: Brown thread.

BODY: Light brown floss.

WINGCASE: Dark brown duck quill section tied in over the thorax.

THORAX: Dubbed seal brown synthetic fur.

LEGS: Dark ginger hackle wrapped through the thorax.

BROWN SHRIMP

HOOK: Mustad 3906, sizes 6-10.

THREAD: Brown.

BODY: Dubbed hot orange synthetic fur.

LEGS: Dark ginger hackle tied Palmer over the body.

BACK AND TAIL: Brown elk hair.

NOTES: When tying this pattern leave a piece of brown tying thread at the rear of the body to tie in elk hair at the rear. After hair is tied in the thread should be ribbed forward and tied off at the head. Clip hackle and legs from the point of the hook to the eye.

BROWN STONE (Acroneuria pacifica)

HOOK: Mustad 38941, sizes 4-8.

THREAD: Brown.

UNDERBODY:Two pieces of lead wire equal in diameter to hook wire and tied in at each side of hook shank.

TAILS: Dark brown saddle hackle stems tied in at each side. Tails should be equal to length of body only. Exclude thorax and head in this measurement.

RIBBING: Dyed brown flat monofilament. Rib body only.

BODY: Dubbed dark brown and seal brown synthetic fur mixed in equal parts.

WINGCASE: Dyed brown mottled cock ringneck pheasant quill section tied in over thorax.

THORAX: Dubbed yellowish brown synthetic fur.

LEGS: Brown hackle wrapped through thorax. Trim hackle barbles from bottom.

HEAD: Dubbed dark brown and seal brown synthetic fur mixed in equal parts.

BUCKSKIN NYMPH

HOOK: Mustad 3906, sizes 12-18.

THREAD: Black.

TAIL: Soft brown hackle fibers.

BODY: Underbody is constructed with lead wire and thread. The outer body is wrapped with a narrow ribbon of buckskin. Buckskin should be wrapped on edge to give the effect of segmentation.

This pattern was sent to me by George Bodmer of Colorado Springs, Colorado. As you can see, George and his friends like their nymphs simple. They usually fish them weighted and deep. They do not like a pattern so complicated to tie that they get emotionally involved when they lose one.

BURKE NYMPH

HOOK: Mustad 3906B, sizes 6-12.

THREAD: Black.

TIP: Flat gold tinsel.

TAIL: Black hackle fibers.

RIBBING: Flat gold tinsel. Rib body only.

BODY: Dubbed dyed black muskrat fur.

WINGCASE: Hen ringneck pheasant quill section tied in over thorax.

THORAX: Dubbed dyed black muskrat fur.

LEGS: Black hackle tied on as a collar and tied back.

An old reliable pattern created by Ed Burke. When tied weighted and fished deep this pattern can really do the trick on larger fish.

BURLAP

This is a very good pattern when fished as a nymph. It was originated as a Steelhead fly and details for its construction are listed under Steelhead Flies.

BURLAP NYMPH

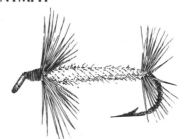

HOOK: Mustad 9671, sizes 4-8.

THREAD: Black.

REAR HACKLE: Dark ginger.

BODY: Burlap fibers wrapped thin.

FRONT HACKLE: Dark ginger.

This pattern was sent to me by Pete Test of Albuquerque, New Mexico. It is a good variation of the Burlap Nymph for their area.

CAREY SPECIAL

HOOK: Mustad 9672, sizes 4-14.

THREAD: Black.

TAIL: Ringneck pheasant rump feather. fibers.

BODY: Your selection.

HACKLE: Ringneck pheasant rump feather.

When you say Carey Special in the Pacific Northwest it can have hundreds of meanings. The original dressings for this pattern are thought to have a brown bear hair tail and body. It is suggestive of the dobson, damsel, and dragon fly larvae found in many lakes. This pattern originated in British Columbia and was popularized by Thomas Carey.

CARROT N BLACK

HOOK: Mustad 3906 B, sizes 10-16.

THREAD: Black.

TAIL: Dark ginger hackle fibers.

BODY: Dark orange floss.

THORAX: Black chenille.

HACKLE: Dark ginger.

Originated by Rube Cross. This is a very good early season pattern which accounts for many fish in either lake or stream.

CARROT NYMPH

HOOK: Mustad 3906, sizes 10-12.

THREAD: Gray.

BODY: Dubbed dark orange synthetic fur.

HACKLE: Gray partridge tied on as a collar and tied slightly back.

CASED CADDIS

HOOK: Mustad 9671, sizes 10-16.

THREAD: Black.

RIBBING: Copper wire.

BODY: First build a tapered underbody of dark brown floss or yarn. Then select a brown and a black saddle hackle and tie in by their tips. Twist the two saddle hackles together and wrap forward. Hackle barbles should then be clipped close.

HEAD: Black ostrich.

This pattern was sent to me by George Bodmer of Colorado Springs, Colorado. He reports that it is a good fly there locally and from the feedback he has been getting it should work well just about any place.

COLORADO CADDIS

HOOK: Mustad 3906B, sizes 8-16.

THREAD: Black.

SHELLBACK: Natural gray goose quill section.

BODY: Pale yellow wool yarn or dubbed synthetic fur.

LEGS: Black hackle tied on as a collar before the shellback is tied in at front. After the hackle is wrapped the back is pulled forward splitting the hackle on top and leaving legs to the sides and underneath.

HEAD: Tied extra large with black tying thread.

Bob Good of Denver, Colorado, originated this pattern. It has no resemblance of anything in the caddis family but there must be something there because of its fish taking ability.

CREAM CADDIS (JONNIE COME LATELY)

HOOK: Mustad 3906B, sizes 14-18.

THREAD: Black.

RIBBING: Gold wire.

BODY: Pale yellow wool yarn or dubbed rabbit or synthetic fur.

THORAX: Dubbed muskrat fur.

A pattern with simple dressings. Originated by Jon Nelson of Colorado Springs, Colorado. About the same design as many caddis larva imitations, but has been extra effective for the Colorado flyfishers.

CREAM CADDIS WORM

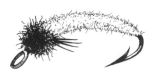

HOOK: Mustad 37140, size 12.

THREAD: Black.

BODY: Dubbed cream synthetic fur. Body should be tied well down into the bend of the hook.

LEGS: Metallic black turkey tail feather fibers tied in at each side and tied short.

HEAD: Dubbed black synthetic fur. Pick out for shaggy appearance.

CREAM NYMPH

HOOK: Mustad 9671, sizes 10-14.

THREAD: White.

TAIL: Barred lemon wood duck fibers.

BODY: Natural white, off white, chenille.

WINGCASE: Barred lemon wood duck fibers tied in over thorax.

THORAX: Natural white, off white, chenille.

LEGS: Cream hackle wrapped through thorax.

DANDY GREEN

HOOK: Mustad 9671, sizes 6-10.

THREAD: Olive.

TAIL: Greenish gray ringneck pheasant body feather fibers.

BODY: Dubbed with a mixture of 50% olive rabbit fur, 30% yellow synthetic fur, and 20% green synthetic fur.

HACKLE: Greenish gray ringneck pheasant body feather fibers tied in at each side and extending to the middle of the body.

NOTES: Body is often ribbed with dyed green flat monofilament.

DARK GREEN DRAKE

HOOK: Mustad 3906B, size 8.

THREAD: Olive.

TAIL: Dark brown peccary, 3-5 fibers.

RIBBING: Heavy dark brown thread.

BODY: Dubbed dyed olive Hare's Ear fur.

WINGCASE: Dyed black goose quill section tied in over the thorax.

THORAX: Dubbed dyed olive Hare's Ear fur.

LEGS: Brown partridge dyed olive. Tie on by the tip and wrap two full turns. Pull back and down and tie in. Clip fibers from the bottom, leaving legs on each side.

NOTES: Art Foam is tied in to form an underbody of this nymph after the tail and ribbing have been tied in. Coats and Clarks Button and Carpet thread in shade no. 51 is the correct thread for ribbing.

An effective Al Troth original to simulate the May Fly nymph, *Ephemerella grandis*.

DARK HENDRICKSON

HOOK: Mustad 3906B, sizes 8-12.

THREAD: Brown.

TAIL: Dark moose body hairs.

BODY: Dark brown ostrich herl with an overlay of dark brown peccary. Ostrich herl should stick through wraps of peccary.

WINGCASE: Dyed black duck quill section tied in over the thorax.

THORAX: Dubbed dark brown rabbit fur.

LEGS: Dyed dark brown barred mallard fibers tied in at throat.

Another Al Troth pattern which works very well in the Rocky Mountain area.

DARK HENDRICKSON

HOOK: Mustad 3906B, sizes 10-18.

THREAD: Black.

TAIL: Blue dun hackle fibers.

BODY: Dark moose mane. An underbody of brown floss should first be wrapped to give a medium taper.

LEGS: Blue dun hackle fibers tied in at throat.

WINGCASE: Dark gray duck shoulder feather tied in at head and extending over a third of the body.

DARK STONE (Acroneuria nigrita)

HOOK:	Mustad 38941, sizes 6-8.
THREAD:	Black.
UNDERBODY:	Two pieces of lead wire equal in diameter to hook wire and tied in at each side of hook shank.
TAILS:	Natural brown hackle stems dyed dark orange and tied in at each side. Tails should be equal in length to body only. Exclude thorax and head in this measurement.
RIBBING:	Dyed black flat monofilament.
BODY:	Dubbed dark brown synthetic fur.
WINGCASE:	Dyed dark brown barred teal tied in over thorax.
THORAX:	Dubbed dark orange and yellow synthetic fur mixed in equal parts.
LEGS:	Black hackle wrapped through thorax. Trim hackle barbles from bottom.
HEAD:	Dubbed black synthetic fur.

DAVE'S SHRIMP

HOOK:	Mustad 7957BX, sizes 8-14.
THREAD:	Olive.
TAIL:	Barred lemon wood duck fibers.
BODY:	Dubbed with a mixture of yellow synthetic fur, olive synthetic fur, bleached beaver belly fur and muskrat belly fur. Blend consists of equal parts of each.
LEGS:	Barred lemon wood duck fibers tied in at throat.

NOTES: Needle-nosed pliers are used to bend hook shank up about one-quarter length behind the eye. Bend should not be sharp, but rounded. Eye should be parallel with hook shank.

A Dave Whitlock pattern which I am using more and more in lake fishing. If I get it to the bottom I usually find fish.

DIRTY OLIVE

HOOK:	Mustad 3906, sizes 8-14.
THREAD:	Brown.
TAIL:	Ringneck pheasant tail feather fibers.
RIBBING:	Dyed orange round monofilament. Rib body only.
BODY:	Dubbed brown olive synthetic fur.
WINGCASE:	Natural gray goose quill section tied in over thorax.
THORAX:	Brown olive synthetic fur.
LEGS:	Dyed brown speckled guinea fibers tied in at throat.

This is a particularly good fly for use in the Yellowstone and Jackson Hole areas. Reports are also good from other areas.

DRAGON

HOOK:	Mustad 9672, size 10.
THREAD:	Black.
LEGS:	Black hackle wrapped through thorax. Trim off top hackle barbles.
BODY:	Dark olive chenille wrapped from front to rear and returned to the front, giving the body a good fat taper.
WINGCASE:	Dark gray duck shoulder feather tied in at head.

NOTES: Wingcase should be prepared in advance of tying the fly. Select a dark gray duck shoulder feather and trim out a center V from the tip of the feather. Coat with a thin vinyl cement and allow to dry. Trim to shape, if needed, and give another coat of thin vinyl cement.

This fly has done very well in lakes having a population of Dragon Flies. It is often a good idea to weight the underbody with lead wire for fishing in the deeper lakes. It does best when put right on the bottom.

DR. WINTERS

HOOK:	Mustad 3906B, sizes 8-12.

THREAD: Black.

SHELLBACK: Black ostrich herl.

RIBBING: Fine silver wire.

LEGS: Black hackle fibers tied in at throat.

BODY: Peacock herl.

DUSTER

HOOK: Mustad 3906, sizes 10-16.

THREAD: Black.

TAIL: Sparse black hackle fibers.

BODY: Select three or four pieces of gray ostrich herl and tie in at tips. Twist around your tying thread and wrap forward. Body should be full and the back trimmed short, about 1/8".

HACKLE: Black hackle tied on as a collar and tied back. Top is clipped off.

A Doug Prince pattern which is popular in many areas of the West Coast.

ELMO NYMPH

HOOK: Mustad 3906B, sizes 8-12.

THREAD: Brown.

TAIL: Dark ginger variant hackle fibers.

SHELLBACK: Dyed brown goose quill section.

RIBBING: Brown thread.

BODY   Dubbed pale yellow synthetic fur.

LEGS: Dyed brown speckled guinea fibers tied in at throat.

EMERGING MARCH BROWN

HOOK: Mustad 3906B, sizes 10-12.

THREAD: Brown.

TAIL: Three ringneck pheasant tail feather fibers.

RIBBING: Gold thread. Rib body only.

BODY: Dubbed Hare's Ear fur.

THORAX: Dubbed Hare's Ear Fur.

COLLAR: Hare's Ear fur equal to the length of body.

WINGCASE: Small bunch of brown partridge fibers tied in at the head and equal to the length of the collar.

HEAD: Dubbed Hare's Ear fur.

A fine Al Troth pattern that should work most any place.

FAIR DAMSEL

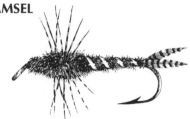

HOOK: Mustad 9672, sizes 6-8.

THREAD: Brown.

TAILS: Dyed brown grizzly hackle tips tied in a V.

RIBBING: Oval gold tinsel.

BODY: Dubbed seal brown and dark brown synthetic fur mixed in equal parts.

HACKLE: Dyed brown grizzly. Strip hackle barbles from side of hackle before wrapping. Wrap with two full turns only.

HEAD: Dubbed seal brown and dark brown synthetic fur mixed in equal parts.

NOTES: Body of the fly is tied with a good taper and large at thorax. Leave some extra room at head as it should be rather large and long. You might picture the finished fly as having the hackle wrapped in the center of the thorax.

This is one of the blessed originals of Charles Brooks. He states that brown mottled fuzzy yarn or fur should be used. We have tried the blend of synthetics as indicated above and have had good results.

FIRE FLY

HOOK: Mustad 7957B, sizes 8-14.

THREAD: Black.

TAIL: Lady Amherst pheasant tippet fibers.

BODY: Dyed black peacock herl with flourescent green floss center joint (Royal Coachman style).

LEGS: Black hackle tied on as a collar and tied back.

WINGCASE: White goose quill fibers taken from back of flight quill and tied in a V over the body.

This is another Doug Prince pattern of merit.

FIVE CARATS

HOOK: Mustad 3906, sizes 10-12.

THREAD: Gray.

RIBBING: Oval silver tinsel. Ribbing should consist of five full turns of tinsel.

BODY: White flourescent floss tied with a full taper and extending well down into the bend of the hook.

HACKLE: Soft blue dun tied long. Hackle should be tied back and extend to the bend of the hook.

FLEDERMAUS

HOOK: Mustad 7957BX, sizes 4-10.

THREAD: Black.

BODY: Dubbed muskrat fur tied full and shaggy. Guard hairs should be left in the dubbing and picked out after body is completed.

WING: Red fox squirrel tail hair tied the length of the body.

Some prefer this fly tied well weighted. It was created some years ago by Jack Schneider. This is one of the flies in your box which represents nothing. As unorthodox as it may appear it is a good one and has produced many large fish. Chalk

up another one for muskrat fur. Some alter the pattern and use gray squirrel for the wing. Among the many conquests accredited this fly is the excellent results it gets the night fly fishermen on Utah's Flaming Gorge Reservoir.

FORKED TAIL NYMPH

HOOK: Mustad 3906B, sizes 6-10.

THREAD: Black.

TAIL: Brown goose quill fibers taken from the back of the flight quill and tied in a V.

RIBBING: Flat silver tinsel.

BODY: Peacock herl.

LEGS: Furnace hackle tied on as a collar and tied back.

WINGCASE: White goose quill fibers taken from the back of the flight quill and tied in a V.

FORKED TAIL NYMPH, BLACK

HOOK: Mustad 9671, sizes 6-10.

THREAD: Black.

TAIL: Black goose quill fibers taken from the back of the flight quill and tied in a V.

RIBBING: Flat silver tinsel.

BODY: Black ostrich herl.

LEGS: Black hackle tied on as a collar and tied back.

WINGCASE: White goose quill fibers taken from back of flight quill and tied in a V.

The creation of the Forked Tail Nymphs is credited to Doug Price of Monterey, California. Doug popularized the patterns but Don and Dick Olson of Bemidji, Minnesota, spawned the idea.

G. B. BLACK STONE

HOOK: Mustad 79580, sizes 4-12.

THREAD: Black.

TAILS: Two fibers of peccary or moose body hair tied in at each side and tide widespread.

RIBBING: Copper wire. Rib body only.

BODY: Dubbed black muskrat fur.

WINGCASE: Natural dark gray goose quill sections. They should be folded to give a fuller effect. The first is tied in at the center of the thorax and the last one is tied in at the front.

THORAX: Dubbed black muskrat fur.

LEGS: Soft black hackle fibers tied in at each side.

G. B. BROWN STONE

HOOK: Mustad 79580, sizes 4-12.

THREAD: Brown.

TAILS: Two fibers of peccary or moose body hair tied in at each side and tied widespread.

RIBBING: Fine oval gold tinsel. Rib body only.

BODY: Dubbed brown beaver and Hare's Ear fur mixed in equal parts.

WINGCASE: Dark brown turkey tail sections. They should be folded to give a fuller effect. The first is tied in at the center of the thorax and the last one is tied in at the front.

THORAX: Dubbed brown beaver and Hare's Ear fur mixed in equal parts.

LEGS: Greenish brown ringneck pheasant body plumage fibers tied in at each side.

G. B. TAN STONE

HOOK: Mustad 79580, sizes 4-12.

THREAD: Tan.

TAILS: Two fibers of peccary or moose body hair tied in at each side and tied widespread.

RIBBING: Brown thread. Rib body only.

BODY: Dubbed tannish gray fox fur.

WINGCASE: Light brown oak turkey quill section. They should be folded to give a fuller effect. The first is tied in at the center of the thorax and the last one is tied in at the front.

THORAX: Dubbed tannish gray fox fur.

LEGS: Greenish brown ringneck pheasant body plumage fibers tied in at each side.

NOTES: When tying the G. B. Stones a small ball of body material is dubbed in at the rear of the hook shank before tying in the tails. When tails are tied in at each side the ball of dubbed fur assists in giving the desired spread to the tails.

George Bodmer of Colorado Springs, Colorado, developed these patterns for his area. The style and colorations are proving to be good anywhere they are used. George ties all of these nymphs weighted to meet the conditions in his area. I have had good luck with his Brown Stone on Idaho's Little Wood River. I am sure it would do well elsewhere.

GINGER MAY FLY

HOOK: Mustad 3906B, sizes 10-14.

THREAD: Tan.

TAIL: Light ginger variant hackle fibers.

RIBBING: Brown thread.

BODY: Tan floss.

WINGCASE: Light brown duck quill section tied in over the thorax.

THORAX: Dubbed tan synthetic fur.

LEGS: Light ginger variant hackle wrapped through the thorax.

GINGER QUILL

HOOK: Mustad 3906B, sizes 10-16.

THREAD: Tan.

TAIL: Ginger hackle fibers.

BODY: Light peacock quill. An underbody of tan floss should first be wrapped to give body a good taper. Reverse wrap the body with fine gold wire.

LEGS: Ginger hackle fibers tied in at each side and extending back to center of body.

GOLDEN QUILL

HOOK: Mustad 3906B, sizes 10-12.

THREAD: Yellow.

TAIL:	Natural gray goose quill fibers taken from the back of flight quill and tied in a V.
BODY:	Dyed golden yellow saddle hackle stem. An underbody of yellow floss should first be wrapped to give slight taper. Reverse wrap the body with fine gold wire.
HACKLE:	Two full turns of brown partridge.

GOLDEN STONE (Acroneuria californica)

HOOK:	Mustad 38941, sizes 2-8.
THREAD:	Yellow.
UNDERBODY:	Two pieces of lead wire equal in diameter to hook wire and tied in at each side of hook shank.
TAILS:	Dyed yellow dark ginger saddle hackle stems tied in at each side. Tails should be equal to length of body only. Exclude thorax and head in this measurement.
RIBBING:	Dyed gold flat monofilament. Rib body only.
BODY:	Dubbed gold synthetic fur.
WINGCASE:	Mottled cock ringneck pheasant quill section dyed dark gold and tied in over thorax.
THORAX:	Dubbed light gold synthetic fur.
LEGS:	Dyed gold grizzly hackle (with fine black barring) wrapped through the thorax. Trim hackle barbles from bottom.
HEAD:	Dubbed gold synthetic fur.

GOLDEN WOODY

HOOK:	Mustad 38941, sizes 8-14.
THREAD:	Brown.

TAIL:	Dyed gold barred teal fibers. Tail should be half as long as body.
RIBBING:	Oval gold tinsel.
BODY:	Dubbed woodchuck fur with guard hairs left in. After fly is finished body should be picked out for shaggy effect.
LEGS:	Dyed gold barred teal fibers tied in at throat.
WINGCASE:	Brown Mallard drake throat feather tied in at front and extending over the body ⅓.

I created this pattern during the 1961 season. Out of desperation we needed something to match the stone fly nymph in the upper Sacramento River above Shasta Lake in Northern California. I had to use what materials I had with me so some dirty looking brown yarn was used on the first flies and it worked great. After a few seasons the yarn was gone and so was the effectiveness of the fly. Later I tried some woodchuck which resembled the yarn. Now I think the fly is even better than it was in its first version. It has been good to me everywhere I have fished it in the west.

GRANDE STONE

HOOK:	Mustad 38941, sizes 6-10.
THREAD:	Brown.
TAILS:	Two brown neck hackle stems tied in a V.
RIBBING:	Oval gold tinsel. Rib body only.
BODY:	Dubbed beaver fur.
WINGCASE:	Brown mottled hen ringneck pheasant quill section tied in over thorax.
THORAX:	Dubbed beaver fur.
LEGS:	Brown hackle wrapped through the thorax.
ANTENNA:	Fashion two from butts of wingcase material. Trim away excess fibers leaving about three of four fibers for each side. Cement fibers together and position in a V of about 50 degrees.

GRAY CADDIS

HOOK:	Mustad 3906, sizes 10-14.
THREAD:	Black.
BODY:	Dubbed beaver fur. Body should be tied well down into the bend of the hook.
WINGCASE:	Two gray duck shoulder feathers trimmed to shape and tied in at each side.
LEGS:	Barred teal tied in at throat.
HEAD:	Peacock herl.

GRAY MAY FLY

HOOK:	Mustad 3906B, sizes 10-14.
THREAD:	Gray.
TAIL:	Grizzly hackle fibers.
RIBBING:	Black thread.
BODY:	Gray floss.
WINGCASE:	Natural dark gray duck quill section tied in over thorax.
THORAX:	Dubbed dark gray synthetic fur.
LEGS:	Grizzly hackle wrapped through the thorax.

GRAY NYMPH

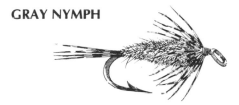

HOOK:	Mustad 3906, sizes 6-12.
THREAD:	Gray.
TAIL:	Grizzly hackle fibers.
BODY:	Dubbed muskrat fur with guard hairs left in. Body should be picked out and given shaggy appearance.
HACKLE:	Soft grizzly hen hackle.

This nationally famous pattern was invented in 1935 by Dee Vissing of Rigby, Idaho. Since the time of its introduction many articles have appeared extolling the usefullness of this pattern. Many substitute badger guard hairs for the tailing material.

GRAY RAT

HOOK:	Mustad 3906, sizes 6-14.

THREAD:	Black.
TAIL:	Dyed light gray elk hair. Three hairs only.
BODY:	Dubbed muskrat and gray synthetic fur mixed in equal parts. Body should be tied with a large fat taper.
LEGS:	Two natural gray duck quill fibers taken from the back of the flight quill and tied in a small V on each side. Legs should extend to the middle of the body.
WINGCASE:	Barred mallard fibers tied in at head, extending over ⅓ of the body and trimmed off.

This is another one of the Gray Nymph type flies which are so effective.

GRAY RUNT

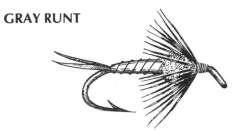

HOOK:	Mustad 3906B, sizes 10-12.
THREAD:	Gray.
TAIL:	Natural gray goose quill fibers taken from the back of the flight quill and tied in a V.
RIBBING:	Black thread.
BODY:	Gray floss.
THORAX:	Gray chenille.
HACKLE:	Grizzly tied on as a collar and tied back.

GREEN CADDIS WORM

HOOK:	Mustad 37140, size 12.
THREAD:	Black.
BODY:	Dubbed caddis green synthetic fur. Body should be tied well down on the bend of hook.
LEGS:	Metallic black turkey tail feather fibers tied in at throat and tied short.
HEAD:	Dubbed black synthetic fur.

GREEN DAMSEL

HOOK:	Mustad 38941, sizes 8-12.

THREAD: Brown.

TAILS: Two narrow brown hackle tips tied in a V.

RIBBING: Fine gold wire. Rib close with about six turns.

BODY: Light olive floss.

WINGCASE: Mottled brown hen ringneck pheasant body feather tied in over thorax.

THORAX: Dubbed olive synthetic fur.

LEGS: Mottled brown hen ringneck pheasant body feather fibers tied in at each side.

GREEN MAY FLY

HOOK: Mustad 3906B, sizes 10-14.

THREAD: Green.

TAIL: Green hackle fibers.

RIBBING: Green thread.

BODY: Light green floss.

WINGCASE: Dark green duck quill section tied in over the thorax.

THORAX: Dubbed green synthetic fur.

LEGS: Green hackle wrapped through the thorax.

GREYS CREEPER

HOOK: Mustad 38941, sizes 6-8.

THREAD: Black.

TAIL: Natural gray goose quill fibers taken from the back of flight quill and tied in a V.

RIBBING: Dyed black round monofilament.

BODY: Dubbed muskrat fur with guard hairs left in.

SHELLBACK: Natural gray goose quill section pulled over back before body is ribbed.

LEGS: Soft black hackle tied on as a collar before shellback is tied in. Shellback should be pulled over the hackle leaving hackle at sides and bottom.

This nymph is reported to be extremely effective on Wyoming's Greys River. It was created by Carl Glisson of Pinole, California, while on one of his annual fishing trips to Wyoming. He reports it works well on many of the larger California and Oregon rivers.

GROVE'S STONE

HOOK: Mustad 79580, sizes 2-10.

THREAD: Brown.

TAILS: Dyed brown round monofilament tied in a V.

BODY: Olive brown wool yarn.

UNDERBODY: Light tan wool yarn.

RIBBING: Dyed brown flat monofilament.

THORAX: Light tan wool yarn.

LEGS: Partridge breast feather divided and cemented into three legs on each side.

FEELERS: Dyed brown round monofilament tied in a V.

Instructions for construction of the Grove's Stone:

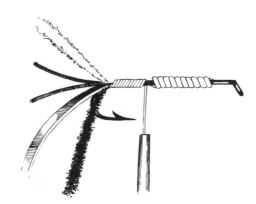

STEP 1: Tie in lead wire if you desire your nymph to be weighted. Tie in brown round monofilament tails. Tie in olive brown wool yarn for body. Then just slightly forward tie in tan wool yarn and flat monofilament.

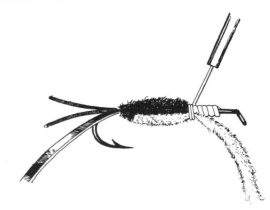

STEP 2: Pull tan wool yarn and flat monofilament forward and wrap one full turn with the olive brown yarn and tie off. This will prevent the

ribbing from slipping off the back of the body when it is wrapped. Wrap olive brown wool yarn forward to the middle of the hook shank and tie in. Pull down on tan wool yarn so it comes out on the body directly on the bottom of the fly. Pull it forward and tie off at the middle of the shank of the hook.

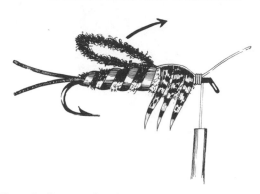

STEP 5: Pull partridge breast feather forward and tie in.

STEP 3: Rib the body and cut off flat monofilament leaving about ¼" protruding. This is tied in under thorax material. (This will prevent ribbing from pulling out when hook is bent). Tie in a loop of olive brown yarn.

STEP 6: Pull olive brown loop of wool yarn forward and tie in for wingcase.

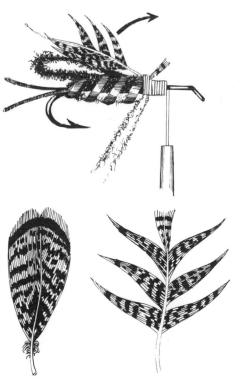

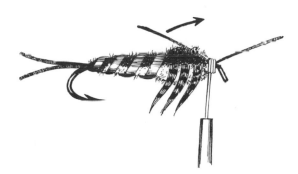

STEP 7: Wrap tying thread to form a large head. Tie in a piece of dyed brown round monofilament for feelers.

STEP 4: Tie in a partridge breast feather for legs. Feather should be tied in so concave side is down when it is pulled over the thorax and tied in. Tie in tan wool yarn for thorax.

STEP 8: Tie off the head and trim feelers so they are of equal length. While your hook is still in the vise bend it so it is offset. Remove the fly from vise and bend body just behind the thorax downward about 30 degrees.

GUNNY SACK

HOOK: Mustad 9671, sizes 8-14.

THREAD: Brown.

TAIL: Grizzly hackle fibers.

BODY: Natural burlap fibers tied with a good taper. Body is then Palmered with a grizzly saddle hackle. Hackle is trimmed into a taper. Hackle should be about ¼'' at front and taper to almost zero at rear.

This is a simple fly to tie and it has proven to be a good fly for both trout and summer run Steelhead.

HALFBACK

HOOK: Mustad 9672, sizes 8-14.

THREAD: Olive.

TAIL: Brown hackle fibers.

BODY: Peacock herl. An underbody of olive wool yarn should be wrapped to give the body a nice full fat taper.

LEGS: Brown hackle fibers tied in at throat.

WINGCASE: Dyed brown barred mallard fibers tied in at head and extending over ⅓ of the body.

HARE'S EAR

HOOK: Mustad 3906B, sizes 8-18.

THREAD: Brown.

TAIL: Brown partridge fibers.

BODY: Dubbed Hare's Ear fur. Body should be picked out and made shaggy.

LEGS: Brown partridge fibers tied in at throat.

There are many variations of the Hare's Ear nymph. Some tyers leave the throat hackle off and pick out the dubbing fur for the legs. The Hare's Ear is also tied with a fine oval gold tinsel rib.

HEATHER NYMPH

HOOK: Mustad 9671, sizes 10-12.

THREAD: Brown.

TAIL: Scarlet red hackle fibers.

RIBBING: Fine oval gold tinsel.

BODY: Dubbed insect green rabbit fur.

THORAX: Peacock herl.

HACKLE: Two turns of soft grizzly hen hackle.

This pattern is very useful during damsel fly hatches on lakes. It was originated by Fenton Roskelley of Spokane, Washington, in 1960.

HELLGRAMMITE

HOOK: Mustad 79580, sizes 4-8.

THREAD: Black.

UNDERBODY: Lead wire and black yarn.

TAILS: Black duck quill fibers taken from back of flight quill.

RIBBING: Dyed brown flat monofilament.

BODY: Dubbed blackish brown synthetic fur.

WINGCASE: Natural dark gray goose quill section.

LEGS: Dyed black ringneck pheasant breast feather divided and cemented into three legs on each side.

THORAX: Dubbed blackish brown synthetic fur.

ANTENNA: Black duck quill fibers taken from back of flight quill.

Instructions for tying the Hellgrammite are:

STEP 1: Tie in a piece of lead wire on each side of the hook shank. Diameter of the lead wire should be equal to wire of hook.

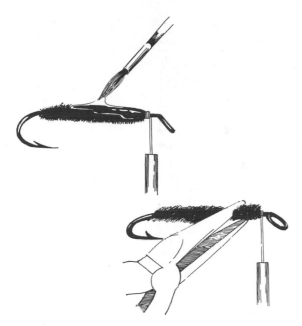

STEP 2: Wrap body with a 4 ply black or dark brown yarn. Wrap from rear to front, back to rear and to the front again. Tie off and clip thread. Soak body with cement and allow to dry 15 or 20 minutes (¾ dry). Flatten body with plain-nosed jeweler's pliers.

STEP 3: Tie in two black duck quill fibers taken from the back of a flight quill both at front and rear. They should be short and tied in a small V. Cement fibers with vinyl cement and allow your half finished bug to dry overnight.

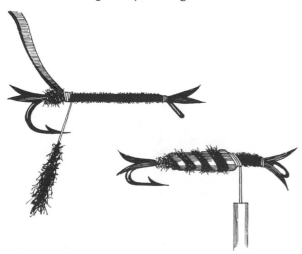

STEP 4: Tie in a small ball of blackish brown synthetic fur in front of rear duck fibers. Tie in a

piece of dyed brown flat monofilament and finish dubbing rear ⅔ of body. Wrap monofilament ribbing forward over dubbed body.

STEP 5: Tie in a section of natural dark gray goose quill section for wingcase. Then tie in a dyed black ringneck pheasant breast feather for legs. Dub the thorax with blackish brown synthetic fur. Pull legs and wingcase over thorax and tie in at head.

STEP 6: Dub head with a small amount of blackish brown synthetic fur and tie off thread under antenna.

This pattern is slow to tie and not something you would want to undertake at streamside. I have been a Hellgrammite freak since I was a boy. I am always in search of good patterns to try and simulate these giant Dobson Fly larvas. After putting everyone's ideas together and a great deal of trial and error I was able to come up with this pattern. The size and overall coloration of this pattern is extremely deadly in rivers where Hellgrammites are present.

HELLGRAMMITE

HOOK:	Mustad 79580, sizes 4-8.
THREAD:	Black.
BODY:	Black chenille.
LEGS:	One black and one brown saddle hackle tied Palmer over the body. Clip hackle barbles off from both top and bottom. Next clip hackle barbles on sides. They should be clipped so they are about ¾" at front and taper to almost zero at rear.

This is a much easier Hellgrammite to tie than the one above and it will often take fish where many of the other patterns do not.

HELLGRAMMITE

HOOK: Mustad 9672, sizes 6-10.

THREAD: Black.

TAIL: Black goose quill fibers taken from the back of flight quill and tied in a V.

RIBBING: Black ostrich herl. Rib body only and clip herl down to about 1/16."

BODY: Black floss.

WINGCASE: Black goose quill section tied in over the thorax.

THORAX: Dubbed black rabbit fur with a strip of red wool yarn pulled across the bottom.

LEGS: Black hackle wrapped through thorax. Also, a black goose quill fiber tied in at each side and tied so tips flare outward.

A very good pattern which was originated by Doug Prince. The ostrich herl ribbing serves to simulate the small legs of the natural but unfortunately it is rather fragile and is usually gone after taking the first fish. This does not seem to affect the fly as the fish often keep on hitting it.

Hellgrammites stay in their larval stage for three years which gives the angler a good range of sizes to tie them in. I only fish the size 4 during high cloudy water conditions. They are too big above size 6 during normal water conditions since the fish have a better chance to look them over. Hellgrammites are best fished in the swift center section of a river or stream. Keep the fly on the bottom and you should have good results. My best luck has been when they are fished at a dead drift.

HENRY'S LAKE NYMPH

HOOK: Mustad 9671, sizes 6-10.

THREAD: Black.

TAIL: Gray squirrel tail hair tied same length as body.

SHELLBACK: Gray squirrel tail hair pulled over the body and tied in at front. Hair at front is then divided and tied into a V.

BODY: Yellow chenille.

Do not limit this fly in just Henry's Lake as it is good in any lake that has fresh water shrimp. When fished with an erratic retrieve the front whiskers give the fly a most desirable effect in the water. Other colors are often used for the body to meet local fishing conditions.

HOWELL MAY FLY NYMPH, BLUE DUN

HOOK: Mustad 3906, sizes 14-16.

THREAD: Gray.

TAIL: Blue dun hackle fibers.

BODY: Dark peacock quill.

THORAX: Blue dun hackle wrapped closely and clipped to form a small rounded thorax. Leave a few hackle barbles extending out from each side for legs.

NOTES: This style of nymph can be tied in as many colors as there are shades of hackle.

The Howell May Fly Nymphs were perfected by the master rod builder Gary Howells of Richmond, California. It was an idea he adapted from an old English method of tying. These nymphs have been effective on flat water and in spring creeks. They should be fished just under the surface.

IDA MAY

HOOK: Mustad 38941, sizes 8-10.

THREAD: Black.

TAIL: Dyed dark green grizzly hackle fibers.

RIBBING: Peacock herl.

BODY: Dubbed black synthetic fur. Pick body out to give a fuzzy appearance. Reverse wrap with fine gold wire after ribbing has been wrapped.

HACKLE: Soft dyed dark green grizzly tied on as collar, one and a half turns, and tied back.

This pattern was created by Charles Brooks of West Yellowstone, Montana.

LADY MONO

HOOK: Mustad 3906B, sizes 10-14.

THREAD: Brown.

BODY: Tapered brown floss with orange floss tied in at rear and pulled up the belly. Body is then wrapped with flat monofilament.

HEAD: Black ostrich herl.

LARGE DARK STONE (Pteronarcys californica)

HOOK: Mustad 79580, sizes 2-8.

THREAD: Black.

UNDERBODY: Two pieces of lead wire equal in diameter to hook wire and tied in at each side of hook shank.

TAILS: Dyed dark brown saddle hackle stems tied in at each side. Tails should be equal to length of body only. Exclude thorax and head in this measurement.

RIBBING: Dyed brown flat monofilament. Rib body only.

BODY: Dubbed blackish brown synthetic fur.

WINGCASE: Natural dark gray goose quill section tied in over the thorax.

THORAX: Dubbed two parts blackish brown and one part dark orange synthetic fur mixed.

LEGS: Dark furnace hackle wrapped through thorax. Trim hackle barbles.

HEAD: Dubbed blackish brown synthetic fur.

LEADWING COACHMAN

HOOK: Mustad 9671, sizes 10-14.

THREAD: Brown.

TAIL: Dark brown hackle fibers.

RIBBING: Copper wire.

BODY: Peacock herl.

LEGS: Dark brown hackle fibers tied in at throat.

WINGCASE: Two gray duck shoulder feathers trimmed to a point.

LEADWING COACHMAN

HOOK: Mustad 3906B, sizes 8-14.

THREAD: Black.

TAIL: Two pieces of peacock herl trimmed short. Bronze mallard fibers should be tied over peacock so they extend slightly over.

BODY: Peacock herl with close dark brown peccary ribbing.

WINGCASE: Black duck quill section tied in over thorax.

THORAX: Dubbed dark brown beaver fur.

LEGS: Bronze mallard fibers tied in at each side.

Al Troth originated this variation of the Leadwing Coachman Nymph. It is probably the best of all the attempts yet made in improving the pattern.

LIEB'S BUG

HOOK: Mustad 9672, sizes 6-12.

THREAD: Black.

TAILS: Brown goose quill fibers taken from the back of flight quill and tied short in a V.

BODY: Peacock herl. Reverse wrap with fine gold wire. Palmer with brown hackle and clip off on top.

LEGS: Brown goose quill fibers tied in at each side so tips flare out.

Originated by Don Lieb. This fly has accounted for many fish. When tied weighted so it will bump along the bottom of a stream it will bring some unexpected results.

LIGHT CAHILL

HOOK:	Mustad 3906B, sizes 12-16.
THREAD:	Tan.
TAIL:	Barred lemon wood duck fibers.
BODY:	Dubbed cream rabbit or synthetic fur.
LEGS:	Light ginger hackle fibers.
WINGCASE:	Barred lemon wood duck fibers tied in at front and extending over ⅓ of body.

LIGHT CREEPER

HOOK:	Mustad 3906B, sizes 10-14.
THREAD:	Black.
TAIL:	Gray squirrel tail hair.
RIBBING:	Flat gold tinsel.
BODY:	Dubbed cream rabbit or synthetic fur.
THORAX:	Peacock herl.
LEGS:	Gray squirrel tail hair tied in at each side and extending ½ the length of body.

LIGHT OLIVE

HOOK:	Mustad 9671, sizes 10-14.
THREAD:	Olive.
TAILS:	Olive saddle hackle stems tied in a V.
RIBBING:	Fine oval gold tinsel.
BODY:	Light olive floss.
WINGCASE:	Natural dark gray duck quill section tied in over thorax.
THORAX:	Dubbed light olive synthetic fur.
LEGS:	Brown hackle wrapped through thorax.

LINDGREN'S DARK MAY

HOOK:	Mustad 3906B, sizes 12-16.
THREAD:	Black.
TAIL:	Black hackle fibers.
RIBBING:	Yellow thread.
BODY:	Black floss.
THORAX:	Peacock herl.
LEGS:	Metallic ringneck pheasant body feather fibers dyed black and tied in at throat.

LINDGREN'S INCH WORM

HOOK:	Mustad 3906B, sizes 8-12.
THREAD:	Black.
TAIL:	Black hackle fibers.
RIBBING:	Black ostrich wrapped rather close.
BODY:	Fluorescent green yarn.
HEAD:	Black ostrich herl.

LINDGREN'S OLIVE

HOOK:	Mustad 3906B, sizes 10-18.
THREAD:	Black.
TAIL:	Black hackle fibers.
RIBBING:	Gold wire.
BODY:	Olive marabou fibers.
THORAX:	Peacock herl.
LEGS:	Black hackle tied on as a collar and clipped off on both top and bottom.

LINDGREN'S PEACOCK

HOOK:	Mustad 3906B, sizes 10-16.
THREAD:	Black.
TAIL:	Black hackle fibers.
BODY:	Peacock herl. Reverse wrap the body with fine silver wire.
LEGS:	Soft black hackle tied on as a collar and clipped off on both top and bottom.

LINDGREN'S WOOD DUCK

HOOK: Mustad 3906B, sizes 12-18.

THREAD: Brown.

TAIL: Barred lemon wood duck fibers.

BODY: Barred lemon wood duck fibers wrapped thin. Reverse wrap the body with fine gold wire.

THORAX: Black ostrich herl.

LEGS: Barred lemon wood duck fibers tied in at each side and extending to the middle of body.

LINDGREN'S YELLOW

HOOK: Mustad 3906, sizes 12-16.

THREAD: Black.

TAIL: Black hackle fibers.

BODY: Yellow marabou fibers wrapped thin. Reverse wrap the body with fine gold wire.

LEGS: Black hackle tied on as a collar and trimmed off on both top and bottom.

These patterns were created by Ira Lindgren. They are all easy to tie and are effective most anywhere.

LITTLE GOOSE

HOOK: Mustad 3906B, sizes 14-18.

THREAD: Gray.

TAIL: Three porcupine bristles.

RIBBING: Copper wire.

BODY: Gray goose quill fibers wrapped thin.

WINGCASE: Gray goose quill section tied in over the thorax.

THORAX: Gray goose down.

LEGS: Fashion two legs for each side from protruding wingcase material. Legs should be clipped off just behind the thorax.

This is an unusually productive pattern. Materials are simple and it is one you should tie and try. Most effective on high mountain lake Brookies.

LITTLE GRAY CADDIS

HOOK: Mustad 9671, sizes 8-10.

THREAD: Black.

RIBBING: Peacock herl.

BODY: Gray spun fur wrapped thin. Reverse wrap the body after ribbing has been wrapped with fine gold wire.

HACKLE: Black. Wrap one full turn only. Hackle should be very soft and short.

NOTES: Peacock herl ribbing should be rather close. About one wrap into the joint of the spun fur body. Hackle should be short with a size 16 hackle suitable for a size 10.

This is another one of the patterns from Charlies Brooks who has been called the master of the unorthodox fraternity of flyfishers.

LITTLE GREEN CADDIS

HOOK: Mustad 3906, sizes 12-14.

THREAD: Black.

BODY: Insect green spun fur or dubbed synthetic fur.

LEGS: Blue dun hackle fibers tied in at throat.

WINGCASE: Two natural gray duck shoulder feathers trimmed to a point and tied in at each side.

HEAD: Black ostrich herl.

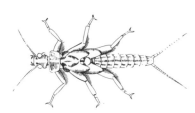

LITTLE YELLOW STONE (*Alloperla isoperla*)

HOOK: Mustad 38941, sizes 8-10.

THREAD: Yellow.

UNDERBODY: Two pieces of lead wire equal in diameter to hook wire and tied in at each side of hook shank.

TAILS: Dyed lemon yellow saddle hackle stems tied in at each side. Tails should be equal to length of body only. Exclude thorax and head in this measurement.

RIBBING: Dyed yellow flat monofilament. Rib body only.

BODY: Dubbed with a mixture of yellow, pale yellow and insect green synthetic fur mixed in equal parts.

WINGCASE: Barred teal dyed lemon yellow and tied in over the thorax.

THORAX: Dubbed pale yellow synthetic fur.

LEGS: Dyed lemon yellow grizzly hackle wrapped through the thorax. Trim hackle barbles from the bottom.

HEAD: Yellow tying thread.

MARABOU NYMPH, BLACK

HOOK: Mustad 3906B, sizes 6-14.

THREAD: Black.

TAIL: Black marabou tied short.

RIBBING: Fine silver oval tinsel.

BODY: Dubbed blackish brown synthetic fur.

WINGCASE: Short bunch of black marabou extending over half of body. Dyed black raffia tied in over the thorax.

THORAX: Dubbed dark gray synthetic fur.

LEGS: Speckled guinea fibers tied in at each side and extending to back of thorax.

MARABOU NYMPH, BROWN

HOOK: Mustad 3906B, sizes 6-14.

THREAD: Brown.

TAIL: Dark brown marabou tied short.

RIBBING: Fine gold oval tinsel.

BODY: Dubbed seal brown synthetic fur.

WINGCASE: Short bunch of dark brown marabou extending over half of body. Dyed dark brown raffia tied in over the thorax.

THORAX: Dubbed seal brown and pale yellow synthetic fur mixed in equal parts.

LEGS: Dyed brown speckled guinea fibers tied in at each side and extending to back of thorax.

MARABOU NYMPH, CREAM

HOOK: Mustad 3906B, sizes 6-14.

THREAD: Light yellow.

TAIL: Pale yellow marabou tied short.

RIBBING: Fine gold oval tinsel.

BODY: Dubbed cream synthetic fur.

WINGCASE: Short bunch of pale yellow marabou extending over half of body. Dyed yellow raffia tied in over the thorax.

THORAX: Dubbed natural white synthetic fur.

LEGS: Dyed yellow speckled guinea fibers tied in at each side and extending to back of thorax.

MARABOU NYMPH, GRAY

HOOK: Mustad 3906B, sizes 6-14.

THREAD: Gray.

TAIL: Gray marabou tied short.

RIBBING: Fine silver oval tinsel.

BODY: Dubbed gray synthetic fur.

WINGCASE: Short bunch of gray marabou extending over half of body. Dyed gray raffia tied in over the thorax.

THORAX: Dubbed light gray synthetic fur.

LEGS: Speckled guinea fibers tied in at each side and extending to back of thorax.

MARABOU NYMPH, OLIVE

HOOK: Mustad 3906B, sizes 6-14.

THREAD: Olive.

TAIL: Olive marabou tied short.

RIBBING: Fine gold oval tinsel.

BODY: Dubbed olive synthetic fur.

WINGCASE: Short bunch of olive marabou extending over half of body. Dyed olive raffia tied in over the the thorax.

THORAX: Dubbed yellowish olive synthetic fur.

LEGS: Dyed olive speckled guinea fibers tied in at each side and extending to back of thorax.

MARABOU NYMPH, TAN

HOOK: Mustad 3906B, sizes 6-14.

THREAD: Tan.

TAIL: Tan marabou tied short.

RIBBING: Fine gold oval tinsel.

BODY: Dubbed tan synthetic fur.

WINGCASE: Short bunch of tan marabou extending over half of body. Dyed tan raffia tied in over the thorax.

THORAX: Dubbed tan and natural white synthetic fur mixed in equal parts.

LEGS: Dyed tan speckled guinea fibers tied in at each side and extending to back back of thorax.

NOTES: Ribbing on the Marabou Nymphs should be confined to only three turns.

I first came in contact with this type of fly while fishing the Bighorn River in Wyoming. We had been fishing most of the day with little success when we came upon an old gentlemen from the area. He had a fish on so we stayed and watched. It was a monster. He beached it finally and released it almost at once. Before we knew it he had another fish on. This was too much. I went over this time and netted his fish for him and started pumping him on the fly he was using. He had an entire fly box filled with varying colors and sizes of nymphs tied in the Marabou style. He called them his "getters," and advised how and why he tied them in the style he did. Like the ordinary dry fly man he watched for the hatches, however, rather than try and match the hatching insects on top he used his patterns to match their emerging counterparts. It worked for him and after I was able to talk him out of some of his nymphs we were also catching fish regularly. For some years now I have been trying various colors and combinations of colors and find the basic six patterns above meet most situations.

MARCH BROWN

HOOK: Mustad 9671, sizes 10-16.

THREAD: Brown.

TAIL: Barred lemon wood duck fibers.

RIBBING: Light yellow thread.

BODY: Dubbed tannish red fox and Hare's Ear fur mixed in equal parts.

LEGS: Barred lemon wood duck fibers tied in at throat.

WINGCASE: Dyed brown ringneck pheasant quill section tied in at front and extending over ⅓ of the body.

NOTES: Wingcase should be made before tying the fly. Select a well marked section of dyed brown ringneck pheasant quill section. Trim a V at the end of the quill section to represent two wing pads. Apply a coat of vinyl cement and allow to dry before tying in.

MARCH BROWN, AMERICAN

HOOK: Mustad 3906B, sizes 8-14.

THREAD: Brown.

TAIL: Three brown elk hairs.

BODY: Brown saddle hackle stem.

WINGCASE: Natural dark gray duck quill section tied in over the thorax.

THORAX: Peacock herl.

LEGS: Brown hackle wrapped through the thorax.

NOTES: An underbody of brown floss should be wrapped to give the body a good natural taper and give the thorax more fullness.

MARTINEZ BLACK NYMPH

HOOK: Mustad 9671, sizes 8-12.

THREAD: Black.

TAIL: Speckled guinea fibers.

RIBBING: Oval gold tinsel.

BODY: Dubbed black muskrat fur. Body should be picked out and made shaggy.

THORAX: Black chenille.

WINGCASE: Green raffia tied in over the thorax.

HACKLE: Gray partridge.

This is another one of Don Martinez's patterns which has become a standard pattern throughout North America.

METALLIC MIDGE

HOOK: Mustad 3906, sizes 14-18.

THREAD: Black.

RIBBING: Black thread. Wrap six turns.

BODY: Gray floss tied well down into bend of hook.

THORAX: Dark metallic turkey tail feather fibers.

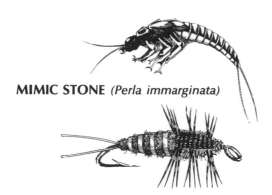

MIMIC STONE (Perla immarginata)

HOOK: Mustad 38941, sizes 6-10.

THREAD: Light yellow.

UNDERBODY: Two pieces of lead wire equal in diameter to hook wire and tied in at each side of hook shank.

TAILS: Dyed yellow saddle hackle stems equal to length of body only. Exclude thorax and head in this measurement.

RIBBING: Dyed yellow flat monofilament. Rib body only.

BODY: Dubbed dark brown and yellow synthetic fur mixed in equal parts.

WINGCASE: Dyed deep yellow barred teal tied in over the thorax.

THORAX: Dubbed yellowish brown synthetic fur.

LEGS: Dyed deep yellow grizzly hackle wrapped through thorax. Trim hackle barbles from bottom.

HEAD: Dubbed dark brown and yellow synthetic fur mixed in equal parts.

NOTES: Dyed grizzly for legs should have a fine black barring.

MIMS SHRIMP

HOOK: Mustad 94838, sizes 8-12.

THREAD: Olive.

TAIL: Dyed yellow bucktail.

SHELLBACK: Dyed yellow bucktail.

NOTES: This special pattern is designed to give the fly an unusual natural action in the water. The deer hair is taken from the back of the tail. Only the lighter hair at the base of the tail is used. Tie hair in with the butts towards the front of the hook. Pull the hair over the back of the hook and tie in at head. Clip off excess hair at front leaving about ⅛" protruding at the head. Butt pieces sticking out at the belly are then trimmed to represent shrimp legs.

This is a very deadly shrimp pattern. Fish it with a wet line and at least a 7 foot leader. Stripping in your line pulls the imitation down and between retrieves the deer hair floats the fly upwards. Even in the hardest fished waters this fly will take fish regularly. This pattern was developed by Mims Barker of Ogden, Utah.

MINK NYMPH

HOOK: Mustad 7957BX, sizes 6-14.

THREAD: Brown.

TAIL: Soft brown hackle fibers.

BODY: Dubbed brown mink fur tied full and shaggy. Leave guard hairs in fur.

LEGS: Dark furnace hackle tied on as a collar and tied back.

This pattern was originated by Doug Prince. This has been an effective pattern on larger streams and rivers for those real big fish. This fly is usually tied weighted.

MIRACLE NYMPH

HOOK: Mustad 3906, sizes 14-20.

THREAD: Black.

RIBBING: Copper wire.

BODY: Construct an underbody of black tying thread. Overwrap with white floss.

NOTE: The idea of this rather simple pattern is that the white floss turns a dirty dun gray when it gets wet. You should avoid getting any cement on the body. It will not change color and will attract fewer fish.

MONTANA STONE

HOOK: Mustad 79580, sizes 4-8.

THREAD: Black.

TAILS: Two black hackle tips tied in a V.

BODY: Black chenille.

WINGCASE: Black chenille.

THORAX: Yellow chenille.

LEGS: Black hackle wrapped through the thorax.

This pattern is also very effective when tied with dark olive chenille rather than black.

MOSQUITO LARVA

HOOK: Mustad 3906B, sizes 14-18.

THREAD: Gray.

TAIL: Grizzly hackle fibers.

BODY: Grizzly saddle hackle stem.

FEELERS: Grizzly hackle fibers tied in over the eye of the hook. Feelers should be about half the length of the body and thorax combined.

THORAX: Grizzly saddle hackle trimmed to shape.

NOTES: Select a saddle hackle with fine textured barbles and minimum web for the thorax. Wrap very close.

I have a high regard for this pattern. It is very good in waters with large mosquito populations. The fish

maintain a steady feeding pace when this larva is emerging. I have been fortunate to be at the right place at the right time and had continuous action from early morning until night using this pattern. Some tyers substitute peacock herl for thorax material which only reduces the effectiveness of the fly and makes it less durable. It is good to experiment but don't go backwards.

MUSKRAT NYMPH

HOOK: Mustad 9671, sizes 10-20.

THREAD: Brown.

TAIL: Soft brown hackle fibers.

RIBBING: Silver wire.

BODY: Dubbed muskrat fur. Leave guard hairs in fur. Body should be tied full and well tapered.

HACKLE: Long soft brown hackle tied on as a collar and tied back.

This is another variation of the muskrat nymphs. It was sent to me by George Bodmer of Colorado Springs, Colorado. It is a good fly as are all of the muskrat nymphs.

NYERGES SHRIMP

HOOK: Mustad 9672, sizes 8-12.

THREAD: Olive.

BODY: Dark olive chenille.

LEGS: Brown hackle wrapped over the body and then clipped off on top and sides to suggest shrimp legs.

This fly was developed by Gil Nyerges. A very easy fly to tie and very good anywhere shrimp are present.

OLIVE AND BROWN

HOOK: Mustad 3906B, sizes 10-16.

THREAD: Black.

TAIL: Peacock sword. Use three pieces.

RIBBING: Oval gold tinsel.

BODY: Dubbed olive synthetic fur.

THORAX: Peacock herl.

HACKLE: Soft furnace tied on as a collar and tied back.

OLIVE MAY FLY

HOOK: Mustad 3906B, sizes 10-14.

THREAD: Olive.

TAIL: Olive hackle fibers.

RIBBING: Yellow thread.

BODY: Olive floss.

WINGCASE: Dark olive duck quill section tied in over thorax.

THORAX: Dubbed olive synthetic fur.

LEGS: Yellow hackle wrapped through thorax.

OLIVE MIDGE PUPA

HOOK: Mustad 94838, sizes 12-16.

THREAD: Olive.

BODY: Peacock herl tied in at butt and olive floss.

FEELERS: Olive hackle fibers tied in over eye of hook.

OLIVE SEDGE

HOOK: Mustad 3906, sizes 10-14.

THREAD: Brown.

BODY: Dubbed olive rabbit and synthetic fur mixed in equal parts.

WINGCASE: Natural gray duck quill sections. Tie a section in at each side with tip of each section pointing downward.

LEGS: Brown partridge tied in at throat.

HEAD: Dubbed Hare's Ear fur. Tie rather large and shaggy.

OLIVE SHRIMP

HOOK: Mustad 3906, sizes 6-10.

THREAD: Olive.

BODY: Dubbed insect green synthetic fur.

LEGS: Olive hackle tied Palmer over the body.

BACK AND TAIL: Olive elk hair.

NOTES: When tying this pattern leave a piece of olive thread at the rear of the body to tie in elk hair at rear. After hair is tied in at the rear thread should be ribbed forward and tied off at the head. Clip hackle from the point of the hook to the eye.

PEACOCK BLUE

HOOK: Mustad 3906, sizes 10-14.

THREAD: Blue.

TAIL: Three peacock blue sword feather fibers.

BODY: Dubbed peacock blend synthetic fur. Tie body with large full taper.

LEGS: Barred teal fibers tied in at each side and extended to the middle of the body.

PEACOCK NYMPH

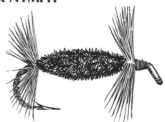

HOOK: Mustad 9671, sizes 4-10.

THREAD: Black.

REAR HACKLE: Dark ginger tied slightly back. Hackle should be rather short and not exceed much past point of hook.

BODY: Peacock herl. Wrap an underbody of dark olive wool yarn to give the body a good fullness. Reverse wrap the body with fine gold wire.

FRONT HACKLE: Dark ginger. Front hackle should match the length of rear hackle.

This pattern was sent to me by Pete Test of Albuquerque, New Mexico. He states this pattern is one of the more productive flies in his area. A variation includes a tail of peacock herl.

PEACOCK SHRIMP

HOOK:	Mustad 94838, sizes 8-14.
THREAD:	Black.
SHELLBACK:	Peacock herl.
RIBBING:	Round clear monofilament.
BODY:	Dubbed yellowish brown synthetic fur.
LEGS:	Brown hackle wrapped over the body. Clip off hackle barbles on top.

PHEASANT TAIL

HOOK:	Mustad 3906, sizes 10-16.
THREAD:	Brown.
TAIL:	Reddish brown cock ringneck pheasant center tail feather fibers.
RIBBING:	Gold wire.
BODY:	Ginger cock ringneck pheasant body feather fibers.
LEGS:	Reddish brown cock ringneck pheasant center tail feather fibers tied in at throat.

PIG NYMPH, BLACK

HOOK:	Mustad 94840, sizes 10-18.
THREAD:	Black.
TAIL:	Three dark peccary fibers.
BODY:	Dyed black peccary.
THORAX:	Black ostrich herl.
LEGS:	Soft black hackle wrapped on as a collar and trimmed off on both top and bottom.

This pattern was created by Doug Prince. This fly is also tied in tan, olive, brown, yellow and gray. Ostrich herl and hackle should be one shade darker than body color. Select tying thread to match the overall coloration of the nymph being tied.

PKCK NYMPH

HOOK:	Mustad 3906B, sizes 8-16.
THREAD:	Black.

TIP:	Flat silver tinsel.
RIBBING:	Dark peacock quill. After the quill is wrapped it is then over-wrapped with a fine silver wire.
BODY:	Dubbed green synthetic fur.
WINGCASE:	Mottled hen ringneck pheasant quill section tied in over the thorax.
THORAX:	Dubbed seal brown synthetic fur.
LEGS:	Black ostrich herl tied in at each side and trimmed off at back of thorax.

Dave Powell and Jim Kilburn developed this pattern. It has been useful in many areas. Size 8 is favored.

PUGET BUG

HOOK:	Mustad 7957BX, sizes 10-14.
THREAD:	Black.
TAILS:	Black goose quill fibers taken from the back of flight quill and tied in a V.
BODY:	One dark and one light moose mane wrapped in alternating bands.
THORAX:	Peacock herl.
HACKLE:	Gray partridge.

This fly was originated by Washington fly-tyer Enos Bradner. It is more than just effective in the Puget Sound area as the name suggests.

PUSSYCAT

HOOK:	Mustad 38941, sizes 6-10.
THREAD:	Gray.
TAIL:	Greenish gray cock ringneck pheasant rump feather fibers.
BODY:	Dubbed muskrat, beaver and olive synthetic fur mixed in equal parts.
LEGS:	Greenish gray cock ringneck pheasant rump feather fibers tied in at throat.
WINGCASE:	Mottled brown cock ringneck pheasant body feather tied in at head and extending over ⅓ of body.

This is a creation of Joseph Miotle. It has been an extremely successful nymph in Utah's Strawberry Reservoir. Also, good reports have come from Idaho's Salmon and Lost Rivers.

RAGGLE BOMB

HOOK:	Mustad 9671, sizes 8-14.
THREAD:	Black.
UNDERBODY:	Dark olive wool yarn wrapped with a large cigar taper.
RIBBING:	Furnace hackle tied Palmer over the body. Tie hackle in by the tip.
BODY:	Peacock herl. Select herl from just below the eye. Reverse wrap the body with fine gold wire after hackle has been wrapped forward.

This bug has proven to be good during the early part of the season.

RENEGADE NYMPH

HOOK:	Mustad 9671, sizes 8-14.
THREAD:	Brown.
TIP:	Flat gold tinsel.
SHELLBACK:	Cock ringneck pheasant tail feather fibers or gray goose quill section.
REAR LEGS:	Soft white hackle.
RIBBING:	Round clear monofilament. (Opt.)
BODY:	Peacock herl.
FRONT LEGS:	Soft brown hackle.

NOTES: In tying this nymph you should tie the shellback so it separates both the front and rear hackle when it is pulled over the back. Ribbing is wrapped forward after the shellback is tied in.

RIFFLE DEVIL

HOOK:	Mustad 79580, size 4.
THREAD:	Olive.
BODY:	Olive chenille. Body should be tied fat and full.

HACKLE:	Dark ginger tied Palmer over the body. Hackle should be tied in by the tip and wrapped so the hackle barbles are pointing to the rear.

Another one of the Charles Brooks patterns.

SAND FLY NYMPH

HOOK:	Mustad 3906, sizes 6-14.
THREAD:	Brown.
TAIL:	White marabou. Tail should be equal to the length of the body.
RIBBING:	Yellow thread.
BODY:	Dark brown floss.
HACKLE:	Dark ginger tied on as a collar and tied back.

This fly was developed some years ago by Terry Bryant of Spokane, Washington.

SAND SEDGE

HOOK:	Mustad 3906B, sizes 12-16.
THREAD:	Brown.
BODY:	Dubbed with two parts pale yellow and one part seal brown synthetic fur mixed.
WINGCASE:	Natural gray duck quill sections tied in at each side and extending to the middle of the body.
LEGS:	Bronze mallard fibers tied in at throat.
HEAD:	Dubbed Hare's Mask fur.

SCUD

HOOK:	Mustad 7957B, sizes 6-12.
THREAD:	Olive.
TAIL:	Olive dun hackle fibers tied in well down on bend of hook.
SHELLBACK:	Clear 4 mil. plastic sheeting.

ANTENNA:	Olive dun hackle fibers.
RIBBING:	Clear round monofilament (size 3X).
BODY:	Dubbed six parts olive, two parts gray, one part red and one part orange synthetic fur.

Originated by Al Troth. Body color can be adjusted to suit your own area.

SHRIMP NYMPH, GOLD

HOOK:	Mustad 94838, sizes 8-14.
THREAD:	Yellow.
TAIL:	Dyed gold teal fibers.
SHELLBACK:	Dyed gold hen ringneck pheasant quill section.
RIBBING:	Gold wire. Rib body only.
BODY:	Dubbed with gold rabbit, gold and yellow synthetic fur mixed in equal parts.

SHRIMP NYMPH, GRAY

HOOK:	Mustad 94838, sizes 8-14.
THREAD:	Gray.
TAIL:	Barred teal fibers.
SHELLBACK:	Natural gray goose quill section.
RIBBING:	Silver wire. Rib body only.
BODY:	Dubbed with gray rabbit and gray synthetic fur mixed in equal parts.

SHRIMP NYMPH, OLIVE

HOOK:	Mustad 94838, sizes 8-14.
THREAD:	Olive.
TAIL:	Dyed olive barred teal fibers.
SHELLBACK:	Dyed olive hen ringneck pheasant quill section.
RIBBING:	Gold wire. Rib body only.
BODY:	Dubbed with olive rabbit and yellowish olive synthetic fur mixed in equal parts.

NOTES: Do not rib the thorax area of the fly. The thorax should be tied fuller than the body and picked out and made shaggy. I recommend lead wire be wrapped through the thorax area before tying the fly. This not only gives the light wire hook an assist in sinking but also gives the thorax the desired fullness. Tails should be tied in well down on the bend of the hook and only about ⅔ the length of the body.

This type of fly was originated by Dave Whitlock. Through the blending of body furs you can match the fresh water shrimp in your own area by using his basic fly design.

SOWBUG

HOOK:	Mustad 3906, sizes 10-16.
THREAD:	Gray.
TAIL:	Natural gray duck quill fibers taken from the back of the flight quill and tied in a V. Tail should be ½ the length of the body.
SHELLBACK:	Clear 4 mil. plastic sheeting.
RIBBING:	Gold wire.
BODY:	Dubbed with muskrat and gray synthetic fur mixed in equal parts.

This is another one of the Dave Whitlock patterns. It is not only easy to tie, it catches fish.

SPECKLED SPINNER

HOOK:	Mustad 9671, sizes 12-16.
THREAD:	Gray.
TAIL:	Three porcupine bristles.
RIBBING:	Gray thread.
BODY:	Dubbed muskrat and light gray synthetic fur mixed in equal parts.
WINGCASE:	Speckled brown hen ringneck pheasant body feather tied in over the thorax.
THORAX:	Dubbed muskrat and light gray synthetic fur mixed in equal parts.
LEGS:	Brown partridge fibers tied in at throat.

SPRUCE NYMPH

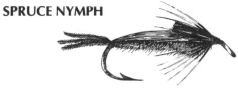

HOOK:	Mustad 9671, sizes 6-10.

THREAD:	Black.
TAIL:	Peacock sword fibers.
SHELLBACK:	Natural gray goose quill section.
RIBBING:	Gold wire. Rib body and thorax.
BODY:	Dubbed pale yellow and scarlet red synthetic fur mixed in equal parts.
THORAX:	Peacock herl.
LEGS:	Soft well marked badger hackle tied on as a collar and tied back.

STONE FLY CREEPER

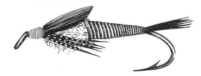

HOOK:	Mustad 38941, sizes 6-8.
THREAD:	Brown.
TAIL:	Reddish brown cock ringneck pheasant center tail feather fibers.
BODY:	Natural brown saddle hackle stem. Wrap a tapered underbody of brown floss before wrapping hackle stem.
THORAX:	Dubbed yellow rabbit and pale yellow synthetic fur mixed in equal parts.
WINGCASE:	Natural gray goose quill section tied in at head and extending over the thorax. Quill section should be folded double to give the wingcase extra fullness.
LEGS:	Dyed brown speckled guinea fibers tied in at each side and extending just past the thorax.

This is one of the better patterns of the many variations of the Stone Fly Creepers. Good most anywhere it is used.

TAINTOR SHRIMP

HOOK:	Mustad 3906, sizes 8-14.
THREAD:	Black.
TAIL:	Reddish brown cock ringneck pheasant center tail feather fibers.
SHELLBACK:	Natural gray goose quill section.
RIBBING:	Grizzly saddle. Select a hackle with extra fine textured barbles and a minimum of web. Also, disregard length of hackle as it is clipped after fly is completed.

BODY:	Fluorescent green yarn tied with extra large taper.

NOTES: Fly is ribbed before shellback is pulled forward and tied in. After fly is completed pull hackle barbles down and clip from the point of the hook to the eye. Shorter end of the taper is at the eye of the hook.

This is the original pattern of the old master Bob Taintor. It has been a good fly over many years. There have been variations from time to time, but everyone seems to go back to the original.

TAN CADDIS LARVA

HOOK:	Mustad 9671, sizes 8-12.
THREAD:	Black.
BODY:	Tan chenille.
THORAX:	Black metallic turkey tail feather section.
LEGS:	Soft brown hackle tied on as a collar and then clipped on both top and bottom.

NOTES: When tying the body wrap the chenille on through the thorax and tie off. Then wrap tying thread back to the rear of the thorax and tie in thorax material. The chenille gives you an under padding for wrapping the thorax material.

TAN SHRIMP

HOOK:	Mustad 3906, sizes 6-10.
THREAD:	Tan.
BODY:	Dubbed pink synthetic fur.
LEGS:	Light ginger hackle tied Palmer over the body.

BACK AND TAIL: Light tan elk hair.

NOTES: When tying, leave a piece of tan thread at the rear. After hair is tied in at rear, the thread should be ribbed forward and tied off at the head. Clip hackle from the point of the hook to the eye.

T.D.C. NYMPH

HOOK:	Mustad 7957B, sizes 10-12.
THREAD:	Black.

RIBBING:	Fine flat silver tinsel, five or six turns.
BODY:	Black wool yarn tied well down on the bend of the hook and tapered towards the head.
THORAX:	Black chenille, two turns.
COLLAR.	White ostrich herl, two turns.

A pattern developed by Dick Thompson of Seattle, Washington, for fishing the lowland lakes of western Washington and Oregon. Dick is a fishery research biologist and developed this nymph to imitate the *chironomid* pupa which emerge from the bottom of the lakes in the west. It is suggested that this pattern be dressed in two versions—one with a rather fat taper and the other with a slender taper. This difference can decide your success from one area to another. Some amateurs tie this pattern with a black chenille body which only reduces its effectiveness. Maybe this is one of those patterns that should not be fooled with and left in its present form. Dick has already done the qualified research on this one for us.

TEENY NYMPH

HOOK:	Mustad 3906B, sizes 4-12.
THREAD:	Brown.
BODY:	Cock ringneck pheasant tail feather fibers tied in two segments.
LEGS:	Cock ringneck pheasant tail feather fibers tied in at the center of the belly and at the throat.

I offer this pattern because of its unusual design. Jim Teeny of Portland, Oregon, originated this style of fly. Jim holds three patent designs on his flies and states that he would rather not share his patterns with us. Is it possible that he is injecting his flies with some secret elixir? I find it perplexing when I see fly-tyers like young Jim taking out patents on their flies. Only when we all share our limited information do these "secret weapons" get tied and tried by the amateur. This generates variations and often some very good standard patterns result. Where would our flies be today if the Gordons and Hewitts of yesterday had not given freely?

TELLICO

HOOK:	Mustad 3906B, sizes 8-14.
THREAD:	Black.

TAIL:	Speckled guinea fibers.
SHELLBACK:	Cock ringneck pheasant tail feather fibers.
RIBBING:	Peacock herl.
BODY:	Dubbed yellow synthetic fur. Body should have a nice full plump taper.
LEGS:	Soft dark brown hackle tied on as a collar, two turns, and tied back.

This pattern originated in the southern United States and was originally tied with a dubbed body of natural wool which was a dirty grayish color. It has been a very good pattern wherever it has been used.

TERRIBLE STONE

HOOK:	Mustad 3665A, sizes 2-4.
THREAD:	Black.
TAIL:	Natural gray goose quill fibers dyed dark brown and tied in a V.
RIBBING:	Black and seal brown synthetic fur twisted on a dubbing loop. Fur should be mixed in equal parts.
BODY:	Dark brown chenille.
LEGS:	Black hackle stems with barbles trimmed off.
THORAX:	Dark brown chenille.
FEELERS:	Natural gray goose quill fibers dyed dark brown and tied in a V.

Instructions for tying the Terrible Stone:

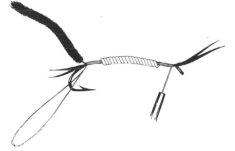

STEP 1: Bend hook shank in the center to about 25-30 degrees. Tie in tail, feelers, chenille and a loop of black tying thread.

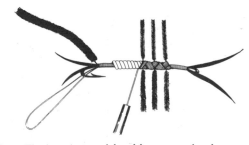

STEP 2: Tie in trimmed hackle stems for legs.

STEP 3: Wrap dark brown chenille to the front.

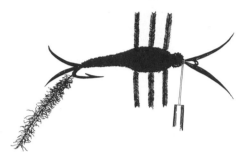

STEP 4: Wrap chenille back through the thorax and back to the head again to give the thorax a fuller effect. Tease synthetic fur into dubbing loop and twist. Rib body and thorax closely with dubbing.

STEP 5: Trim dubbing from top and bottom of fly to give it a flattened effect. Bend joints into the legs and place a drop of vinyl cement in each joint so they will hold their shape.

This pattern was sent to me by Al Troth. When I opened the box that it came in I about jumped out of my skin. A very realistic and deadly imitation of the Stone Fly, *Pteronarcys californica*.

THUNDERBERG

HOOK: Mustad 38941, sizes 6-10.
THREAD: Gray.
TAIL: Black bear hair tied equal to ½ the length of the body.

RIBBING: Copper wire.
BODY: Dubbed with beaver and dark gray synthetic fur mixed in equal parts. Leave guard hairs in the beaver fur and pick out the thorax area to simulate the legs.

This pattern was developed by Gene Snow of Salt Lake City, Utah. I have seen the same pattern in many other states in the west all tied the same but known under other names.

TROTH LEECH

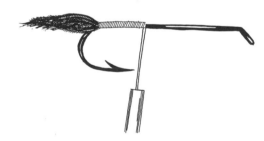

HOOK: Mustad 79580, size 4.
THREAD: Black.
TAIL: Dark brown marabou.
BODY: Dark brown marabou.

Instructions for tying the Troth Leech:

STEP 1: Tie in a small bunch of dark brown marabou.

STEP 2: Wrap the body closely with marabou hackle. Normally it takes two or three hackles to cover the entire body.

STEP 3: Clip marabou off on both top and bottom.

STEP 4: Finished fly should look like sample above. To obtain the desired natural ends of the marabou fibers and have correct taper you can pinch off the ends of the marabou.

TRUEBLOOD'S BLUE GRAY

HOOK: Mustad 3906B, sizes 8-16.

THREAD: Gray.

TAIL: Brown partridge fibers.

BODY: Dubbed dark muskrat fur taken from the back of the muskrat. Leave the guard hairs in the fur and pick out and make shaggy.

LEGS: Brown partridge fibers tied in at throat.

TRUEBLOOD'S CADDIS

HOOK: Mustad 7957BX, sizes 8-12.

THREAD: Black.

TAIL: Green floss extending just past the bend of the hook.

SHELLBACK: Peacock herl.

RIBBING: Oval silver tinsel. Ribbing is tied over the shellback.

BODY: Green floss tied with a large taper.

LEGS: Barred mallard fibers tied in at the throat.

TRUEBLOOD'S MAY FLY

HOOK: Mustad 9671, sizes 14-16.

THREAD: Black.

BODY: Dark peacock quill.

THORAX AND FEELERS: Fine barred and fine textured fox squirrel tail hair tied in at rear of thorax. Tie in with butt toward front of hook. Clip off butts and form a thread under-thorax by over-wrapping the butts. Pull the hair forward and tie in at head. Separate the ends of the hair and form feelers tied in a V of about 50 degrees.

NOTES: Squirrel hair taken from the base of the tail is best suited for tying this nymph.

TRUEBLOOD'S SHRIMP NYMPH

HOOK: Mustad 3906, sizes 8-12.

THREAD: Brown.

TAIL: Brown partridge fibers.

BODY: Dubbed otter and cream seal fur mixed in equal parts.

LEGS: Brown partridge fibers tied in at throat.

NOTES: Mink fur and cream synthetic fur can be substituted for body material.

This pattern is sometimes called Otter Nymph.

TRUEBLOOD'S STONE FLY

HOOK: Mustad 38941, sizes 6-12.

THREAD: Black.

TAILS: Natural gray goose quill fibers taken from the back of flight quill and tied in a V.

BODY: Dark brown chenille.

WINGCASE: Two strands of dark brown chenille tied in over the thorax.

THORAX: Dark orange chenille.

LEGS: Black hackle wrapped through the thorax.

Ted Trueblood's first Stone Fly Nymphs appeared in several other color combinations. After years of trial and extensive use by fly fishermen everywhere this one was resolved to be the best of the lot.

WALKER'S NYMPH

HOOK: Mustad 3906B, sizes 6-10.

THREAD: Brown.

TAIL: Dyed gold goose quill fibers taken from the back of the flight quill and tied in a V.

BODY: Dubbed golden brown synthetic fur.

LEGS: Dark ginger hackle tied in as a collar behind and in front of the thorax.

THORAX: Dubbed golden brown and yellow synthetic fur mixed in equal parts.

The Walker's Nymph was developed by Mike Walker of Portola, California, for fishing the upper portion of the Feather River. This nymph is exceptionally good wherever the stone fly, *Acroneuria californica,* is present.

WHISKER NYMPH

HOOK: Mustad 3906, sizes 8-14.

THREAD: Black.

TAIL: Black hackle fibers.

BODY: Two dark and one light moose mane hairs wrapped together.

THORAX: Dubbed black muskrat fur.

LEGS: Black hackle tied in as a collar then trimmed off on both top and bottom.

A pattern perfected by Bill Powell of Seattle, Washington, during the 1940s. It is still in use in many areas.

WHITE CADDIS WORM

HOOK: Mustad 37140, size 12.

THREAD: Black.

BODY: Dubbed natural white synthetic fur. Tie body well down on bend of hook.

LEGS: Metallic black turkey tail feather fibers tied in at each side and tied short.

HEAD: Dubbed black synthetic fur tied shaggy.

WONDER NYMPH

HOOK: Mustad 9671, sizes 6-12.

THREAD: Black.

TAIL: Three black porcupine bristles.

RIBBING: Blue dun and brown saddle hackle wrapped together, four turns, over body. Clip hackle down to about 1/16''.

BODY: Dubbed muskrat fur.

HEAD: Black ostrich herl.

YELLOW CADDIS WORM

HOOK: Mustad 37140, size 12.

THREAD: Black.

BODY: Dubbed pale yellow synthetic fur. Tie body well down on bend of hook.

LEGS: Metallic black turkey tail feather fibers tied in at each side and tied short.

HEAD: Dubbed black synthetic fur tied shaggy.

YELLOW MIDGE PUPA

HOOK: Mustad 9671, sizes 10-14.

THREAD: Brown.

BUTT: Three turns of gray ostrich.

RIBBING: Peacock herl.

BODY: Yellow floss. Reverse wrap the body with fine gold wire after ribbing has been wrapped.

LEGS: Soft cree hackle tied on as a collar and tied back.

HEAD: Dubbed Hare's Ear fur.

An Al Troth pattern which is a very good lake fly.

YELLOW STONE

HOOK: Eagle Claw 1197B, size 6.

THREAD: Yellow.

TAIL: Natural gray and white turkey quill fibers taken from the back of the flight quill and dyed gold.

BODY: Woven with J. and P. Coats Mercerized Cotton Floss. Use Shade 214 Warm Beige for back and Shade 10-A Canary Yellow for the belly.

WINGCASE: Mottled brown turkey quill section.

FEELERS: Coarse brown bear hairs tied in a V.

HACKLE: Dyed tan grizzly.

Instructions for tying the Yellow Stone:

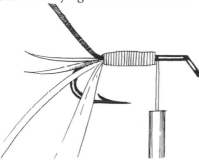

STEP 1: Tie in the dyed gold turkey quill fibers. They should be tied in a V about 5/8'' long. Tie in floss. Tan floss should be on the side of the hook away from you and the yellow on the side facing you. Cut a piece of yellow 1/8'' thick Art Foam about 3/16'' wide and 4'' long. Tie in the Art Foam at the rear of the hook.

STEP 2: Wrap Art Foam forward to form an underbody.

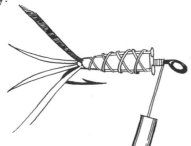

STEP 3: Tie in dressmaker's pins at each side. Pins should be about 5/8'' long after they have been cut off.

STEP 4: Tie in another strip of Art Foam at rear of body and wrap over the pins.

STEP 5: Tie off your tying thread at front and clip. Turn your vise so that the eye of the hook is facing you. The weaving is a simple overhand knot.

STEP 6: Slip the knot over the hook. Pull up tight and repeat this operation until there is a small space still left in back of the pin heads.

STEP 7: Tie the floss in behind the pin heads.

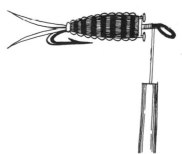

STEP 8: Make stripes on the top side with a black waterproof fine tipped marking pen.

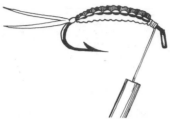

STEP 9: Bend the hook shank to give the body a more natural curve. Coat the heads of the dressmaker's pins with yellow lacquer.

STEP 10: Clip a section of turkey with a V at the end and tie in with windings slightly ahead of the center of the body. The tips of the wingcase should extend slightly to the rear of the center of the body. Lift the turkey quill wingcase and tie in the hackle feather.

STEP 11: Wrap three full turns of the hackle and tie in just behind the heads of the dressmaker's pins. Tie down the wingcase at the head of the fly and clip hackle barbles from the belly.

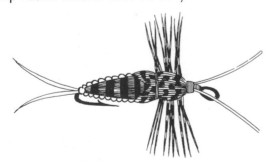

STEP 12: Tie in the feelers and tie off the head of the fly.

As you might have guessed, only Al Troth could have worked out such an ideal imitation. This is a rather slow fly to tie; however, when you get it to the stream you will be very happy you took the time to put it all together. This is one that you just cannot run down to your local tackle shop and expect to pick-up.

ZERO

HOOK:	Mustad 3906, sizes 12-16.
THREAD:	Gray.
TAIL:	Barred mallard fibers.
BODY:	Dubbed dark gray synthetic fur.
WINGCASE:	Black raffia tied in over thorax.
THORAX:	Dubbed dark gray and olive synthetic fur mixed in equal parts.
LEGS:	Grizzly hackle tied through the thorax.

ZUG BUG

HOOK:	Mustad 9671, sizes 8-14.
THREAD:	Black.
TAIL:	Three peacock herl fibers. Clip down so tail is equal to ⅔ the length of the body.
RIBBING:	Oval silver tinsel.
BODY:	Peacock herl.
WINGCASE:	Barred lemon wood duck fibers tied in at front. Clip fibers so they extend over the body ⅓.
HACKLE:	Two turns of soft long furnace tied on as a collar and tied back.

This nymph is also known as the Davis Special or Kemp's Bug. Eastern fly-tyer Cliff Zug got to working on the original versions and came up with today's more accepted variation.

I prefer using peacock sword fibers rather than clipped peacock for the tail on the Zug Bug. I feel that the natural curved tips of the peacock sword fibers gives the bug more life-like action in the water.

DRY FLIES

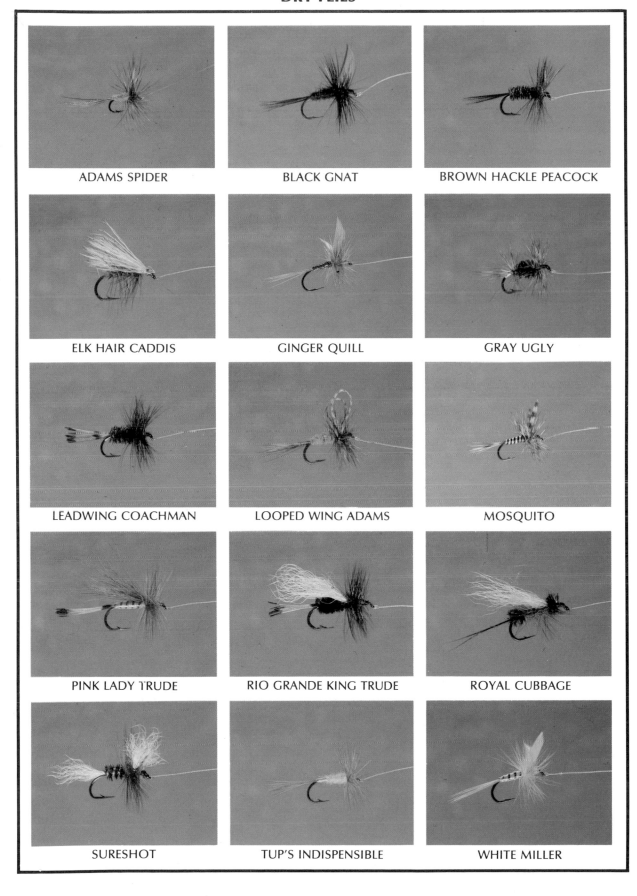

ADAMS SPIDER	BLACK GNAT	BROWN HACKLE PEACOCK
ELK HAIR CADDIS	GINGER QUILL	GRAY UGLY
LEADWING COACHMAN	LOOPED WING ADAMS	MOSQUITO
PINK LADY TRUDE	RIO GRANDE KING TRUDE	ROYAL CUBBAGE
SURESHOT	TUP'S INDISPENSIBLE	WHITE MILLER

DRY FLIES

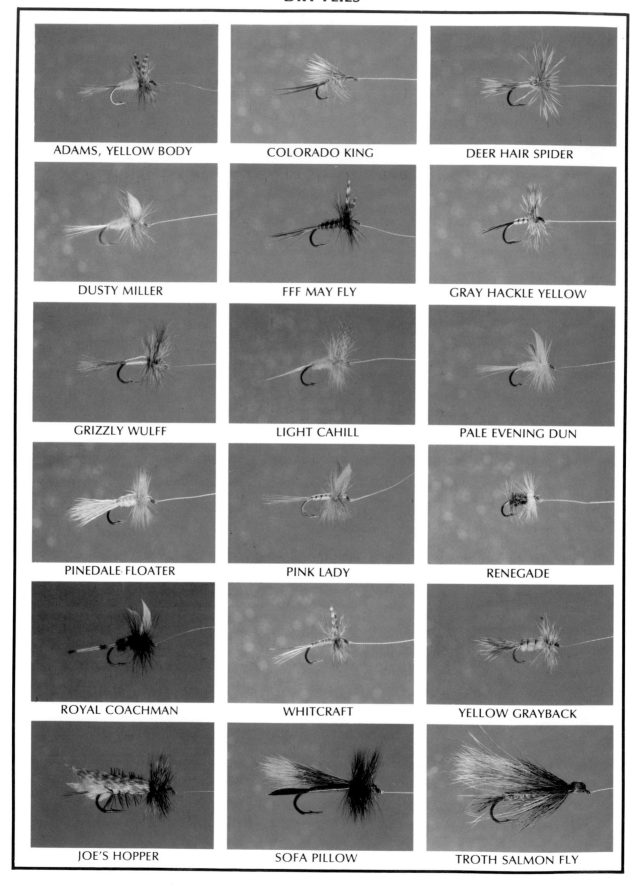

ADAMS, YELLOW BODY   COLORADO KING   DEER HAIR SPIDER

DUSTY MILLER   FFF MAY FLY   GRAY HACKLE YELLOW

GRIZZLY WULFF   LIGHT CAHILL   PALE EVENING DUN

PINEDALE FLOATER   PINK LADY   RENEGADE

ROYAL COACHMAN   WHITCRAFT   YELLOW GRAYBACK

JOE'S HOPPER   SOFA PILLOW   TROTH SALMON FLY

WATERWALKERS

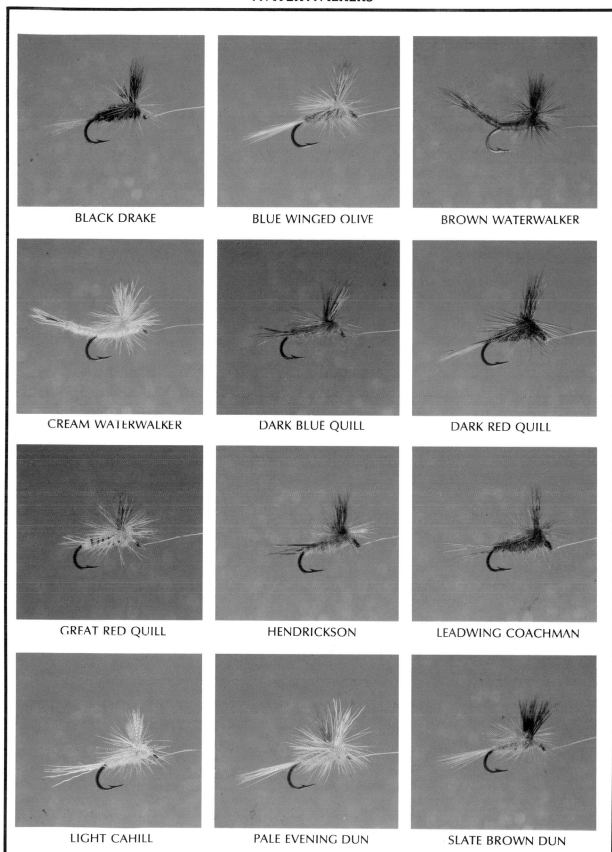

BLACK DRAKE

BLUE WINGED OLIVE

BROWN WATERWALKER

CREAM WATERWALKER

DARK BLUE QUILL

DARK RED QUILL

GREAT RED QUILL

HENDRICKSON

LEADWING COACHMAN

LIGHT CAHILL

PALE EVENING DUN

SLATE BROWN DUN

NYMPHS

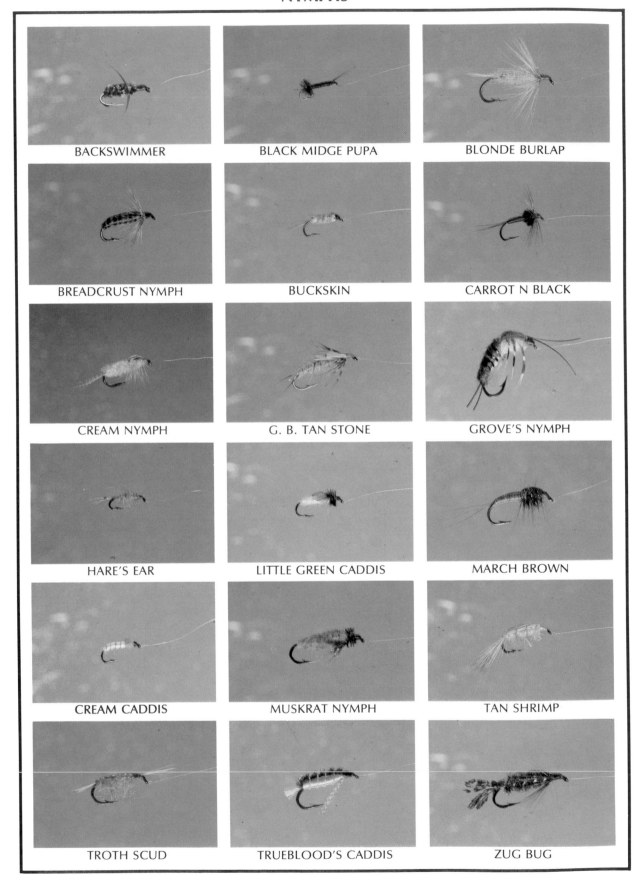

BACKSWIMMER

BLACK MIDGE PUPA

BLONDE BURLAP

BREADCRUST NYMPH

BUCKSKIN

CARROT N BLACK

CREAM NYMPH

G. B. TAN STONE

GROVE'S NYMPH

HARE'S EAR

LITTLE GREEN CADDIS

MARCH BROWN

CREAM CADDIS

MUSKRAT NYMPH

TAN SHRIMP

TROTH SCUD

TRUEBLOOD'S CADDIS

ZUG BUG

NYMPHS

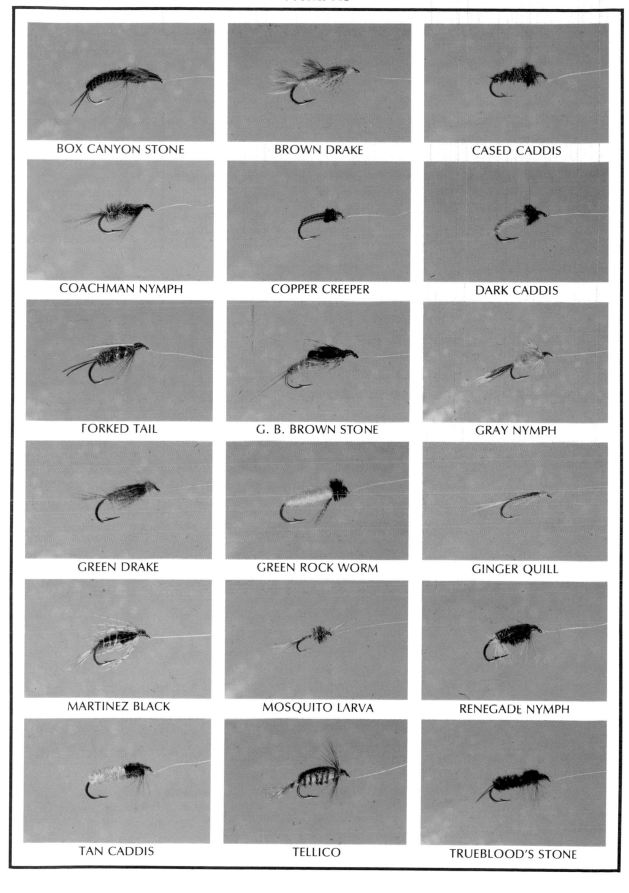

BOX CANYON STONE	BROWN DRAKE	CASED CADDIS
COACHMAN NYMPH	COPPER CREEPER	DARK CADDIS
FORKED TAIL	G. B. BROWN STONE	GRAY NYMPH
GREEN DRAKE	GREEN ROCK WORM	GINGER QUILL
MARTINEZ BLACK	MOSQUITO LARVA	RENEGADE NYMPH
TAN CADDIS	TELLICO	TRUEBLOOD'S STONE

NYMPHS

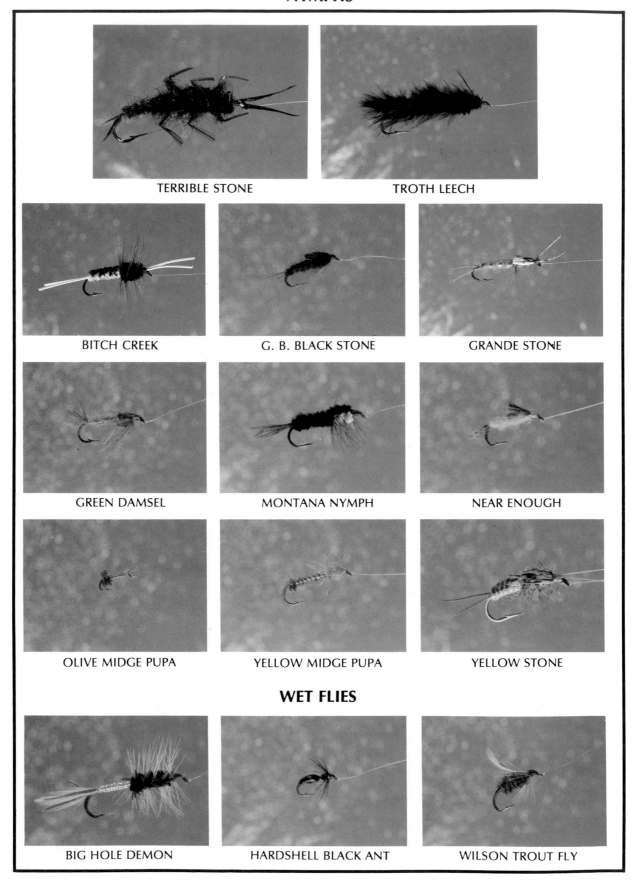

TERRIBLE STONE

TROTH LEECH

BITCH CREEK

G. B. BLACK STONE

GRANDE STONE

GREEN DAMSEL

MONTANA NYMPH

NEAR ENOUGH

OLIVE MIDGE PUPA

YELLOW MIDGE PUPA

YELLOW STONE

WET FLIES

BIG HOLE DEMON

HARDSHELL BLACK ANT

WILSON TROUT FLY

STREAMERS

BLACK BEAR

BLACK GHOST

HORNBERG

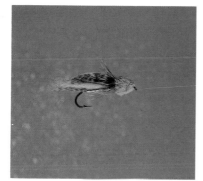

MUDDLER MINNOW

PARTRIDGE SCULPIN

PLATTE RIVER SPECIAL

REDSIDED SHINER

TROTH BULLHEAD

ROYAL COACHMAN

SILVER SPRUCE

SPRUCE MATUKA

STEELHEAD FLIES

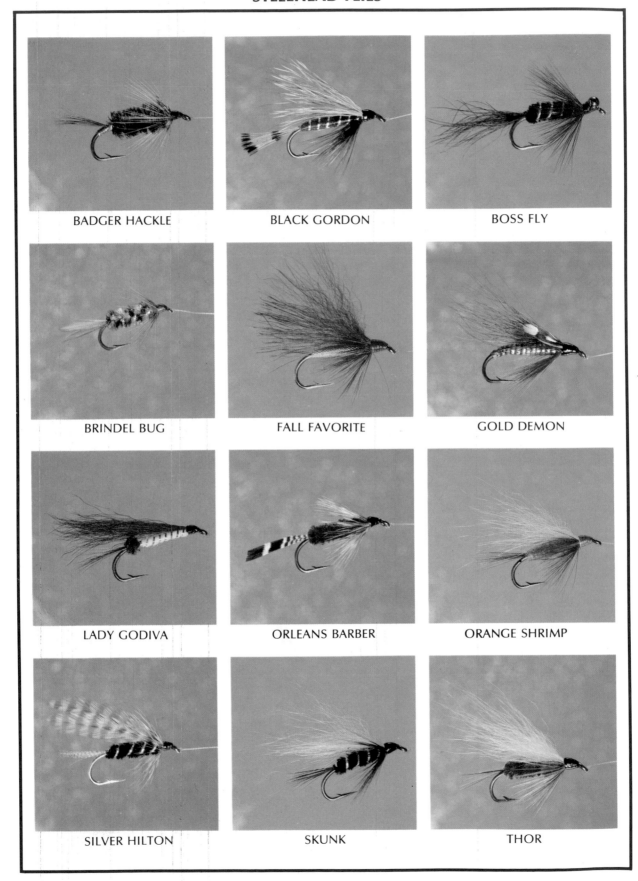

BADGER HACKLE

BLACK GORDON

BOSS FLY

BRINDEL BUG

FALL FAVORITE

GOLD DEMON

LADY GODIVA

ORLEANS BARBER

ORANGE SHRIMP

SILVER HILTON

SKUNK

THOR

WET FLIES

The Wet Flies are some of the most overlooked flies, yet they are among the most effective. They are generally dressed rather sparsely in order to sink quickly. They can be tied using many of the dry fly patterns previously listed. Many of the wets are tied as attractor type flies and represent nothing; however, many of the patterns represent either drowned insects, emerging nymphs and larvas, or submerged insects which are in the process of laying their eggs. It is a mistake to over-hackle any wet fly and, whenever possible, the use of soft hen neck hackle is encouraged. Stiff rooster hackle does not give the fly the desired action and greatly reduces its effectiveness. In view of the bewildering array of dry flies and nymphs that many of us already carry with us it may sound rather foolish for me to even suggest that you add some wet flies to your collection and further clutter your fly boxes. You need not start out your adventures in wet fly fishing with a large assortment of patterns, hoping to later narrow it down to what works best in your own area. I have found that if you have a particular dry fly that works well for you, excluding the Humpies, Irresistibles, and other hair type flies with good floating qualities of course, that most often the same pattern tied wet will also be useful. During the period of many of the hatches I have seen trout tailing and giving the impression that they are feeding on surface insects when actually they are feeding on the emergers. This is when the wet fly is probably at its very best. At least this has been what I have experienced. Some of the most successful fly fishermen that I know are seldom caught using anything but a wet fly. All too often a wet fly bumping along the bottom is the only fly capable of bringing any action whatsoever. If your fishing is confined to floating a piece of steel and feather then you are missing a great part of the action. The following patterns are some of the more popular wet flies, and if you combine this with the dry flies that can be tied wet then you have a very lengthy selection of patterns to choose from.

109

Instructions for tying a conventional wet fly:

STEP 1: Tie in the tail, the ribbing material and the body material.

STEP 2: Wrap body material forward and tie off at front. Body materials like floss and yarn are usually tied in at front first and then wrapped to the back and back to the front, forming a tapered body. Next wrap the ribbing forward. Tradition dictates four turns of ribbing.

STEP 3: Tie in your hackle. Hen hackle if possible.

STEP 4: Wrap hackle (two or three turns) on as a

collar and tie back and down. On wet flies without wings hackle is normally just tied back.

STEP 5: Tie in wings. Wings should extend to the bend in the hook.

STEP 6: Tie off the head with a nice clean taper.

ALDER

HOOK:	Mustad 3906, sizes 8-14.
THREAD:	Black.
TIP:	Flat gold tinsel.
TAIL:	Golden pheasant tippet fibers.
BODY:	Peacock herl. Reverse wrap the body with fine gold wire.
HACKLE:	Black.
WINGS:	Mottled dark brown turkey tail feather sections tied on edge over the body.

This is a very productive pattern wherever it is used. It is also tied without a tail.

ALEXANDRA

HOOK:	Mustad 3906 B, sizes 8-12.
THREAD:	Black.
TIP:	Red floss.

TAIL: Three peacock sword fibers.

BODY: Embossed silver tinsel.

HACKLE: Black.

WING: Five peacock sword fibers tied over the body.

This is a modified English fly pattern which is extremely successful when used for Brookies.

BIG HOLE DEMON, GOLD

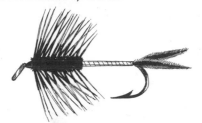

HOOK: Mustad 9672, sizes 2-10.

THREAD: Black.

TAIL: Furnace hackle tips tied in a V.

REAR BODY HALF: Oval gold tinsel.

FRONT BODY HALF: Black chenille.

HACKLE: Furnace wrapped through chenille portion of body.

BIG HOLE DEMON, SILVER

HOOK: Mustad 9672, sizes 2-10.

THREAD: Black.

TAIL: Badger hackle tips tied in a V.

REAR BODY HALF: Oval silver tinsel.

FRONT BODY HALF: Black chenille.

HACKLE: Badger wrapped through chenille portion of body.

NOTES: When tying the Demons, hackle should be tied in by the tip so it will have a tapering effect.

The Big Hole Demons were originated in Montana. Dan Bailey states they have taken more trout from the Big Hole River than any other fly. They have proven to be real good on many others rivers as well.

BLACK ANT

HOOK: Mustad 3906, sizes 10-12.

THREAD: Black.

BODY: Black chenille tied in at butt with a black floss body.

HACKLE: Black.

WINGS: Dark grizzly hackle tips tied on edge over the body.

BLACK ANT, HARDSHELL

HOOK: Mustad 3906B, sizes 10-18.

THREAD: Black.

BODY: Black size A tying thread wrapped in two distinctive lumps to simulate an ant's body. After thread underbody is formed it is coated with a black lacquer and allowed to dry. An additional coat may be necessary if first coat is thin and penetrates the thread.

HACKLE: Black tied on as a collar and tied back.

This is one of the most durable flies that you can tie. This particular pattern has taken more fish for me when the weather has warmed and the ants are out than any ant pattern. I do not consider it a standby but rather a pattern to start out with then change if things are slow.

BLOODY BUTCHER

HOOK: Mustad 3906, sizes 8-12.

THREAD: Black.

TAIL: Scarlet red hackle fibers.

BODY: Silver embossed tinsel.

HACKLE: Scarlet red.

WINGS: Black duck quill sections tied on edge over the body.

Very good early season fly to use when waters are high and cloudy.

BLUE BOTTLE

HOOK: Mustad 3906, sizes 10-14.

THREAD: Black.

TIP: Flat gold tinsel.

TAIL: Black hackle fibers.

BODY: Dark blue floss.

HACKLE: Black.

WINGS: Natural dark gray duck quill
             sections tied on edge over the body.

BLUE DUN, MARTINEZ

HOOK: Mustad 7957BX, sizes 8-14.

THREAD: Gray.

TAIL: Blue dun hackle fibers.

RIBBING: Oval gold tinsel.

BODY: Dubbed muskrat fur with guard hairs
             removed.

HACKLE: Blue dun.

WING: Gray squirrel tail hair tied
             over the body.

A Don Martinez pattern which is very good in
larger rivers. When tied on the heavy wire 7957BX
hook it gets down to the bottom and can really
bring fish to the landing net.

BROWN BOMBER

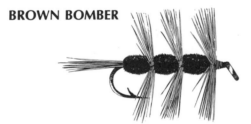

HOOK: Mustad 9672, sizes 6-10.

THREAD: Brown.

TAIL: Scarlet red hackle fibers.

BODY: Black chenille tied in three
             separate steps. See illustration
             above.

HACKLE: Brown tied in at each joint
             in the body and in front.

This Woolly Worm type fly will often be the answer.
I have taken summer-run Steelhead on it when they
are ignoring everything else.

CALIFORNIA COACHMAN

HOOK: Mustad 3906, sizes 8-14.

THREAD: Brown.

TAIL: Golden pheasant tippet fibers.

BODY: Peacock herl with a yellow
             floss center band. Reverse wrap
             the body with fine gold wire.

HACKLE: Brown.

WINGS: White duck quill sections tied on
             edge over the body.

This fly can also be tied with a white calf tail hair
wing. Very popular in many areas along the West
Coast.

CAPTAIN

HOOK: Mustad 3906, sizes 8-14.

THREAD: Black.

TIP: Flat gold tinsel.

TAIL: Golden pheasant tippet fibers.

BODY: Black floss.

HACKLE: Brown.

WINGS: Natural gray duck quill sections
             tied on edge over the body.

This is an old reliable wet fly pattern with many
variations. Wings are sometimes white and often
the tail is omitted.

CONWAY

HOOK: Mustad 3906, sizes 8-10.

THREAD: Black.

TIP: Oval gold tinsel.

TAIL: Scarlet red and white hackle fibers
             mixed.

RIBBING: Oval gold tinsel.

BODY: Dark orange floss.

HACKLE: Orange tied Palmer over the body.
             Also, two turns of scarlet red hackle
             at front.

WINGS:	White goose quill sections tied on edge over the body and extending to the middle of the tail. Married red and yellow duck quill fibers are tied in along the side of each wing and extend ¾ the length of the wing.
HEAD:	Peacock herl.

This attractor pattern was originated by a one armed fly-tyer by the name of Dan Conway. Although this pattern was originally intended for sea-run Cutthroat it is very effective in high mountain lakes for Brookies. It has also proven a good pattern on Wyoming's Golden trout.

COWDUNG

HOOK:	Mustad 3906, sizes 10-16.
THREAD:	Brown.
TIP:	Flat gold tinsel.
BODY:	Dark olive floss.
HACKLE:	Dark ginger.
WINGS:	Natural gray duck quill sections tied on edge over the body.

DUSTY MILLER

HOOK:	Mustad 3906, sizes 10-14.
THREAD:	Gray.
TIP:	Flat gold tinsel.
TAIL:	Brown hackle fibers.
BODY:	Dubbed muskrat fur. Pick out the body and make it shaggy.
HACKLE:	Cree.
WINGS:	Cock ringneck pheasant quill sections tied on edge over the body.

FLIGHT'S FANCY

HOOK:	Mustad 3906, sizes 10-14.

THREAD:	Tan.
TAIL:	Brown hackle fibers.
RIBBING:	Flat gold tinsel.
BODY:	Light yellow floss.
HACKLE:	Light ginger.
WINGS:	Natural gray duck quill sections tied on edge over the body.

This is a old English pattern which has proven to be successful over a period of many years.

GIRDLE BUG

HOOK:	Mustad 9672, sizes 6-10.
THREAD:	Black.
TAIL:	White rubber hackle tied in a V.
BODY:	Black chenille.
LEGS:	White rubber hackle.

NOTES: When tying a Girdle Bug it is easier to tie in the tail and then the legs first; then wrap the chenille over the body and position the legs.

These are some very easy flies to tie and they are useful wherever they are used. They are also tied with gray, yellow, brown and olive chenille bodies.

GOLDEN PHEASANT

HOOK:	Mustad 3906, sizes 6-10.
THREAD:	Orange.
TAIL:	Golden pheasant tippet fibers.
RIBBING:	Oval gold tinsel.
BODY:	White floss.
HACKLE:	Lemon yellow.
WINGS:	Ringneck pheasant neck feather tied on edge over the body.

Another good attractor type pattern which is good in high mountain lakes. This pattern was originally tied for use in Northern California's High Sierra country. I first came in contact with it in a small shop in Portola, California. I had the opportunity to try it out a few days later and have been carrying it with me since.

GRANNOM

HOOK:	Mustad 3906, sizes 10-14.
THREAD:	Brown.
TAIL:	Ginger variant hackle fibers.
BODY:	Dubbed Hare's Ear fur with a green floss egg sac tied in at the butt.
HACKLE:	Ginger variant.
WINGS:	Hen ringneck pheasant quill sections tied on edge over the body.

This is the female variation of the many Grannom patterns. I have used this pattern with or without the green sac and find that the little bit of green always makes the fly much more effective.

GRAY SEDGE

HOOK:	Mustad 7957B, sizes 8-12.
THREAD:	Black.
TAIL:	Crimson red hackle fibers.
BODY:	Gray chenille.
HACKLE:	Badger.
WINGS:	Barred mallard fibers tied over the body.

GRIZZLY KING

HOOK:	Mustad 3906, sizes 10-14.
THREAD:	Gray.
TAIL:	Scarlet red hackle fibers.
RIBBING:	Flat gold tinsel.
BODY:	Green floss.
HACKLE:	Grizzly.
WINGS:	Barred mallard fibers tied over the body.

HARE'S EAR

HOOK:	Mustad 3906, sizes 8-14.
THREAD:	Brown.
TAIL:	Bronze mallard fibers.
BODY:	Dubbed Hare's Ear fur. Pick out the body and make shaggy.
WINGS:	Hen ringneck pheasant quill sections tied over the body.

KING OF WATERS

HOOK:	Mustad 3906, sizes 10-14.
THREAD:	Red.
TIP:	Embossed silver tinsel.
BODY:	Red floss.
HACKLE:	Brown tied Palmer over the body.
WINGS:	Barred mallard fibers tied over the body

McGINTY

HOOK:	Mustad 3906, sizes 10-14.
THREAD:	Black.
TAIL:	Crimson hackle and barred teal fibers mixed.
BODY:	Alternating bands of black and yellow chenille. There are two bands of each color with black starting at the back.
HACKLE:	Brown.
WINGS:	White tipped mallard secondary quill section tied on edge over the body.

MORMON GIRL

HOOK:	Mustad 3906, sizes 8-14.

THREAD: Black.

TIP: Red floss.

BODY: Yellow floss.

HACKLE: Grizzly tied Palmer over the body.

WINGS: Barred mallard fibers tied over the body.

ORANGE FISH HAWK

HOOK   Mustad 3906, sizes 10-14.

THREAD: Black.

TIP: Flat gold tinsel.

BODY: Dubbed orange synthetic fur.

HACKLE: Badger.

PACIFIC KING

HOOK: Mustad 3906, sizes 8-14.

THREAD: Black.

TAIL: Black hackle fibers.

RIBBING: Brown thread.

BODY: Light green floss with brown floss tied in at back and pulled over the back. Ribbing is completed after shellback is tied in.

HACKLE: Black.

WING: Black calf tail tied over the body.

This pattern was originated by Roy Patrick for fishing in Northern California. Since the time of its origination some 25 years ago it has been fished in most parts of the west with success.

PARMACHENIE BELLE

HOOK: Mustad 7957B, sizes 8-12.

THREAD: White.

TAIL: Scarlet red and white hackle fibers mixed.

RIBBING: Oval gold tinsel.

BODY: Dubbed yellow synthetic fur.

HACKLE: Scarlet red and white mixed.

WING: White calf tail.

TOPPING: Red Lady Amherst pheasant crest feather.

PICKET PIN

HOOK: Mustad 9671, sizes 4-10.

THREAD: Black.

TAIL: Golden pheasant tippet fibers.

BODY: Oval gold tinsel.

WING: Gray squirrel tail hair tied over the body and extending to the end of the tail.

HACKLE: Brown tied on as a collar in front of the wing.

HEAD: Peacock herl.

There are a number of Picket Pin variations. They include tying the hackle Palmer style over the body and altering the body colors. These are some very popular flies for Montana fishing.

RED ANT

HOOK: Mustad 3906, sizes 10-14.

THREAD: Black.

TAIL: Golden pheasant tippet fibers.

BODY: Red floss with peacock herl tied in at the butt.

HACKLE: Brown.

WINGS: Natural gray duck quill section tied on edge over the body.

RENEGADE

HOOK:	Mustad 3906B, sizes 6-14.
THREAD:	Black.
TIP:	Flat gold tinsel.
REAR HACKLE:	White.
BODY:	Peacock herl. Reverse wrap the body with fine gold wire.
FRONT HACKLE:	Brown.

This pattern is also referred to as the Reversed Renegade.

RENEGADE, DOUBLE

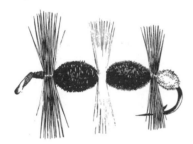

HOOK:	Mustad 9672, sizes 4-12.
THREAD:	Black.
TIP:	Red chenille tied in as an egg sac.
REAR HACKLE:	Brown.
BODY:	Peacock herl.
CENTER HACKLE:	White.
FRONT HACKLE:	Brown.

This is a very popular fly in many parts of the Rocky Mountain area. The variations of the Renegade pattern are endless. Some anglers feel that a significant difference is made by just changing the color of tying thread.

RUBE WOOD

HOOK:	Mustad 3906, sizes 10-14.
THREAD:	Brown.
TIP:	Red floss.
BODY:	White chenille.
HACKLE:	Brown.
WINGS:	Barred mallard fibers tied over the body.

SILVER DOCTOR

HOOK:	Mustad 3906B, sizes 8-12.
THREAD:	Black.
TAIL:	Lady Amherst pheasant tippet fibers.
BODY:	Embossed silver tinsel.
HACKLE:	Light blue.
WINGS:	Dark brown mottled turkey tail feather sections tied on edge over the body. Also, blue and yellow calf tail hair mixed and tied in over the wing.
TOPPING:	Red Lady Amherst pheasant crest feather.

SPECIAL RED ANT

HOOK:	Mustad 3906, sizes 10-14.
THREAD:	Brown.
BODY:	Dubbed black synthetic fur at rear and red synthetic fur at front. Body should be tied in two distinctive lumps to simulate an ant's body.
HACKLE:	Furnace.

The Special Red Ant will pick up a lot of fish for you during spring run off when the banks of most rivers are full. The extra little flash of red usually does the trick.

WESTERN BEE

HOOK:	Mustad 3906B, sizes 10-14.
BODY:	Alternating band of orange and black chenille. There are two bands of each color with orange starting at the back.
HACKLE:	Brown.

WINGS: Natural gray duck quill sections tied on edge over the body.

WHITE MILLER

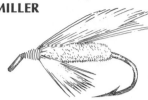

HOOK: Mustad 3906, sizes 10-14.

THREAD: White.

TIP: Flat silver tinsel.

BODY: White chenille.

HACKLE: White.

WINGS: White duck quill section tied on edge over the body.

WILSON

HOOK: Mustad 3906, sizes 8-14.

THREAD: Orange.

BODY: Dubbed orange synthetic fur.

HACKLE: Orange.

WING: One green winged teal breast feather with a single dot in it. Tie with concave up.

WILSON ANT

HOOK: Mustad 3906, sizes 8-14.

THREAD: Brown.

BODY: Dubbed brown synthetic fur with a peacock herl butt.

HACKLE: Brown.

WING: One brown duck breast feather tied with concave up.

WILSON'S MORMON GIRL

HOOK: Mustad 3906, sizes 8-14.

THREAD: Gray.

TIP: Red floss.

BODY: Yellow floss.

HACKLE: Grizzly.

WING: One gray duck shoulder feather tied with concave side up.

WILSON'S RED ANT

HOOK: Mustad 3906, sizes 8-14.

THREAD: Black.

TIP: Red floss.

TAIL: Three peacock sword fibers.

BODY: Red floss.

HACKLE: Ginger.

WING: One green winged teal breast feather with a single dot in it. Tie with concave up.

WILSON'S TROUT FLY

HOOK: Mustad 3906, sizes 6-14.

THREAD: Black.

TIP: Red floss.

RIBBING: Red thread.

BODY: Peacock herl.

HACKLE: Ginger.

WING: One green winged teal breast feather with a single dot in it. Tie with concave up.

WILSON'S TROUT KILLER

HOOK: Mustad 3906, sizes 6-14.

THREAD: Yellow.

TIP: Red floss.

RIBBING: Peacock herl.

BODY: Yellow floss. Reverse wrap the body with fine gold wire.

HACKLE: Grizzly.

WING: One green winged teal breast feather with a single dot in it. Tie with concave up.

The Wilson patterns have become a legend among many of the old time flyfishers and they are still just as effective as they were some decades ago when they were first tied. They were originated by a fly-tyer named Wilson from North Ogden, Utah. These flies are as remarkable as their originator who had but one arm. Their wing is tied with the concave side up which gives them an unusual vibrating action when worked through the water.

WOOLLY WORM

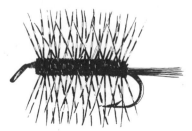

HOOK: Mustad 9671, sizes 2-12.

THREAD: Black.

TAIL: Crimson red hackle fibers.

HACKLE: Grizzly saddle hackle tied Palmer over the body. Hackle should be tied so barbles slant forward. This gives the fly better action in the water.

BODY: Black chenille.

As with all good fish-taking flies there are endless variations of the Woolly Worms. Don Martinez probably should get the most credit for popularizing the Woolly Worm type fly, however angling history records similar flies during the 1800s. Woolly Worms are tied with or without a tail. Some prefer a red tag of yarn rather than a tail. Also, they are sometimes ribbed with tinsel. Sparkle chenille is also often used for the bodies. I like to carry with me a selection of weighted Woolly Worms and I tie in a narrow band of 6/0 red thread on the head for easy identification of my weighted flies. Mustad 9672 and 79580 hooks are also used for longer bodies. Some of the more useful color combinations are:

BODY/HACKLE	BODY/HACKLE
Red/Grizzly	Black/Black
Gray/Black	Black/Badger
Yellow/Badger	Yellow/Brown
Orange/Brown	Brown/Black
Olive/Black	Red/Badger
Brown/Brown	Dark Gray/Badger
Tan/Brown	Gray/Grizzly
Olive/Brown	Black/Furnace

WOOLLY WORM, DAVE'S

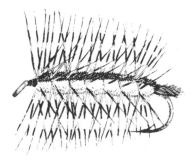

HOOK: Mustad 9672, sizes 4-12.

THREAD: Black.

TAG: Red wool yarn.

HACKLE: Grizzly tied Palmer over the body.

BODY: Yellow chenille with peacock herl tied in over the back.

A more recent newcomer to the Woolly Worm family is this creation of Dave Whitlock.

YELLOW JACKET

HOOK: Mustad 3906, sizes 10-14.

THREAD: Brown.

RIBBING: Black floss.

BODY: Yellow floss tied with a large full taper.

HACKLE: Dark ginger variant.

WINGS: Cree hackle tips tied flat and in a slight V over the body.

ZULU

HOOK: Mustad 3906, sizes 10-14.

THREAD: Black.

TAG: Red wool yarn.

HACKLE: Black tied Palmer over the body.

BODY: Peacock herl.

STREAMERS

As a rule, streamers or bucktails are designed to simulate various kinds of minnows or bait fish. Some, however, are tied as attractor type lures. The idea of this style of fly originated in Maine around 1900. Fly-tyer Herbert L. Welch is credited with the first streamer patterns. The word "streamer" generally applies to the feather winged patterns; but for the sake of organization all of the minnow type imitations have been grouped together. Many fly fishermen specialize in the use of the streamer type flies and consider them to be the total answer to seducing large fish. Undoubtedly these flies are used more in the New England states, but they can be successful most any place if they are properly fished. I have had most of my success in the fall when large trout are feeding heavily on bait fish just before winter sets in. For the fly fisherman who can think more than just trout, these flies are very deadly on bass and other types of game fish.

BLACK BEAR

HOOK:	Mustad 79580, sizes 4-10.
THREAD:	Black.
TAIL:	Gray squirrel tail hair. Tail should be ½ the length of the body.
HACKLE:	Black tied Palmer over the body.
BODY:	Black chenille.
WING:	Gray squirrel tail hair tied over the body.

BLACK GHOST

HOOK:	Mustad 79580, sizes 4-10.
THREAD:	Black.
TAIL:	Yellow hackle fibers. Tail should be ⅓ the length of the body.
RIBBING:	Flat silver tinsel.
BODY:	Black floss.
HACKLE:	Yellow hackle fibers tied in at throat.
WINGS:	Four white saddle hackles.
CHEEKS:	Jungle Cock or substitute.

BLACK NOSED DACE

HOOK: Mustad 38941, sizes 4-8.

THREAD: Black.

TAG: Very short piece of red wool yarn.

RIBBING: Oval silver tinsel.

BODY: Flat silver tinsel.

WING: White bucktail tied on bottom, black bucktail in the middle and natural brown bucktail on top. The black bucktail should only be about ¾ the length of the white and brown.

This pattern was created by Art Flick and has become popular throughout North America.

BROWN BEAR

HOOK: Mustad 79580, sizes 4-10.

THREAD: Brown.

TAIL: Fox squirrel tail hair. Tail should be ½ the length of the body.

HACKLE: Brown tied Palmer over the body.

BODY: Seal brown chenille.

WING: Fox squirrel tail hair tied over the body.

Both of the bear flies have accounted for some very large fish, especially on Wyoming's North Platte River.

BROWN BUCKTAIL

HOOK: Mustad 38941, sizes 4-14.

THREAD: Brown.

RIBBING: Oval silver tinsel.

BODY: Flat silver tinsel.

HACKLE: Crimson red hackle fibers tied in at throat. Should be tied short.

WING: Natural brown bucktail.

This is a very effective pattern and when used in the smaller sizes it gives the appearance of many of the tinier minnows and brings very good results.

BULLHEAD

HOOK: Mustad 36890, sizes 3/0-6.

THREAD: White.

TAIL: White bucktail.

UPPER TAIL AND BACK: Black ostrich.

BODY: Dubbed cream fur.

GILLS: Dubbed red fur.

HEAD AND HACKLE: Natural deer body hair.

Instructions for tying the Bullhead:

STEP 1: Tie in the tail. Also, leave about 1 foot of tying thread at rear.

STEP 2: Dub the body with cream fur.

STEP 3: Tie in several strands of black ostrich herl. The number of strands will depend on the size being tied.

STEP 4: Pull ostrich herl firmly down over the back and tie in at rear. Dub in a small collar of red fur at front for gills.

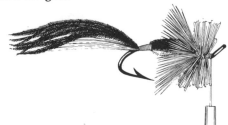

STEP 5: Tie in a large bunch of light tannish gray deer body hair. Allow hair to spin around the hook shank to form the hackle. Tie in additional deer hair, as necessary, and spin on for head.

STEP 6: Clip the head down to shape and darken the top of the head with a black waterproof felt tipped marking pen.

A great pattern developed by Al Troth of Dillon, Montana. This fly has also proven to be a good salt water pattern. I have learned that everytime I see a pattern with the name Troth attached to it that I had better give it a try. I have seldom been disappointed.

DARK SPRUCE

HOOK:	Mustad 9672, sizes 4-10.
THREAD:	Black.
TAIL:	Four peacock sword fibers.
BODY:	Rear ⅓ red floss and front ⅔ peacock herl. Reverse wrap peacock with fine gold wire.
WINGS:	Two furnace neck hackles tied back over the body.
HACKLE:	Furnace tied on as a collar.

EDSON TIGER, DARK

HOOK:	Mustad 38941, sizes 4-10.
THREAD:	Yellow.
TIP:	Flat gold tinsel.
TAIL:	Two small yellow neck hackle tips tied in a slight V.
BODY:	Yellow chenille.
HACKLE:	Tie in the tips of two crimson red hackle at throat.
WING:	Dyed yellow natural brown bucktail. This is the hair taken from a bucktail which has been dyed yellow. Wing should only extend to the bend of the hook.

EDSON TIGER, LIGHT

HOOK:	Mustad 38941, sizes 4-10.

THREAD:	Black.
TIP:	Flat gold tinsel.
TAIL:	Barred lemon wood duck with black bar.
BODY:	Peacock herl. Reverse wrap the body with fine gold wire.
WING:	Yellow bucktail. Wing should only extend to the bend of the hook.
TOPPING:	Two crimson red hackle tips tied on top of the wing and extending back over the wing ⅓.

NOTES: Many tyers dress these patterns with Jungle Cock or a suitable substitute, however, their originator William R. Edson used small gold metal cheeks and eyes on these two patterns. Today gold mylar sheeting can be used successfully to fashion small gold cheeks for these flies.

FOX SQUIRREL

HOOK:	Mustad 38941, sizes 4-14.
THREAD:	Brown.
RIBBING:	Oval silver tinsel.
BODY:	Flat silver tinsel.
HACKLE:	Crimson red hackle fibers tied in at throat.
WING:	Fox squirrel tail hair.

GRAY GHOST

HOOK:	Mustad 9672, sizes 4-10.
THREAD:	Black.
TIP:	Flat silver tinsel.
RIBBING:	Flat silver tinsel.
BODY:	Orange floss tied in a thin taper.
THROAT:	First tie in a golden pheasant crest feather. It should extend to the point of the hook and the tip of the feather should curve upward. Next tie in a small bunch of white bucktail. The bucktail should extend along the bottom of the fly to just past the bend in the hook. Over this is tied four or five pieces of peacock herl which extend slightly past the white bucktail.

WINGS: Four olive dun saddle hackles
                tied on edge over the body.
                A silver pheasant body feather
                is then tied in along each
                side of the saddle hackles. They
                should extend ⅓ the length of the
                saddle hackles.

CHEEKS: Jungle Cock or substitute.

TOPPING: Golden pheasant crest feather.

HEAD: Whip finish a small band of
                red tying thread on the head.

This streamer has gained universal popularity since
it was originated in 1924 by Carrie Stevens. Mrs.
Stevens is responsible for many of the streamer
patterns that we have today.

GRAY SQUIRREL

HOOK: Mustad 38941, sizes 4-14.

THREAD: Black.

RIBBING: Oval silver tinsel.

BODY: Flat silver tinsel.

HACKLE: Small bunch of crimson
                red hackle fibers tied in at throat.

WING: Gray squirrel tail hair.

HORNBERG

HOOK: Mustad 9672, sizes 4-14.

THREAD: Brown.

BODY: Flat silver tinsel.

WINGS: Tie in a small bunch of yellow
                bucktail. Over this tie in a pair
                of well matched barred mallard
                flank feathers at the sides.

CHEEKS: Jungle Cock or substitute.

HACKLE: Brown and grizzly mixed and tied
                on as a full collar.

NOTES: Hackle is not tied back and should be
tied rather full, as if you were tying a dry fly.

This pattern was originated by Frank Hornberg.
When used in the smaller sizes it is often fished as
a dry fly. I use barred lemon wood duck with the
heavy black bar at the tip as a substitute for Jungle
Cock and find it most satisfactory.

INTEGRATION FLY

HOOK: Mustad 79580, sizes 2-10.

THREAD: Black.

BODY: Silver mylar piping. Wrap an
                underbody of floss or yarn
                to give it fullness and taper.

THROAT: White bucktail.

WING: Equal portion of black and
                white bucktail with the black
                tied in on top.

NOTES: I recommend you tie off the rear of the
body with red tying thread. This added flash of
red often makes the fly a bit more effective.

This fly was created by Ted Trueblood and is a
good producing attractor type streamer pattern.
This fly has also proven to be a successful salt
water fly. The combination of basic black and
white in any fishing lure has always proven to be
good.

LITTLE BROOK TROUT

HOOK: Mustad 79580, sizes 4-12.

THREAD: Black.

TAIL: Green bucktail tied short.

TAG: Red floss tied in over the tail.

RIBBING: Flat silver tinsel.

BODY: Dubbed cream rabbit fur.

HACKLE: Orange hackle fibers tied
                in at throat.

WING: Small bunches of white bucktail,
                then orange bucktail, then green
                bucktail and badger guard hairs tied
                in on top.

LITTLE BROWN TROUT

HOOK: Mustad 79580, sizes 4-12.

THREAD: Black.

TAIL: Small cock ringneck pheasant breast feather. The dark center of the feather is clipped out and the feather is tied in so that it curves upward.

RIBBING: Copper wire.

BODY: Dubbed white rabbit fur.

WING: Small bunches of yellow bucktail, then hot orange bucktail, then dark gray squirrel tail hair and dark fox squirrel tail hair tied in on top.

LITTLE RAINBOW TROUT

HOOK: Mustad 79580, sizes 4-12.

THREAD: Black.

TAIL: Green bucktail tied short.

RIBBING: Flat silver tinsel.

BODY: Dubbed with pink and white rabbit fur mixed in equal parts.

HACKLE: Pink hackle fibers tied in at throat.

WING: Small bunches of white bucktail, then pink bucktail, then green bucktail and badger guard hairs tied in on top.

The three Little Trout patterns listed above are some of the better minnow imitations available to the fly fisherman today. They were created by Samuel Slaymaker II of Gap, Pennsylvania.

MALLARD MINNOW

HOOK: Mustad 79580, sizes 4-10.

THREAD: Red.

BODY: Silver mylar piping.

WINGS: First tie in a small bunch of orange bucktail. Then tie in a grizzly neck hackle at each side of bucktail. Tips of hackle should curve inwards. Next tie in a pair of well matched mallard flank feathers at each side.

CHEEKS: Small brown mallard breast feathers.

HACKLE: Furnace tied on as a collar and tied back.

MARABOU, BLACK

HOOK: Mustad 9672, sizes 4-10.

THREAD: Black.

TAIL: Crimson red hackle fibers tied short.

BODY: Silver tinsel chenille.

HACKLE: Crimson red hackle fibers tied in at throat.

WING: Black marabou.

TOPPING: Six strands of peacock herl.

MARABOU, BROWN

HOOK: Mustad 9672, sizes 4-10.

THREAD: Brown.

TAIL: Orange hackle fibers tied short.

BODY: Silver tinsel chenille.

HACKLE: Crimson red hackle fibers tied in at throat.

WING: Brown marabou.

TOPPING: Six strands of peacock herl.

MARABOU, WHITE

HOOK: Mustad 9672, sizes 4-10.

THREAD: Black.

TAIL: Scarlet red hackle fibers tied short.

BODY: Silver tinsel chenille.

HACKLE: Scarlet red hackle fibers tied in at throat.

WING: White marabou.

TOPPING: Six strands of black ostrich herl.

MARABOU, YELLOW

HOOK: Mustad 9672, sizes 4-10.

THREAD: Yellow.

TAIL: Scarlet red hackle fibers tied short.

BODY: Silver tinsel chenille.

HACKLE: Scarlet red hackle fibers tied in at throat.

WING: Yellow marabou.

TOPPING: Six strands of peacock herl.

MATUKA, BLUE DUN

HOOK: Mustad 79580, sizes 4-10.

THREAD: Gray.

RIBBING: Dyed gray flat monofilament.

BODY: Dubbed muskrat fur.

WINGS: Dyed blue dun badger neck hackles.

HACKLE: Dyed blue dun badger tied on as a collar and tied back.

MATUKA, BRUCE'S

HOOK: Mustad 79580, sizes 4-10.

THREAD: Brown.

RIBBING: Oval gold tinsel.

BODY: Wrap an underbody of tan floss, then over-wrap with a strip of chamois skin.

WINGS: Cree neck hackles.

HACKLE: Cree tied on as a collar and tied back.

Originated by Bruce Barker of Ogden, Utah. The coloration of this streamer when it is wet has proven to be very attractive to fish.

MATUKA, GREEN WEENY

HOOK: Mustad 79580, sizes 4-10.

THREAD: Olive.

RIBBING: Oval gold tinsel.

BODY: Dubbed olive rabbit fur.

WINGS: Dyed olive grizzly neck hackles.

HACKLE: Dyed olive grizzly tied on as a collar and tied back.

MATUKA, GRIZZLY

HOOK: Mustad 79580, sizes 4-10.

THREAD: Black.

RIBBING: Oval silver tinsel.

BODY: Dubbed muskrat fur.

WINGS: Grizzly neck hackles.

HACKLE: Grizzly tied on as a collar and tied back.

MATUKA, GRIZZLY KING

HOOK: Mustad 79580, sizes 4-10.

THREAD: Black.

RIBBING: Oval gold tinsel.

BODY: Green floss.

WINGS: Grizzly neck hackles

HACKLE: Grizzly tied on as a collar and tied back.

MATUKA, PLATTE RIVER SPECIAL

HOOK: Mustad 79580, sizes 4-10.

THREAD: Brown.

RIBBING: Oval gold tinsel.

BODY: Brown chenille.

WINGS: Brown neck hackles with a pair of yellow neck hackles tied in the middle.

HACKLE: Brown and yellow mixed. Tie on as a collar but do not tie back.

MATUKA, SPRUCE

HOOK: Mustad 79580, sizes 4-10.

THREAD: Black.

RIBBING: Oval silver tinsel.

BODY: Rear half red floss and front half peacock herl.

WINGS: Badger neck hackles.

HACKLE: Badger tied on as a collar and tied back.

The Matuka streamer design came to us from New Zealand. It is hard to say how old they are but recently I saw them in the pages of a 1925 issue of a Hardy tackle catalogue.

Instructions for tying the Matukas:

STEP 1: Tie in ribbing material at rear of hook. Next tie in body material and complete it as you would any other streamer fly. Do not rib the body.

STEP 2: Select a pair of matched neck hackles. They should be wide and soft and equal to twice the length of the hook shank. Tie in by the butt. The bright side of the hackles should be on the outside.

STEP 3: Bend the hackle barbles on the top of the body area up to a 90 degree angle and wrap ribbing forward. Ribbing should consist of six or seven turns and be wrapped tightly as this is the only means of securing the wing over the body.

STEP 4: Tie on hackle. Except for the Platte River Special Matuka the hackle of the Matukas is generally tied on as a collar, five or six turns and then tied back.

MICKEY FINN

HOOK: Mustad 38941, sizes 4-12.

THREAD: Black.

RIBBING: Oval silver tinsel.

BODY: Flat silver tinsel.

WING: Small bunches of yellow bucktail, then red bucktail in the middle and yellow bucktail on top.

NOTES: The wing of the Mickey Finn should consist of two smaller bunches of red and yellow bucktail on the bottom with the top bunch being equal to both the red and yellow on the bottom.

The originator of the Mickey Finn is unknown, however, John Alden Knight is responsible for popularizing it and Gregory Clark is responsible for the name it has today.

MUDDLER MINNOW

HOOK: Mustad 9672, sizes 2-10.

THREAD: Brown.

TAIL: Mottled brown turkey quill section.

BODY: Flat gold tinsel.

WINGS: Tie in a small bunch of brown and white bear hair. Hair should be mixed. Mottled brown turkey quill sections are then tied in on edge over the body. Wing should only extend to the bend in the hook with the hair portion extending to the center of the tail.

HACKLE: Spin on a collar of natural deer body hair.

HEAD: Spin on natural deer body hair and clip to shape.

NOTES: I have found it much easier to clip the hair off on both ends when spinning on hair for Muddler heads. I simply hold a small bunch between my thumb and index finger and clip the protruding ends. This gives you a shorter hair to spin and allows the hair to flair rather than get tied down when being spun.

The original Muddler Minnow was created by Don Gapen; however, when it reached the west Dan Bailey improved on it and is credited with its popularity today.

MUDDLER MINNOW, BROWN

HOOK: Mustad 9672, sizes 2-10.

THREAD: Brown.

TAIL: Dyed brown goose quill section.

BODY: Brown wool yarn.

WINGS: Tie in a small bunch of brown bear hair. Dyed brown goose quill sections are then tied in on edge over the body. Wing should only extend to the bend of the hook with the hair portion extending to the center of the tail.

HACKLE: Spin on a collar of dyed brown deer body hair.

HEAD: Spin on dyed brown deer body hair and clip to shape.

Of all the Muddler patterns I favor this one. It has been responsible for many large fish being beached over the years.

MUDDLER MINNOW, WHITE

HOOK: Mustad 9672, sizes 2-10.

THREAD: White.

TAIL: Light mottled brown turkey quill section.

BUTT: Red chenille.

RIBBING: Flat silver tinsel.

BODY: White wool yarn.

WINGS: Tie in a small bunch of white calf tail hair. Tie in a pair of barred teal sections on each side of the hair. Both the hair and teal should extend to the center of the tail. Light mottled brown turkey quill sections are then tied in on edge over the body. They should only extend to the bend of the hook.

HACKLE: Spin on a collar of white deer body hair.

HEAD: Spin on white deer body hair and clip to shape.

The White Muddler is also known as the Mizoolain Spook.

MUDDLER MINNOW, YELLOW

HOOK: Mustad 9672, sizes 2-10.

THREAD: White.

TAIL: Dyed yellow mottled brown turkey quill section.

BODY: Flat gold tinsel.

WINGS: Tie in a small bunch of brown calf tail. Tie in a small bunch of yellow calf tail over the brown. Dyed yellow mottled brown turkey quill sections are then tied in on edge over the body. Wing should only extend to the bend in the hook with the hair portion extending to the center of the tail.

HACKLE: Spin on a collar of natural deer body hair.

HEAD: Spin on natural deer body hair and clip to shape.

The Yellow Muddler is also known as the Gordon Dean.

BULLET HEAD MUDDLERS

Paul Drake and George Bodmer of Colorado Springs, Colorado, have come up with an interesting variation of the Muddler patterns. They use a Mustad 79580 hook and tie patterns as listed above, however, they stop at the point when it comes to tying in the hackle. They crimp on a split shot behind the eye of the hook (leaving a small space between the eye and split shot). They then spin on deer hair in front of the shot and fold it back over the shot forming both the head and the hackle. A rod ferrule works great for folding the hair back. Use red thread when tying this type of fly as the red band behind the head is suggestive of minnow gills. The weight up front makes these flies dip and dart well when given rod action.

MUDDLER MINNOW, BLACK MARABOU

HOOK: Mustad 9672, sizes 4-10.

THREAD: Black.

TAIL: Crimson red hackle fibers tied short.

BODY: Silver tinsel chenille.

WINGS: Tie in a small bunch of gray squirrel tail hair and over that tie in black marabou.

TOPPING: Six strands of peacock herl.

HACKLE: Spin on a collar of natural deer body hair.

HEAD: Spin on natural deer body hair and clip to shape.

MUDDLER MINNOW, BROWN MARABOU

HOOK: Mustad 9672, sizes 4-10.

THREAD: Brown.

TAIL: Scarlet red hackle fibers tied short.

BODY: Gold tinsel chenille.

WINGS: Tie in a small bunch of yellow calf tail hair and over that tie in brown marabou.

TOPPING: Six strands of peacock herl.

HACKLE: Spin on a collar of natural deer body hair.

HEAD: Spin on natural deer body hair and clip to shape.

MUDDLER MINNOW, GRAY MARABOU

HOOK: Mustad 9672, sizes 4-10.

THREAD: Gray.

TAIL: Scarlet red hackle fibers
             tied short.

BODY: Silver tinsel chenille.

WINGS: Tie in a small bunch of gray
             squirrel tail hair and over
             that tie in gray marabou.

TOPPING: Six strands of peacock herl.

HACKLE: Spin on a collar of natural gray
             deer body hair.

HEAD: Spin on natural gray deer body hair
             and clip to shape.

MUDDLER MINNOW, OLIVE MARABOU

HOOK: Mustad 9672, sizes 4-10.

THREAD: Brown.

TAIL: Crimson red hackle fibers tied short.

BODY: Gold tinsel chenille.

WINGS: Tie in a small bunch of fox squirrel
             tail hair and over that tie in olive
             marabou.

TOPPING: Six strands of peacock herl.

HACKLE: Spin on a collar of dyed brown
             body hair.

HEAD: Spin on dyed brown deer body
             hair and clip to shape.

MUDDLER MINNOW, WHITE MARABOU

HOOK: Mustad 9672, sizes 4-10.

THREAD: White.

TAIL: Scarlet red hackle fibers tied short.

BODY: Silver tinsel chenille.

WINGS: Tie in a small bunch of gray squirrel
             tail hair and over that tie
             in white marabou.

TOPPING: Six strands of peacock herl.

HACKLE: Spin on a collar of tannish
             gray deer body hair.

HEAD: Spin on white deer body hair and
             clip to shape.

MUDDLER MINNOW, YELLOW MARABOU

HOOK: Mustad 9672, sizes 4-10.

THREAD: Brown.

TAIL: Scarlet red hackle fibers tied short.

BODY: Gold tinsel chenille.

WINGS: Tie in a small bunch of brown
             calf tail hair and over that
             tie in yellow marabou.

TOPPING: Six strands of peacock herl.

HACKLE: Spin on a collar of dyed brown
             deer body hair.

HEAD: Spin on dyed brown deer body hair
             and clip to shape.

PARTRIDGE SCULPIN

HOOK: Mustad 79580, sizes 2-10.

THREAD: Brown.

RIBBING: Oval gold tinsel.

BODY: Dark brown wool yarn.

WING: Tie in a single brown partridge
             tail feather. Strip the fibers
             off from the area that contacts
             the body.

FINS: Tie in a brown partridge feather at
             each side. Tips of these
             feathers should curve outwards.

HACKLE: Spin on a collar of dyed brown deer
             body hair. Clip on top and bottom
             so the hair has more of a flair to
             each side.

HEAD: Spin on dyed brown deer
             body hair and clip to shape.

This is one of the better, if not the best, sculpin patterns available to the fly fisherman today. It was originated by Frank Johnson, Mr. Waterwalker, during 1974 and since that time has accounted for some very nice catches.

PLATTE RIVER SPECIAL

HOOK: Mustad 38941, sizes 4-10.

THREAD: Brown.

RIBBING: Embossed gold tinsel.

BODY: Brown floss.

WINGS: Two yellow neck hackles with
            a brown neck hackle tied in
            at each side. Tips of the
            hackles should curve outward.

HACKLE: Brown and yellow mixed and
            wrapped on as a collar.

This very popular Colorado pattern has many
variations. It is often tied without any body. I have
used it many times over the years and have taken all
species of trout on it.

REDSIDED SHINER

HOOK: Mustad 79580, sizes 2-6.

THREAD: White.

BODY: Silver mylar piping. Wrap an
            underbody of floss or yarn
            to give fullness and taper. Tie off
            rear of body with red tying thread.

WING: Bottom wing is hot orange bucktail
            with dark brown bear hair
            extending slightly past the first
            wing. Top wing is a small bunch of
            yellow bucktail with a larger bunch
            of black skunk tail hair tied
            in on top.

HEAD: Apply black enamel over the top of
            the head. Leave a white throat.

EYES: Yellow with a black center.

The Redsided Shiner is only found in Utah,
Colorado, Wyoming, Idaho, and the Columbia
River basin. When I first became aware of the little
guys I immediately went through my library of fly
fishing books to try and find a pattern which would
simulate them. Nothing. So I started from scratch
and tied this pattern using collected samples as a
guide in determining correct coloration. Success
from the very start. Although the above pattern
catches these little fish in their bright spawning
colors it works well at any time of the year. When
you locate schools of these shiners fish your fly off
to the side of the school and be prepared for some
real action. Large fish prey on the strays.

ROYAL COACHMAN

HOOK: Mustad 9672, sizes 4-10.

THREAD: Brown.

TAIL: Golden pheasant tippet fibers.

BUTT: Peacock herl.

BODY: Red floss.

SHOULDER: Peacock herl.

HACKLE: Brown.

WING: White calf tail hair.

This great old pattern can also be tied with two or
even four white saddle hackles substituted for hair
wings.

SILVER DARTER

HOOK: Mustad 9672, sizes 4-10.

THREAD: Black.

TAIL: Silver pheasant quill section.

RIBBING: Flat silver tinsel.

BODY: White floss.

HACKLE: Four peacock sword feather
            fibers tied in at throat.

WINGS: Two badger saddle hackles.

SPRUCE

HOOK: Mustad 9672, sizes 4-12.

THREAD: Black.

TAIL: Three peacock sword feather fibers.

BODY: Rear ⅓ red floss and front ⅔
            peacock herl. Reverse wrap
            peacock herl with fine gold wire.

WINGS: Two badger neck hackles.

HACKLE: Badger tied on as a collar.

The Spruce originated in Oregon and was created
by a fly-tyer by the name of Godfrey. It has been
around many years and has gained national
popularity. One of the many variations of this
pattern which is good on Brookies has the entire
body tied with red wool yarn. Both patterns should
be tied with a silvery badger hackle for maximum
effectiveness. Make sure that the wings are tied
with the tips turned outward, and fish the fly with a
slow, jerky retrieve.

SPUDDLER

HOOK:	Mustad 79580, sizes 2-10.
THREAD:	Brown.
TAIL:	Brown bear hair.
BODY:	Dubbed cream synthetic fur.
WINGS:	Tie in a small bunch of brown bear hair. Tie in four dyed brown grizzly neck hackles. Tips of hackles should curve inward.
GILLS:	Red yarn. Wrap yarn over the wing tie-off.
OVERWING:	Red fox squirrel tail hair. This wing should extend over the underwing about one third and be spread so that it forms a cape over the fly which extends down to each side of the body.
HEAD:	Spin on reddish brown antelope hair and clip to shape.

NOTES: Head should be trimmed spoon shaped and flat on the bottom. Use 3 parts no. 20 Cocoa Brown and 1 part no. 25 Dark Brown Rit dye to dye grizzly neck hackles. I also dye the antelope hair with the same dye mixture. This gives the finished fly a more natural color. Red Monical of Dan Bailey's Fly Shop and Don Williams are responsible for the development of this pattern.

SUPERVISOR

HOOK:	Mustad 9672, sizes 4-10.
THREAD:	Black.
TAG:	Red wool yarn.
RIBBING:	Oval silver tinsel.
BODY:	Flat silver tinsel.
HACKLE:	White hackle fibers tied in at throat.
WINGS:	Tie in a small bunch of long white bucktail. Over this tie in four light blue saddle hackles and then a light green saddle hackle at each side extending ⅔ the length of the blue saddles.
TOPPING:	Six strands of peacock herl.
CHEEKS:	Jungle Cock or substitute.

STEELHEAD FLIES

I have had a passion for tying Steelhead flies since my youth. Being raised on the West Coast with some very fine water near by only stimulated my interests in tying and fishing these flies. I will always remember the fall trips down the Trinity River Canyon and seeing the Steelhead and Salmon laying in the large clear pools of the river like cord wood. As any dedicated Steelheader will tell you, this brand of fishing is strictly for the patient and the hardy. In addition to the many fishless days one can always expect a cold penetrating mist in the morning hours which as likely as not will turn into rain and last for days. But it becomes worthwhile when the day finally arrives that you hook into one of the monsters. The thrill of seeing 9 pounds of silver fish walking across the water on its tail brings an excitement like no other. Those past days of what appeared to be nothing more than casting practice sessions and the loss of a few dozen flies on the bottom are all erased. The only thoughts I have at moments like this are "which way is he going—up or down stream? I wonder if I have enough backing? Can I get around those roots if he makes a run down stream? Wherever will I be able to beach him?" Then my last collective thought is "oh what the heck, at least I'll get to play him for awhile and that's enough for me."

I have seen a few gifted anglers take and release more than 1,000 Steelhead per season. They are not just lucky either. These few gentlemen are rare, but it makes me really wonder. I fish just as hard as the rest of them but my all-time season high has only been 21 fish. In my opinion there is no more rewarding sport than the pursuit of the Steelhead with a fly. Unfortunately, only about 25 percent of the Steelheaders today have experienced the beaching of a Steelhead with a fly rod. One forms a great respect and develops a certain kinship with these migratory devils like with no other fish.

The following patterns all basically have been generated on the West Coast. With the advent of Steelheading in the Great Lakes area in recent years we are certain to see some changes in patterns for use in that area. Many of the patterns included are also effective on Sea-run Cutthroat and a few have even been responsible for taking Salmon. Both of these fish are that extra reward that the Steelheader enjoys.

ALASKA MARY ANN

HOOK:	Eagle Claw 1197N, sizes 2-6.
THREAD:	White.
TAIL:	Scarlet red hackle fibers.
RIBBING:	Oval silver tinsel.
BODY:	Cream, off white, chenille.
WING:	Natural creamy white polar bear hair.
CHEEKS:	Jungle Cock or suitable substitute.

Originated by Frank Dufresne in 1922 while he was in Alaska. The Steelhead dressing is an altered version of his original streamer pattern.

ALGAN

HOOK:	Mustad 7957BX, sizes 4-8.
THREAD:	Black.
TAIL:	Hot orange hackle fibers.
RIBBING:	Embossed silver tinsel.
BODY:	Black chenille.
HACKLE:	Black and claret mixed. Wrap hackle on as a collar and then tie back and down.
WING:	Black calf tail.

AL'S SPECIAL

HOOK:	Eagle Claw 1197N, sizes 2-6.
THREAD:	Yellow.
TAIL:	Scarlet red hackle fibers.
RIBBING:	Flat silver tinsel.
BODY:	Yellow chenille.
HACKLE:	Yellow tied on as a collar and tied back.
WING:	White polar bear hair.

ATOM BOMB

HOOK:	Eagle Claw 1197N, sizes 1-8.
THREAD:	Black.
TAILS:	Two lemon yellow hackle tips tied in a V. Wrap a few turns of thread under the tails so they slant upwards.
BODY:	Silver mylar piping.
HACKLE:	Dark ginger hackle fibers tied in at throat.
WING:	Lemon yellow marabou with a small bunch of white bucktail tied in on top.
TOPPING:	Six strands of peacock herl.

This pattern came out of the Portland, Oregon area several years ago. Has proven to be a very good winter run fly.

BABINE SPECIAL

HOOK:	Eagle Claw 1197N, sizes 2-6.
THREAD:	Red.
BODY:	Hot pink fluorescent chenille wrapped in two rather large distinctive lumps.
CENTER HACKLE:	Scarlet red.
HACKLE:	White.

This pattern originated in British Columbia. This fly has a number of variations in both body colors and hackle.

BADGER HACKLE PEACOCK

HOOK:	Eagle Claw 1197B, sizes 2-8.
THREAD:	Black.
TAIL:	Crimson red hackle fibers.
TIP:	Fine oval gold tinsel. Wrap five turns under the tail and two full turns above the tail. Use the tinsel to position the tail upward.
BODY:	Peacock herl. Wrap an underbody of olive yarn to give the peacock a more full appearance. Reverse wrap the body with fine gold wire.
HACKLE:	Badger tied on as a collar and tied back.

E. H. "Polly" Rosborough of Chiloquin, Oregon did not originate this pattern but he is responsible for improving upon it and showing us just how effective it can be for Steelhead.

BADGER PALMER

HOOK:	Eagle Claw 1197B, sizes 4-6.
THREAD:	Black.
TAILS:	Dyed scarlet red badger hackle tips tied in a V. Tie in on edge with concave side out.
BODY:	Fluorescent yellow chenille.
HACKLE:	Badger tied Palmer over the body. Hackle should be tied in by the tip and wrapped so hackle barbles slant to the rear.

BADGER AND RED

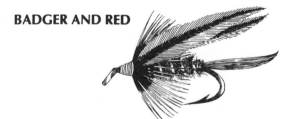

HOOK:	Eagle Claw 1197B, sizes 1-6.
THREAD:	Red.
TAIL:	Dyed crimson red goose quill section.

RIBBING:	Oval silver tinsel.
BODY:	Dubbed crimson red rabbit fur. Pick out the body and make it extra shaggy.
WINGS:	Two badger neck hackles tied in on edge with concave side out. Wrap a few turns in behind the wings so they slant upward.
HACKLE:	Badger tied on as a collar and tied back.

This pattern originated in British Columbia. This fly is a good choice when the water is off color.

BAIR'S BLACK

HOOK:	Eagle Claw 1197B, sizes 2-6.
THREAD:	Red.
TIP:	Red floss.
TAIL:	Scarlet red hackle fibers.
BODY:	Black chenille.
HACKLE:	Black tied on as a collar and tied back.
WING:	White calf tail with a small bunch of fluorescent red bucktail tied in on top.

BARBER'S POLE

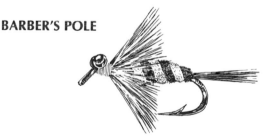

HOOK:	Eagle Claw 1197N, sizes 1-6.
THREAD:	White.
TIP:	Embossed silver tinsel.
TAIL:	Scarlet red and white hackle fibers mixed.
BODY:	Red and white chenille wrapped together.
HACKLE:	Scarlet red and white mixed. Wrap on a collar and tie back.
EYES:	Silver bead chain.

BELLAMY

HOOK: Eagle Claw 1197B, sizes 2-6.

THREAD: Black.

TAIL: Crimson red calf tail.

BODY: Copper wire.

WING: White bucktail with a small bunch of dyed yellow natural brown bucktail tied in at top.

Originated by Pete Schwab while he was residing in Yreka, California. Fly was named after George Bellamy who was particularly responsible for its origination. This pattern was originally created for use on Northern California's Klamath River as were the other wire bodied patterns which follow. They all get down deep and are most effective in many of the larger rivers.

Instructions for tying the wire bodied style Steelhead flies.

STEP 1: Wrap a thin floss underbody. The underbody should taper down sharply at both ends. Copper, brass and silver wire are used for these flies. Select a floss of a color which most closely matches the color of the wire being used. This gives you a better looking finished body should any of the underbody show through after the wire is wrapped.

STEP 2: Before wrapping wire body pull the piece of wire to be used through some fine sand paper or steel wool to remove any oxidation. Starting at the rear of the body, wrap the wire tightly over the underbody. Clip off both ends and press the remaining protruding ends down in tightly. It is advisable to file off the sharp clipped ends of wire. This saves cutting your thread later. Cover the entire body with a thin coat of lacquer. The lacquer fuses the body to the hook and prevents the wire from tarnishing. It should be applied very generously so it penetrates well into the underbody. Allow to dry for at least 30 minutes. You should select the correct wire size to match the size hook you are tying on. Use .018 for size 6 hooks, .023 for size 4 hooks, and .025 for size 2 and larger.

STEP 3: Wrap a thread base at rear of body and tie in the tail.

STEP 4: If the pattern you are tying requires a center wing you next wrap another thread base over the wire in the center of the body and tie in the center wing.

STEP 5: Next tie in a bunch of hackle at the throat if required. Tie in your front wing. Both the center and the front wings have thread wrapped in behind the wing to raise it up to an angle of about 40 to 45 degrees. This is the key to tying this style of fly. The raised wing gives the fly a good action in the water. You might want to try it with any of the other patterns listed. The fact is, Steelhead flies are not just another streamer type or wet fly. They are in a category of their own.

BENCH MARK

HOOK: Eagle Claw 1197N, sizes 1-6.

THREAD: White.

TAIL: Hot orange calf tail.

RIBBING: Embossed silver tinsel.

BODY: Fluorescent orange floss.

HACKLE: Hot orange tied on as a collar and tied back.

WING: White calf tail.

This fly originated in British Columbia. It was first tied using orange surveyor's tape for the body. Karl Mausser is credited with its origination.

BLACK BEAUTY

HOOK: Mustad 7957BX, sizes 4-8.

THREAD: Red.

TAIL: Black calf tail.

BODY: Fluorescent orange chenille.

HACKLE: Black tied on as a collar and tied back.

NOTES: This fly is also sometimes tied on an Eagle Claw 1197N hook and silver bead chain eyes are used.

BLACK DEMON

HOOK: Eagle Claw 1197G, sizes 2-8.

THREAD: Black.

TAIL: Barred lemon wood duck with black and white bar on tip.

BODY: Oval gold tinsel. Wrap an underbody of yellow floss to give the body a good taper. Wrap five turns of the tinsel under the tail for the tip.

HACKLE: Orange tied on as a collar and tied back.

WING: Black bear hair.

BLACK GORDON

HOOK: Eagle Claw 1197B, sizes 4-8.

THREAD: Black.

RIBBING: Narrow oval gold tinsel.

BODY: Rear ⅓ red floss and front ⅔ black floss.

HACKLE: Black tied on as a collar and tied back.

WING: Black bucktail.

BLACK JOE

HOOK: Eagle Claw 1197B, sizes 4-8.

THREAD: White.

TAIL: Black hackle fibers.

BODY: Black chenille.

HACKLE: Black tied on as a collar and tied back and down.

WING: White calf tail.

BLACK O'LINDSAY

HOOK: Mustad 7957BX, sizes 4-8.

THREAD: Black.

TAIL: Dyed blue barred teal and brown hackle fibers.

RIBBING: Oval gold tinsel.

BODY: Dubbed yellow synthetic fur.

HACKLE: Dark brown tied on as a collar and tied back and down. Also, dyed blue barred teal fibers are tied in at throat.

WINGS: Underwing of six strands of peacock sword. Middle wing of a small bunch of dyed teal blue barred teal fibers. Top wing is a distinctly marked barred teal feather tied flat over the top of the body.

NOTES: This pattern is also tied with two sections of barred teal tied tent style over the body.

BLACK OPTIC

HOOK: Mustad 7970, size 2.

THREAD: Black.

BODY: Oval gold tinsel.

HACKLE: Black tied in at throat.

WING: Black bucktail.

HEAD: Black.

EYES: Yellow with a black center.

NOTES: Head is formed by using a ¼'' split brass bead.

Jim Pray of Eureka, California, originated the Optic Steelhead flies. Jim was once regarded as the ''Wizard'' of Steelhead flies and we are still using many of his creations today.

BLACK PRINCE

HOOK: Eagle Claw 1197B, sizes 4-8.

THREAD: Black.

TAIL: Scarlet red hackle fibers tied short.

RIBBING: Oval silver tinsel.

BODY: Rear ⅓ dubbed yellow synthetic fur and front ⅔ black chenille.

HACKLE: Black tied on as a collar and tied back.

WING: Black calf tail.

BLACK SPOOK

HOOK: Eagle Claw 1197B, sizes 4-8.

THREAD: Black.

TAIL: Black hackle fibers.

RIBBING: Oval gold tinsel.

BODY: Dubbed scarlet red synthetic fur. Pick out and make the body rather shaggy after the ribbing has been wrapped.

WING: White calf tail.

HACKLE: Black tied on as a collar and tied back. Hackle is put on in front of the wing.

BLOODY BUTCHER

HOOK: Eagle Claw 1197B, sizes 4-6.

THREAD: Black.

TAIL: Scarlet red and yellow hackle fibers.

BODY: Gray chenille.

HACKLE: Scarlet red and yellow tied Palmer over the body.

WING: Gray squirrel tail.

The Bloody Butcher originated in England in 1838 and you might say it has been butchered ever since its beginning. This is the Steelhead version of the pattern which has been in use for more than 40 years and it should not be confused with the many others which are used for trout.

BLUE CHARM

HOOK: Eagle Claw 1197N, sizes 1-8.

THREAD: Black.

TIP: Oval silver tinsel.

TAIL: Golden pheasant crest feather.

RIBBING: Oval silver tinsel.

BODY: Black floss tied in a thin taper.

HACKLE: Deep blue tied on as a collar and tied back and down.

WING: Dark brown calf tail.

TOPPING: Golden pheasant crest feather.

NOTES: Cheeks of Jungle Cock or a suitable substitute are sometimes used on this pattern but it really does not make any real difference one way or the other.

Thanks to our good friends to the north in British Columbia we have today an Atlantic Salmon pattern modified down to where it is a real Steelhead producer.

BOBBY DUNN

HOOK:	Eagle Claw 1197B, sizes 2-6.
THREAD:	Black.
TAIL:	Crimson red calf tail.
BODY:	Copper wire.
WING:	White bucktail with a small bunch of tied in on top.

NOTES: Crimson red hackle fibers are sometimes tied in at the throat. See Bellamy for tying instructions.

BOSQUITO

HOOK:	Eagle Claw 1197N, sizes 2-6.
THREAD:	White.
TAIL:	Two scarlet red hackle tips tied in a small V.
RIBBING:	Oval gold tinsel.
BODY:	Yellow chenille.
HACKLE:	Black tied on as a collar and tied back and down.
WING:	White calf tail.

BOSS

HOOK:	Eagle Claw 1197B, sizes 2-6.
THREAD:	Orange.
TAIL:	Black Ringtail Cat hair tied twice the length of the body.
RIBBING:	Flat silver tinsel.
BODY:	Black chenille.
HACKLE:	Fluorescent orange tied on as a collar and tied back.
EYES:	Silver bead chain.

BRAD'S BRAT

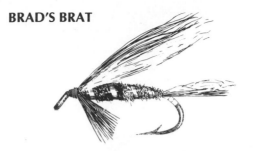

HOOK:	Eagle Claw 1197B, sizes 4-8.
THREAD:	White.
TIP:	Flat gold tinsel.
TAIL:	Orange bucktail with white bucktail tied in on top.
RIBBING:	Flat gold tinsel.
BODY:	Rear ½ orange wool yarn and front ½ red wool yarn.
HACKLE:	Dark brown tied on as a collar and tied back and down.
WING:	Bottom half white bucktail and top half orange bucktail.

Originated by Enos Bradner of Seattle, Washington.

BRASS HAT

HOOK:	Mustad 38941, sizes 2-6.
THREAD:	Black.
TAIL:	Yellow calf tail.
BODY:	Brass wire.
CENTER WING:	White bucktail.
WING:	Yellow bucktail with a small bunch of black bucktail tied in on top.

NOTES: See Bellamy for tying instructions.

BRIGHT DELIGHT

HOOK:	Eagle Claw 1197N, sizes 1-8.
THREAD:	White.
TAIL:	Purple hackle fibers with white calf tail tied on top.
RIBBING:	Fine oval silver tinsel wrapped closely.
BODY:	White floss.
HACKLE:	Purple with white in front. Wrap both hackles on individually as a collar and tie back. Do not mix as the white should vein the purple.
EYES:	Silver bead chain.

BRIGHT EMBER

HOOK:	Eagle Claw 1197G, sizes 2-8.
THREAD:	Red.
TAIL:	Fluorescent orange marabou with a small bunch of fluorescent yellow marabou tied in on top.
BODY:	Copper wire.
HACKLE:	Small bunch of black marabou tied in at throat.
WINGS:	Underwing—a small bunch of fluorescent yellow marabou. Middle wing—a bunch of fluorescent orange marabou. Top wing—a small bunch of black marabou.
CHEEKS:	Short bunch of fluorescent orange marabou tied in at each side.
HEAD:	Fluorescent red lacquer.

NOTES: Wire body is tied in at rear and then wrapped without a taper. See Dark Ember for illustration.

The Bright Ember was originated by California fly-tyer Darwin Atkin. His use of marabou and wire bodies gives his flies an unbeatable combination.

BRINDLE BUG

HOOK:	Eagle Claw 1197B, sizes 1-8.
THREAD:	Brown.
TAILS:	Two brown hackle tips tied in a V.
RIBBING:	Oval silver tinsel.

BODY:	Black and yellow variegated chenille.
HACKLE:	Brown tied on as a collar and tied back.

The Brindle Bug is not only a good Steelhead fly but is also a most productive trout fly. I have had many people relay some very high compliments for this fly when it has been used in the Rocky Mountain area. Sizes 8 and 10 are generally used for trout fishing.

BROWN DRAKE

HOOK:	Mustad 7957BX, sizes 6-8.
THREAD:	Black.
TAIL:	Barred teal fibers.
RIBBING:	Heavy black thread.
BODY:	Light olive floss.
HACKLE:	Furnace tied on as a collar and tied back and down.
WINGS:	Barred teal feather tied flat over the body with a small bunch of brown bear hair tied in over the top.

A good pattern for summer runs. This fly was given to me by Carl Glisson of Pinole, California. He states that it is the only fly for the west side of Victoria Island, British Columbia. I have had success with it in Oregon.

BURLAP

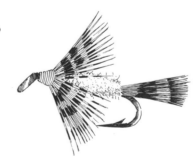

HOOK:	Eagle Claw 1197B, sizes 1-8.
THREAD:	Gray.
TAIL:	Coastal blacktail deer body hair. Tie the tail very heavy.
BODY:	Burlap jute fibers wrapped over an underbody of lead wire. Body should be well tapered and shaggy.
HACKLE:	Grizzly tied on as a collar and tied back.

NOTE: This fly must almost always have the lead wire underbody to sink it properly. Otherwise the heavy deer hair tail floats it, not allowing it to reach the bottom as it should.

CALDWELL

HOOK:	Eagle Claw 1197N, sizes 2-6.
THREAD:	Red.
TIP:	Flat silver tinsel.
TAIL:	Scarlet red hackle fibers.
RIBBING:	Flat silver tinsel.
BODY:	Fluorescent pink wool yarn.
HACKLE:	Scarlet red tied on as a collar and tied back.
WING:	White calf tail with crimson red calf tail tied on top. Both wing colors should be in equal amounts.

A British Columbia pattern which was originated by Lou Caldwell. Has proven to be very good in both California and Oregon.

CANARY

HOOK:	Eagle Claw 1197G, sizes 1-6.
THREAD:	Brown.
TIP:	Flat gold tinsel.
TAIL:	Small bunch of brown marabou.
RIBBING:	Flat gold tinsel.
BODY:	Dubbed yellow synthetic fur.
WING:	Yellow marabou with brown tied in on top. Both wing colors should be in equal amounts.
CHEEKS:	Brown mallard drake neck feathers tied in at each side.

CARSON

HOOK:	Eagle Claw 1197B, sizes 1-8.
THREAD:	Red.
TAIL:	Golden pheasant tippet fibers.
BODY:	Peacock herl with a red floss center band in the middle (Royal Coachman style). Reverse wrap the body with fine gold wire.
HACKLE:	Dark ginger tied on as a collar and tied back and down.
WING:	White calf tail with a small bunch of fluorescent red calf tail tied in on top.
CHEEKS:	Jungle Cock or suitable substitute.

CARTER'S DIXIE.

HOOK:	Eagle Claw 1197G, sizes 4-6.
THREAD:	White.
TAIL:	Fluorescent yellow hackle fibers.
BODY:	Oval gold tinsel. Wrap an underbody of yellow floss to give the body a good taper. Wrap four turns of the tinsel under the tail for the tip.
HACKLE:	Scarlet red tied on as a collar and tied back.
WING:	White bucktail.

CHAPPIE

HOOK:	Eagle Claw 1197B, sizes 1-6.
THREAD:	Orange.
TAILS:	Two grizzly hackle tips tied in a V. Hackle tips should be tied with concave side out.
BODY:	Dubbed orange synthetic fur.
HACKLE:	Grizzly tied on as a collar and tied back and down. Hackle should be long enough to reach the rear of the body.
WINGS:	Two grizzly neck hackle tips tied in a V. Hackle tips should be tied with concave side out and be widespread and high.

Possibly this fly should have been listed with the streamers since it has taken more trout and bass for me than it has ever taken steelhead. Many swear by it though and I cannot argue with the success of others. It was originated by C. L. Franklin of Los Angeles, about 1945.

CHIEF

HOOK: Eagle Claw 1197B, sizes 2-8.

THREAD: Brown.

TAIL: Crimson red hackle fibers.

RIBBING: Oval silver tinsel.

BODY: Dubbed raccoon fur.

HACKLE: Black tied on as a collar and tied back and down.

WING: Natural dark brown bucktail.

CHIQUITA

HOOK: Eagle Claw 1197G, sizes 2-8.

THREAD: Red.

TAIL: White marabou with a small bunch of flourescent yellow marabou tied in on top.

BODY: Brass wire.

HACKLE: Small bunch of fluorescent yellow marabou tied in at throat.

WING: Fluorescent yellow marabou.

CHEEKS: Short bunch of fluorescent orange marabou tied in at each side.

HEAD: Fluorescent red lacquer.

NOTES: Wire body is tied in at rear and then wrapped without a taper.

CHUB

HOOK: Eagle Claw 1197N, sizes 1-4.

THREAD: White.

BODY: White wool yarn with a fluorescent red strip of yarn woven along the belly.

HACKLE: White tied on as a collar and tied back and down.

WING: White calf tail.

A very good pattern originated by Larry Hicks of Tacoma, Washington.

CLEAR CREEK SPECIAL

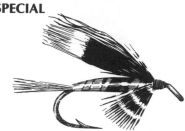

HOOK: Eagle Claw 1197B, sizes 2-8.

THREAD: Black.

TAIL: Yellow hackle fibers.

RIBBING: Flat gold tinsel.

BODY: Rear ⅓ yellow floss, center ⅓ black floss and front ⅓ red floss.

HACKLE: Grizzly tied on as a collar and tied back.

WING: Gray squirrel tail.

TOPPING: Small bunch of yellow bucktail.

Perfected by Bill Kennerly of Happy Camp, California for use on the Klamath River.

COCK ROBIN

HOOK: Mustad 7970, size 2.

THREAD: Black.

BODY: Oval silver tinsel.

HACKLE: Orange tied in at throat.

WING: Badger hair.

HEAD: Black.

EYES: Yellow with a black center.

NOTE: Head is formed by using a ¼'' split brass bead.

Developed in 1940 by Jim Pray of Eureka, California. This optic pattern is considered by many to be one of his best.

COLES COMET

HOOK:	Eagle Claw 1197G, sizes 2-6.
THREAD:	Orange.
TAIL:	Orange calf tail.
BODY:	Oval gold tinsel. **Wrap an underbody of yellow floss to give the body a slight taper.**
HACKLE:	Yellow and hot orange mixed. Wrap on as a collar and tie back.
EYES:	Brass bead chain.

COMET

HOOK:	Eagle Claw 1197N, sizes 2-6.
THREAD:	Yellow.
TAIL:	Orange calf tail.
BODY:	Oval silver tinsel. Wrap an underbody of white floss to give the body a slight taper.
HACKLE:	Yellow and orange mixed. Wrap on as a collar and tie back.
EYES:	Silver bead chain.

The Coles Comet and the Comet are often referred to as the Gold Comet and the Silver Comet. These two highly successful patterns naturally have a number of variations.

COPPER DEMON

HOOK:	Eagle Claw 1197B, sizes 1-6.
THREAD:	Black.
TAIL:	Small bunch of hot orange marabou tied short.
BODY:	Oval copper tinsel. Wrap an underbody of orange floss to give the body a full taper.

HACKLE:	Hot orange tied on as a collar and tied back.
WING:	Hot orange calf tail.

CUMING'S SPECIAL

HOOK:	Eagle Claw 1197B, sizes 4-8.
THREAD:	Black.
RIBBING:	Fine oval gold tinsel.
BODY:	Rear ⅓ yellow wool yarn and front ⅔ claret wool yarn.
HACKLE:	Claret tied on as a collar and tied back and down.
WING:	Natural dark brown bucktail.
CHEEKS:	Jungle Cock or suitable substitute.

CUTTHROAT

HOOK:	Eagle Claw 1197N, sizes 4-8.
THREAD:	Red.
TAIL:	Crimson red hackle fibers.
RIBBING:	Oval silver tinsel.
BODY:	Yellow wool yarn.
HACKLE:	Crimson red tied on as a collar and tied back and down.
WING:	Scarlet red bucktail with a small bunch of white bucktail tied in on top.

Created by Al Knudson for sea run Cutthroat.

DAISY

HOOK:	Eagle Claw 1197G, sizes 2-8.
THREAD:	Red.
TAIL:	White marabou with a small bunch of fluorescent yellow tied in on top.
BODY:	Gold mylar. Wrap an underbody of yellow floss to give the body a slight taper. Also, this pattern is often weighted with lead wire.
HACKLE:	Small bunch of fluorescent yellow marabou tied in at throat.
WINGS:	White marabou with a small bunch of fluorescent yellow marabou tied in on top.

CHEEKS: Short bunch of fluorescent orange marabou tied in at each side.

HEAD: Fluorescent red lacquer.

DARK EMBER

HOOK: Eagle Claw 1197G, sizes 2-8.

THREAD: Red.

TAIL: Small bunch of fluorescent orange marabou.

BODY: Copper wire.

HACKLE: Small bunch of black marabou tied in at throat.

WINGS: Fluorescent orange marabou with black marabou tied in on top. Wing color should be half and half of each color. A small bunch of fluorescent orange marabou is then tied on top.

CHEEKS: Short bunch of fluorescent orange marabou tied in at each side.

HEAD: Fluorescent red lacquer.

Both of the above patterns were created by Darwin Atkin.

DONNELLY'S PARTRIDGE

HOOK: Eagle Claw 1197B, sizes 6-8.

THREAD: Brown.

TAIL: Golden pheasant tippet fibers.

RIBBING: Embossed gold tinsel.

BODY: Yellow wool yarn.

HACKLE: Brown partridge fibers tied in at throat.

WING: Large bunch of brown partridge fibers.

Has proven to be a productive summer run pattern and is especially good in British Columbia.

DR. SPRATLEY

HOOK: Mustad 7957BX, sizes 4-10.

THREAD: Black.

TAIL: Barred mallard fibers.

RIBBING: Oval silver tinsel.

BODY: Black wool yarn.

HACKLE: Grizzly tied on as a collar and tied back and down.

WING: Bunch of ringneck pheasant center tail fibers.

DURHAM RANGER

HOOK: Eagle Claw 1197B, sizes 1-8.

THREAD: Black.

TAIL: Golden pheasant tippet fibers.

RIBBING: Oval gold tinsel.

BODY: Peacock herl tied in at the butt and red floss.

HACKLE: Scarlet red tied on as a collar and tied back and down.

WINGS: Two golden pheasant tippet feathers tied on edge over the body.

CHEEKS: Jungle Cock or suitable substitute.

DUSTY MILLER

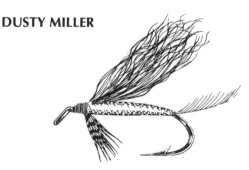

HOOK: Eagle Claw 1197N, sizes 1-8.

THREAD: Black.

TAIL: Lady Amherst pheasant crest feather.

BODY: Embossed silver tinsel. Wrap an underbody of white floss to give the body a slight taper.

HACKLE: Brown partridge fibers tied in at the throat.

WING: Brown calf tail.

EEL BEAUTY

HOOK: Eagle Claw 1197N, sizes 1-8.

THREAD: Black.

TIP: Embossed silver tinsel.

TAIL: Crimson red hackle fibers.

RIBBING: Embossed silver tinsel.

BODY: Dubbed red synthetic fur. Pick out and make shaggy.

WINGS: Two dyed crimson red badger neck hackle tied in a V over the body.

HACKLE: Dyed crimson red badger tied on as a collar and tied back.

A good pattern for winter run Steelhead which has proven productive from California to British Columbia.

FALL FAVORITE

HOOK: Eagle Claw 1197N, sizes 1-6.

THREAD: Red.

BODY: Embossed silver tinsel. Wrap an underbody of white floss to give the body a full taper.

HACKLE: Scarlet red tied on as a collar and tied back and down.

WING: Hot orange calf tail.

This fly was originated by Butch Wilson of Arcata, California, for fishing the winter runs in Northern California rivers; however, it is now used wherever Steelhead run.

FEATHER MERCHANT

HOOK: Eagle Claw 1197B, sizes 2-6.

THREAD: Black.

TAIL: Golden pheasant tippet fibers.

RIBBING: Oval silver tinsel. Rib peacock portion of body only.

BODY: Red floss at butt and peacock herl over the remainder of the body.

HACKLE: Orange tied on as a collar and tied back.

WING: Crimson red calf tail.

CHEEKS: Jungle Cock or suitable substitute.

Designed by Ted Trueblood. This fly is not only a thing of beauty, it takes fish with regularity.

FLAME

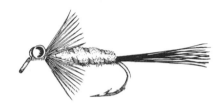

HOOK: Eagle Claw 1197B, sizes 4-6.

THREAD: Orange.

TAIL: Black skunk tail hair.

RIBBING: Oval silver tinsel.

BODY: Fluorescent red wool yarn.

HACKLE: Orange tied on as a collar and tied back.

EYES: Silver bead chain.

Originated in 1960 for use on the Russian River.

FOOL'S GOLD

HOOK: Eagle Claw 1197B, sizes 1-6.

THREAD: Black.

TAIL: Golden pheasant tippet fibers tied short.

BODY: Peacock herl tied in at butt and oval gold tinsel wrapped over the remainder of the body. Body is not tapered.

HACKLE: Dark ginger.

WING: Natural brown bucktail.

Originated by Mike Kennedy of Lake Oswego, Oregon. Mike is considered by many steelheaders as the expert's expert.

GOLDEN BEAR

HOOK:	Eagle Claw 1197G, sizes 1-6.
THREAD:	Brown.
TAIL:	Crimson red hackle fibers.
BODY:	Rear half reddish brown wool yarn and front half gold tinsel chenille.
HACKLE:	Dark brown tied on as a collar and tied back.
WING:	Dark brown bear hair.

GOLDEN DEMON

HOOK:	Eagle Claw 1197G, sizes 1-6.
THREAD:	Black.
TAIL:	Golden pheasant crest feather.
BODY:	Oval gold tinsel. Wrap an underbody of yellow floss to give the body a full taper.
HACKLE:	Orange tied on as a collar and tied back and down.
WING:	Well marked coastal blacktail deer body hair.
CHEEKS:	Jungle Cock or suitable substitute.

The Golden Demon was altered by Jim Pray of Eureka, California from a streamer pattern in 1935.

GOLDEN ROGUE

HOOK:	Eagle Claw 1197G, sizes 1-6.
THREAD:	Brown.
TAIL:	Two small golden pheasant tippet feathers tied on edge.
BODY:	Oval gold tinsel. Wrap an underbody of yellow floss to give the body a full taper.
HACKLE:	Brown tied Palmer over the body.
WING:	Fox squirrel tail hair.

Originated by J. Duckett of the former Cascade Tackle Company of Medford, Oregon.

GRAY HACKLE, YELLOW

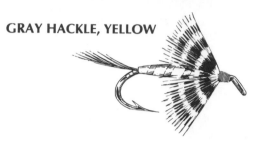

HOOK:	Eagle Claw 1197G, sizes 1-8.
THREAD:	Black.
TIP:	Flat gold tinsel.
TAIL:	Lady Amherst pheasant crest feather.
RIBBING:	Flat gold tinsel.
BODY:	Yellow floss.
HACKLE:	Grizzly tied on as a collar and tied back.

GRIZZLY KING

HOOK:	Eagle Claw 1197B, sizes 4-6.
THREAD:	Gray.
TIP:	Oval gold tinsel.
TAIL:	Scarlet red hackle fibers.
RIBBING:	Oval gold tinsel.
BODY:	Green floss.
HACKLE:	Grizzly tied on as a collar and tied back.
WING:	Gray squirrel tail.

HORNER'S SILVER SHRIMP

HOOK:	Eagle Claw 1197N, sizes 2-8.
THREAD:	Black.
TAIL:	Gray deer body hair.
BACK:	Gray deer body hair.

BODY:	Oval silver tinsel. Wrap an underbody of white floss to give the body a full taper.
HACKLE:	Grizzly tied Palmer over the body. Wrap hackle before back is pulled over and tied in at head.
EYES:	White with black centers.

This shrimp pattern was originated by Jack Horner of San Francisco, California. Good on all migratory species and has been very good in the smaller sizes for lakes having a shrimp population.

HORRIBLE MATUKA

HOOK:	Eagle Claw 1197B, sizes 1-6.
THREAD:	Black.
RIBBING:	Oval silver tinsel.
BODY:	Fluorescent orange chenille.
WINGS:	Two dyed hot orange badger neck hackle tied over the body Matuka style.
HACKLE:	Dyed hot orange badger tied on as a collar and tied back.

Originated by Harry Darbee of Livingston Manor, New York, for Atlantic Salmon. Since its introduction to the West Coast during the 1974 Steelhead season it has become a highly reliable Steelhead fly.

HOT ORANGE

HOOK:	Eagle Claw 1197B, sizes 1-8.
THREAD:	Red.
TAIL:	Hot orange hackle fibers.
RIBBING:	Oval gold tinsel. Wrap three or four turns under the tail for tip and to raise the tail.
BODY:	Dubbed hot orange synthetic fur.
HACKLE:	Hot orange tied on as a collar and tied back.
WING:	Hot orange calf tail with a small bunch of crimson red calf tail tied in on top.

HUMBOLDT RAILBIRD

HOOK:	Eagle Claw 1197B, sizes 2-6.
THREAD:	Black.
TAIL:	Claret hackle fibers.
BODY:	Claret wool yarn with claret hackle tied Palmer over the body.
HACKLE:	Yellow tied on as a collar and tied back and down.
WING:	Gray squirrel tail.
CHEEKS:	Jungle Cock or suitable substitute.

IMPROVED GOVERNOR

HOOK:	Eagle Claw 1197B, sizes 2-6.
THREAD:	Black.
BODY:	Rear 1/3 red floss. Floss should be wrapped partially down into the bend of the hook and then ribbed with fine oval gold tinsel. Front 2/3 dark olive chenille.
TAIL:	Crimson red hackle fibers. Tail is tied in forward of the red floss portion of body.
HACKLE:	Dark brown tied on as a collar and tied back.
WING:	Dark brown bear hair.
CHEEKS:	Jungle Cock or suitable substitute.

INDIAN FLY

HOOK:	Mustad 7957BX, sizes 4-8.
THREAD:	Brown.
TAIL:	Yellow calf tail.
BODY:	Rear half yellow wool yarn and front half red wool yarn.
HACKLE:	Dark ginger tied on as a collar and tied back.
WING:	Fox squirrel tail.

JEAN BUCKTAIL

HOOK:	Eagle Claw 1197B, sizes 1-6.
THREAD:	Black.
TAIL:	Scarlet red hackle fibers.
BODY:	Embossed gold tinsel. Body is not tapered.
HACKLE:	Yellow tied on as a collar and tied back and down.
WING:	Under wing of blue dun bucktail, center wing orange bucktail and top wing blue dun bucktail. Each bunch of bucktail should be rather small as finished wing should be sparse. A very small Jungle Cock body feather is sometimes tied in at each side. This can be substituted with a number of other feathers such as starling.
CHEEKS:	Jungle Cock or suitable substitute.

A very good pattern which originated in British Columbia many years ago. It is also an effective pattern when dressed as a streamer and has accounted for many pounds of trout in the Rocky Mountain area.

JOCK SCOTT

HOOK:	Eagle Claw 1197B, sizes 1-8.
THREAD:	Black.
TAIL:	Golden pheasant tippet fibers.
RIBBING:	Oval gold tinsel.
BODY:	Rear half yellow wool yarn and front half black wool yarn.
HACKLE:	Speckled guinea fibers tied in at throat.
WING:	Gray squirrel tail with small bunches of scarlet red, blue and yellow bucktail mixed and tied in on top.

JOE O'DONNELL

HOOK:	Eagle Claw 1197B, sizes 2-6.
THREAD:	Red.
TAIL:	Scarlet red and yellow hackle fibers mixed.
BODY:	Cream, off white, chenille.
WINGS:	Two badger neck hackles tied in a V with concave side out.

HACKLE:	Scarlet red and yellow wrapped together as a collar and tied slightly back. Hackle is tied on in front of wings.

KALAMA SPECIAL

HOOK:	Eagle Claw 1197B, sizes 4-8.
THREAD:	Black.
TAIL:	Scarlet red hackle fibers.
BODY:	Yellow wool yarn.
HACKLE:	Badger tied Palmer over the body. Also, an additional badger hackle is tied on in front and tied back.
WING:	White calf tail.

KENNEDY SPECIAL

HOOK:	Eagle Claw 1197N, sizes 2-8.
THREAD:	Red.
TAIL:	Crimson red hackle fibers.
BODY:	Embossed silver tinsel. Wrap an underbody of white floss to give the body a full taper.
HACKLE:	Crimson red tied on as a collar and tied back and down.
WING:	Black bear hair.
CHEEKS:	Jungle Cock or suitable substitute.

KISPIOX

HOOK:	Eagle Claw 1197B, sizes 1-6.
THREAD:	White.
TAIL:	Hot orange marabou.
BODY:	Hot orange wool yarn.
HACKLE:	Crimson red tied on as a collar and tied back and down.
WING:	White calf tail.

Developed for the Kispiox River in British Columbia but has been good elsewhere when used in sizes 4 and 6.

LADY CLARET

HOOK:	Eagle Claw 1197B, sizes 4-8.
THREAD:	Black.
TAIL:	Light blue hackle fibers.
RIBBING:	Oval silver tinsel.
BODY:	Dubbed claret synthetic fur.
HACKLE:	Light blue tied on as a collar and tied back and down.
WING:	Coastal blacktail deer body hair.

LADY GODIVA

HOOK:	Eagle Claw 1197N, sizes 1-6.
THREAD:	Black.
TAIL:	Scarlet red and yellow hackle fibers mixed.
RIBBING:	Flat silver tinsel. Rib closely.
BODY:	White wool yarn with red chenille tied in at butt.
WING:	Scarlet red calf tail.

This is a very good pattern. The lack of hackle, hence the name, allows this fly to sink more readily.

MAD RIVER

HOOK:	Eagle Claw 1197N, sizes 4-6.
THREAD:	Red.
TAIL:	Scarlet red hackle fibers.

BODY:	Dubbed red and yellow synthetic fur mixed in equal amounts.
HACKLE:	Scarlet red tied on as a collar and tied back and down.
WING:	Yellow calf tail with a small bunch of brown calf tail tied in on top.

MATTOLE'S REGRET

HOOK:	Eagle Claw 1197N, sizes 2-6.
THREAD:	White.
TAIL:	Claret hackle fibers.
RIBBING:	Embossed silver tinsel.
BODY:	Dubbed pale yellow synthetic fur. Pick out and make shaggy.
HACKLE:	Claret tied on as a collar and tied back.
WING:	Coastal blacktail deer body hair.

McGINTY

HOOK:	Eagle Claw 1197B, sizes 2-6.
THREAD:	Black.
TAIL:	Speckled guinea with a small bunch of scarlet red hackle fibers tied in on top.
BODY:	Black and yellow chenille wrapped in four distinctive joints.
HACKLE:	Brown tied on as a collar and tied back and down.
WING:	Gray squirrel tail.

McLEOD'S BUCKTAIL

HOOK:	Eagle Claw 1197B, sizes 1-6.
THREAD:	Black.
TAIL:	Scarlet red hackle fibers.
BODY:	Black chenille.

HACKLE: Hot orange tied Palmer over the body. Also, an additional grizzly hackle it tied in at the front and tied back.

WING: Black skunk tail.

McLEOD'S UGLY

HOOK: Eagle Claw 1197B, sizes 1-6.

THREAD: Black.

TAIL: Small bunch of hot orange marabou.

BODY: Black chenille.

HACKLE: Grizzly tied Palmer over the body. Also, an additional grizzly hackle is tied in at the front and tied back.

WING: Dark moose body hair.

Both of the above patterns were developed by George McLeod of Seattle, Washington.

MICKEY FINN

HOOK: Eagle Claw 1197N, sizes 1-8.

THREAD: Red.

BODY: Embossed silver tinsel. Wrap an underbody of white floss to give the body a full taper.

WING: Under wing yellow, middle wing crimson and top wing yellow.

Wing is of calf tail or polar bear hair if you can get it. Unlike the bucktail streamer version, the wing should be in three equal portions of color.

NIGHT OWL

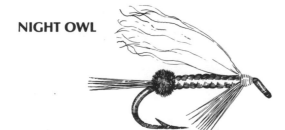

HOOK: Eagle Claw 1197B, sizes 1-8.

THREAD: White.

TAIL: Yellow hackle fibers.

BODY: Oval silver tinsel with red chenille tied in at butt. Do not taper body.

HACKLE: Orange tied on as a collar and tied back and down.

WING: White calf tail.

Originated by Lloyd Silvius of Eureka, California. As far as Steelhead flies are concerned you might say that Lloyd picked up where Jim Pray left off. Lloyd has been filling the need in the Eureka area since Jim Pray's passing.

NORTON'S SPECIAL

HOOK: Eagle Claw 1197N, sizes 4-6.

THREAD: White.

TAIL: Fluorescent orange calf tail.

RIBBING: Embossed silver tinsel.

BODY: Dubbed hot orange synthetic fur.

HACKLE: Fluorescent orange tied on as a collar and tied back.

EYES: Silver bead chain.

Developed by California fly-tyer Howard Norton. This has become one of my favorite patterns for winter runs in the Klamath.

NORWEGIAN MOUSTACHE

HOOK: Eagle Claw 1197G, sizes 4-6.

THREAD: Red.

TAIL: Golden pheasant tippet fibers.

RIBBING: Fine oval gold tinsel.

BODY: Flat gold tinsel. Wrap an underbody of yellow floss so body is slightly fuller towards the front.

HACKLE: Orange tied on as a collar and tied back and down.

WINGS: Two small bunches of bucktail, natural brown at the right and white at the left. Wing is tied in a V over the body with wings at approximately 30 degrees to each other.

Originated by Morley Griswold, ex-governor of Nevada, for fishing in Oregon. The Norwegian Moustache has accounted for many large fish. I have seen many knowledgable and mature men try and hold back their grins, smiles, giggles and laughs when they see this fly. After they have tied it and seen its action in the water they quickly find another type of delight. The wing can also be tied by combining the wings with white on the bottom and brown on the top.

ORANGE BUCKTAIL

HOOK: Eagle Claw 1197B, sizes 2-6.

THREAD: White.

TAIL: Scarlet red hackle fibers with a small bunch of white hackle fibers tied in on top.

SHELLBACK: White bucktail.

RIBBING: Heavy black thread.

BODY: Dubbed orange synthetic fur.

WING: White bucktail.

CHEEKS: A short strand of red wool yarn tied in at each side.

ORANGE DEMON

HOOK: Mustad 7957BX, sizes 4-8.

THREAD: Orange.

TAIL: Hot orange hackle fibers.

BODY: Fluorescent green wool yarn.

HACKLE: Hot orange tied on as a collar and tied back.

WING: Black bear hair.

ORANGE OPTIC

HOOK: Mustad 7970, size 2.

THREAD: Black.

BODY: Oval silver tinsel.

HACKLE: Scarlet red tied in at throat.

WING: Orange bucktail.

HEAD: Black.

EYES: White with a red center.

NOTE: Head is formed by using a ¼'' split brass bead.

ORANGE SHRIMP

HOOK: Eagle Claw 1197B, sizes 1-8.

THREAD: Orange.

TAIL: Scarlet red hackle fibers.

BODY: Dubbed dark orange synthetic fur.

HACKLE: Orange tied on as a collar and tied back and down.

WING: White calf tail.

CHEEKS: Jungle Cock or suitable substitute.

NOTE: An embossed gold tinsel tip is often incorporated into this pattern.
Also, the cheeks are often omitted. See color plate.

ORANGE STEELHEADER

HOOK: Eagle Claw 1197N, sizes 1-4.

THREAD: Black.

TAIL: Hot orange calf tail.

BODY: Silver wire.

WING: Orange calf tail with an equal bunch of hot orange calf tail tied in on top.

NOTES: See Bellamy for tying instruction.

The Orange Steelheader was created by Fred Reed of Nevada City, California.

ORLEANS BARBER

HOOK: Eagle Claw 1197B, sizes 2-6.

THREAD: Black.

TAIL: Section of barred lemon wood duck with black and white barring at tip.

BODY: Red chenille.

HACKLE: Grizzly tied on as a collar and tied back.

Originated by Jim Pray and named after a barber in the now deserted town of Orleans, California.

PAINT BRUSH

HOOK: Mustad 38941, sizes 2-6.

THREAD: Black.

TAIL: Crimson red bucktail.

BODY: Silver wire.

CENTER WING: Scarlet red bucktail.

WING: Yellow bucktail with a small bunch of scarlet red bucktail tied in on top. Also, a very small bunch of natural brown bucktail is tied in on top of the red.

NOTES: See Bellamy for tying instructions.

A Pete Schwab pattern developed in 1927. Still good.

PAINT POT

HOOK: Eagle Claw 1197N, sizes 1-6.

THREAD: Red.

TAIL: Crimson red hackle fibers.

BODY: Embossed silver tinsel. Wrap an underbody of white floss to give the body a slight taper towards the front.

HACKLE: Crimson red tied on as a collar and tied back and down.

WING: Dyed yellow gray squirrel tail.

Originated by Ralph Wahl who has created a number of good Steelhead patterns through the years.

PARMACHENE BELLE

HOOK: Eagle Claw 1197N, sizes 2-6.

THREAD: White.

TAIL: Scarlet red and yellow hackle fibers mixed.

RIBBING: Flat silver tinsel.

BODY: Dubbed yellow synthetic fur.

HACKLE: Scarlet red and yellow wrapped together as a collar and tied back.

WING: White calf tail with a small bunch of crimson red calf tail tied in on top.

PINK LADY

HOOK: Eagle Claw 1197G, sizes 4-8.

THREAD: Tan.

TAIL: Lady Amherst pheasant tippet fibers.

RIBBING: Embossed gold tinsel.

BODY: Dubbed dark pink synthetic fur.

HACKLE: Light ginger tied on as a collar and tied back and down.

WING: Dyed fluorescent gray bucktail.

PINK SHRIMP

HOOK: Eagle Claw 1197N, sizes 4-6.

THREAD: White.

TAIL: Fluorescent pink hackle fibers.

SHELLBACK: Fluorescent pink bucktail.

BODY: Oval silver tinsel.

HACKLE: Fluorescent pink tied Palmer over the body before shellback is pulled forward and tied in at head.

NOTE: You may want to tie the head rather large on this pattern and place two dots of red enamel on each side for eyes.

POLAR SHRIMP

HOOK: Eagle Claw 1197B, sizes 1-8.

THREAD: White.

TAIL: Scarlet red hackle fibers.

BODY: Orange chenille.

HACKLE: Orange tied on as a collar and tied
             back and down.

WING: White calf tail.

POLE-KAT

HOOK: Eagle Claw 1197N, sizes 2-8.

THREAD: Red.

TAIL: White marabou.

BODY: Silver mylar. Wrap a lead wire
             underbody.

HACKLE: Black marabou tied in at throat.

WING: Black marabou with a small bunch of
             white marabou tied in on top.

CHEEKS: Short bunch of fluorescent orange
             marabou tied in at each side.

HEAD: Fluorescent red lacquer.

Designed by Darwin Atkin. In my judgement it is
one of his better patterns. The contrasting colors
of black and white have always proven to be very
good.

PRAWN FLY

HOOK: Eagle Claw 1197G, sizes 2-6.

THREAD: Orange.

TIP: Embossed gold tinsel.

RIBBING: Embossed gold tinsel.

BODY: Dubbed hot orange synthetic fur.
             Pick out after ribbing has been
             wrapped to make shaggy.

HACKLE: Hot orange tied Palmer over the
             body.

NOTE: Hackle should be tied in by the tip and
wrapped so hackle barbles slant forward. This gives
the fly more action in the water.

PRICHARD'S ROCKET

HOOK: Eagle Claw 1197N, sizes 2-6.

THREAD: Black.

TAIL: Hot orange calf tail.

RIBBING: Oval gold tinsel.

BODY: Dubbed black synthetic fur.

WING: Hot orange calf tail.

PROFESSOR

HOOK: Eagle Claw 1197G, sizes 4-8.

THREAD: Black.

TAIL: Scarlet red hackle fibers.

RIBBING: Embossed gold tinsel.

BODY: Dubbed yellow synthetic fur.

HACKLE: Dark ginger tied on as a collar and
             tied back and down.

WING: Gray squirrel tail.

NOTE: Winging material is taken from the base of
the tail where the hair has a finer barring.

PURPLE COMET

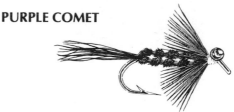

HOOK: Eagle Claw 1197N, sizes 2-8.

THREAD: White.

TAIL: Black skunk hair.

RIBBING: Oval silver tinsel.

BODY: Purple chenille.

HACKLE: Purple tied on as a collar and tied
             back.

EYES: Silver bead chain.

An extremely good dirty water pattern. This fly
was developed by Andre' Puyans of Walnut Creek,
California. Andre' has the unusual talent for always
coming up with a good pattern when the going

starts to get rough and you think that there is no other fly to try.

PURPLE PERIL

HOOK:	Eagle Claw 1197B, sizes 1-6.
THREAD:	Black.
TAIL:	Purple hackle fibers.
RIBBING:	Flat silver tinsel.
BODY:	Purple wool yarn.
HACKLE:	Purple tied on as a collar and tied back.
WING:	Coastal blacktail deer body hair.

QUEEN BESS

HOOK:	Eagle Claw 1197B, sizes 2-6.
THREAD:	Black.
TAIL:	Gray squirrel tail.
BODY:	Silver wire.
HACKLE:	Golden pheasant tippet fibers tied in at throat.
WING:	Yellow bucktail with a small bunch of gray squirrel tail tied in on top.

NOTE: See Bellamy for tying instructions. A Pete Schwab pattern with a well-deserved reputation.

RED ANT

HOOK:	Eagle Claw 1197B, sizes 4-8.
THREAD:	Black.
TAIL:	Crimson red hackle fibers.
BODY:	Crimson red wool yarn with black chenille tied in at butt.
HACKLE:	Dark ginger tied on as a collar and tied back.
WING:	Natural brown bucktail.

REDBUTTED RHESUS

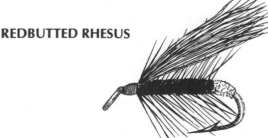

HOOK:	Eagle Claw 1197B, sizes 1-6.
THREAD:	Black.
TIP:	Fluorescent red chenille.
BODY:	Black chenille.
HACKLE:	Black tied Palmer over the body.
WING:	Black bear hair.

RED DRAGON

HOOK:	Eagle Claw 1197N, sizes 2-8.
THREAD:	Red.
TAIL:	Crimson red calf tail.
BODY:	Rear ⅔ embossed silver tinsel and front ⅓ dubbed red synthetic fur.
HACKLE:	Badger tied on as a collar and tied back and down.
WING:	Gray squirrel tail with a small piece of red wool yarn tied at each side.

RED OPTIC

HOOK:	Mustad 7970, size 2.
THREAD:	Black.
BODY:	Oval silver tinsel.
WING:	Crimson red bucktail.
HEAD:	Black.
EYES:	Yellow with black centers.

Another of the patterns perfected by Jim Pray. All of the Optic patterns will certainly get down on the bottom where they need to be.

RINGOLD

HOOK:	Eagle Claw 1197N, sizes 4-8.
THREAD:	White
TAIL:	Scarlet red hackle fibers.
RIBBING:	Flat gold tinsel.
BODY:	White chenille.
HACKLE:	Scarlet red tied on as a collar and tied back and down.
WING:	White calf tail.

ROGUE RIVER SPECIAL

HOOK: Eagle Claw 1197B, sizes 2-8.

THREAD: White.

TAIL: Two orange hackle tips tied in a V.

RIBBING: Oval gold tinsel.

BODY: Rear ⅓ pale yellow wool yarn and front ⅔ red wool yarn.

WINGS: Two bunches of white bucktail tied in a V over the body.

CHEEKS: Jungle Cock or suitable substitute.

NOTE: As with many of the flies used on the Rogue River this fly is often tied on a Mustad 3582 Double hook in sizes 4-10.

SALMON FLY

HOOK: Eagle Claw 1197N, sizes 2-6.

THREAD: White.

TAIL: White bucktail.

BODY: Embossed silver tinsel.

HACKLE: Fluorescent red tied on as a collar and tied back.

EYES: Silver bead chain.

SILVER ANT

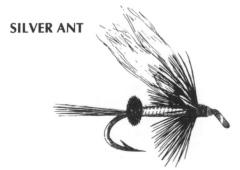

HOOK: Eagle Claw 1197B, sizes 4-6.

THREAD: Black.

TAIL: Crimson red hackle fibers.

BODY: Oval silver tinsel with black chenille tied in at butt.

WINGS: White bucktail tied in a V.

CHEEKS: Jungle Cock or suitable substitute.

HACKLE: Black tied on as a collar and tied back.

NOTES: The wings of this fly are tied upright and divided like a Wulff, however, they slant towards the back. Cheeks should be tied on parallel to the wings. Hackle is tied in last.

This variation of the Silver Ant is a creation of Russ Tower of Coos Bay, Oregon. It has very effective action in the water as evidenced by the many fish Russ has beached from the Rogue River.

SILVER DEMON

HOOK: Eagle Claw 1197N, sizes 2-8.

THREAD: Black.

TAIL: Orange hackle fibers.

BODY: Oval silver tinsel. Wrap an underbody of white floss to give the body a full taper. Wrap tinsel under the tail for tip before wrapping body.

HACKLE: Orange tied on as a collar and tied back and down.

WING: Gray squirrel tail.

SILVER DOCTOR

HOOK: Eagle Claw 1197N, sizes 1-6.

THREAD: Black.

TAIL: Scarlet red hackle fibers with peacock sword fibers tied in on top.

BODY: Embossed silver tinsel with red wool yarn tied in at butt.

HACKLE: Light blue tied on as a collar and tied back and down. Also tie in a small bunch of speckled guinea fibers at throat.

WING: Brown calf tail with peacock sword fibers tied in on top.

This is the Jim Pray variation of the Silver Doctor which he originated for Steelhead.

SILVER HILTON

HOOK: Eagle Claw 1197N, sizes 1-8.

THREAD: Black.

TAIL: Small bunch of barred mallard tied short.

RIBBING: Oval silver tinsel.

BODY: Black chenille.

WINGS: Grizzly neck hackle tips tied in a V over the body. The concave side of the hackle tips should be facing outward.

HACKLE: Grizzly tied on as a collar and tied back.

SILVER ROGUE

HOOK: Eagle Claw 1197N, sizes 1-6.

THREAD: Black.

TAIL: Lady Amherst pheasant tippet fibers.

BODY: Oval silver tinsel. Body is not tapered.

HACKLE: Grizzly tied Palmer over the body.

WING: Gray squirrel tail.

Originated by Jim Duckett of Medford, Oregon. Jim favored the Rogue and Klamath Rivers and few steelheaders will ever be able to match his record pound for pound.

SKUNK

HOOK: Eagle Claw 1197B, sizes 1-6.

THREAD: Black.

TAIL: Crimson red hackle fibers.

RIBBING: Oval silver tinsel.

BODY: Black chenille.

HACKLE: Black tied on as a collar and tied back.

WING: Black skunk tail with a small bunch of white skunk tail tied in on top.

SKYKOMISH SUNRISE

HOOK: Eagle Claw 1197B, sizes 1-6.

THREAD: Red.

TAIL: Scarlet red and yellow hackle fibers mixed.

RIBBING: Flat silver tinsel.

BODY: Red chenille.

HACKLE: Scarlet red and yellow tied on as a collar and tied back and down.

WING: White calf tail.

SKYKOMISH YELLOW

This pattern is the same as the Skykomish Sunrise except yellow chenille and tying thread are used.

SOL DUC

HOOK: Eagle Claw 1197B, sizes 2-8.

THREAD: Red.

RIBBING: Dyed scarlet red flat monofilament.

BODY: Dubbed pale yellow synthetic fur.

HACKLE: Orange tied on as a collar and tied back and down.

WING: Crimson red calf tail with a small bunch of white calf tail tied in on top.

First used on Washington's Sol Duc River, it has taken fish wherever used.

STREAKER

HOOK: Eagle Claw 1197G, sizes 2-8.

THREAD: Red.

TAIL: White marabou with a small bunch of fluorescent yellow marabou tied in on top.

BODY:	Gold mylar. Wrap a lead wire underbody.
HACKLE:	White marabou tied in at throat.
WING:	White marabou.
CHEEKS:	Short bunch of fluorescent orange marabou tied in at each side.
HEAD:	Fluorescent red lacquer.

See Dark Ember for illustration.

SUN BURST

HOOK:	Eagle Claw 1197G, sizes 2-8.
THREAD:	Red.
TAIL:	Fluorescent orange and yellow marabou mixed.
BODY:	Brass wire.
HACKLE:	Fluorescent orange and yellow marabou mixed and tied in at throat.
WING:	Fluorescent orange and yellow marabou mixed with a small bunch of fluorescent orange tied in on top.
CHEEKS:	Short bunch of fluorescent yellow marabou tied in at each side.
HEAD:	Fluorescent red lacquer.

Both of the above patterns are the work of Darwin Atkin.

SURESTRIKE COACHMAN

HOOK:	Mustad 7957BX, sizes 2-8.
THREAD:	Black.
TAIL:	Lady Amherst pheasant crest feather.
RIBBING:	Oval silver tinsel.
BODY:	Peacock herl. Wrap an underbody of olive wool yarn to give the body a full taper.
HACKLE:	Dark brown tied on as a collar and tied back and down.
WING:	White calf tail.
TOPPING:	Lady Amherst pheasant crest feather.

A good pattern almost anywhere. The added touch of red given by the incorporation of the Lady Amerst pheasant crest feathers has an unusually seductive effect. In addition to Steelhead and Cutthroat, this fly has accounted for many large trout elsewhere.

THOR

HOOK:	Eagle Claw 1197B, sizes 1-8.
THREAD:	Black.
TAIL:	Orange hackle fibers.
BODY:	Red chenille.
HACKLE:	Brown tied on as a collar and tied back and down.
WING:	White calf tail.

This is another one of the Jim Pray patterns which has remained popular over a number of decades.

TIGER

HOOK:	Eagle Claw 1197G, sizes 2-6.
THREAD:	Black.
TAIL:	Dyed yellow grizzly hackle fibers.
RIBBING:	Fine black chenille.
BODY:	Yellow chenille.
HACKLE:	Dyed yellow grizzly tied on as a collar and tied back.
WING:	Black calf tail.

TRINITY TORCH

HOOK:	Eagle Claw 1197N, sizes 2-8.
THREAD:	White.
TAIL:	Fluorescent pink hackle fibers.
RIBBING:	Embossed silver tinsel.
BODY:	Fluorescent pink chenille.
WING:	Crimson red calf tail.
HACKLE:	Fluorescent pink tied on as a collar and tied slightly back.

Originated in 1949 by Gene Anderson of Redding, California.

UMPQUA

HOOK: Eagle Claw 1197B, sizes 2-8.

THREAD: Red.

TAIL: White calf tail.

RIBBING: Oval silver tinsel.

BODY: Rear ⅓ yellow wool yarn and front ⅔ red chenille.

HACKLE: Brown tied on as a collar and tied back and down.

WING: White calf tail.

NOTES: The hackle is sometimes tied in last and tied back.

WIND RIVER

HOOK: Eagle Claw 1197B, sizes 4-8.

THREAD: Black.

TIP: Embossed gold tinsel.

TAIL: Barred lemon wood duck fibers.

RIBBING: Embossed gold tinsel.

BODY: Dubbed muskrat fur.

HACKLE: Badger tied on as a collar and tied back.

WING: Gray squirrel.

FLY PATTERNS OF A MASTER

A man should not bandy about the word "master" when talking of a fly-tyer. But in Chiloquin, Oregon, there lives a man who is a master. He is E. H. "Polly" Rosborough, whose accomplishments in the realm of tying flies simply permit no other designation. Polly, now at age 74, is still going strong. I first became aware of Polly when he was western editor for the *Fishing Tackle Digest* and I read some of his western how to and what to in a 1949 issue. I was a boy in those days and really just getting started in fly tying and fishing. In later years I had the opportunity to correspond with Polly, and to this day I have always found him ready and willing to share his knowledge with me. This remarkable man has devoted his life to professional fly tying. He has taken time out to do an article now and then and in 1965 he published a book *Tying and Fishing the Fuzzy Nymphs*. Initially, this book brought criticisms from many corners. At that time far too many of us, myself included, had Hewitt, Blades and others ingrained into our minds and were missing the "Fuzzy Nymph" meaning that he had given us. Today, however, his nymphs are used wherever a fly is cast and Polly, even with the help of others, has a difficult time supplying the demand. Many only know of Polly's nymphs and are unaware of any of his other very successful patterns. He does not try to publicize his other patterns because he just does not have the time to tie and supply them. It is for this reason that I felt it necessary to include for you all of Polly's patterns. You just cannot buy them and try to duplicate them.

DRY FLIES

BIG YELLOW MAY

HOOK: Mustad 38941, size 8.

THREAD: Yellow 2780 Nymo.

WINGS: Pale yellow hackle tips tied upright and divided.

TAIL: Barred lemon wood duck fibers.

BODY: Yellow synthetic yarn tied with a good full taper.

HACKLE: Yellow and light ginger mixed.

NOTES: When hackling this fly at least ten turns of hackle are required to float it properly. Indian Saddle is highly recommended.

BLACK DRAKE

HOOK: Mustad 94840, sizes 8-10.

THREAD: Black.

TAIL: Purplish dun gray hackle fibers.

RIBBING: Gray 2712 Nymo.

BODY: Purplish brown synthetic yarn.

HACKLE: Purplish dun gray.

NOTES: Hackle and tailing material colors are obtained by tinting dyed gray hackle with purple dye. Yarn for the body is obtained by dying brown yarn in the same manner. Use a synthetic yarn as it does not take the dye well and it is much easier to get the desired purplish tint.

CARPENTER ANT

HOOK: Mustad 38941, size 10.

THREAD: Black.

BODY: Black polypropylene yarn wrapped in two distinctive lumps to simulate an ant's body.

HACKLE: Narrow black hackle is wrapped in the center joint.

NOTES: Polly ties this pattern with an extra large lump at the rear. Apply a coat of head cement between each wrap of yarn.

This may appear to be just another ant pattern to many but it has some features most of the others do not. The poly yarn allows the fly to be suspended about three inches under the surface which is an extremely enticing offering.

DARK STONE

HOOK: Mustad 38941, size 8.

THREAD: Black.

RIBBING: Dark furnace hackle tied Palmer over the body.

BODY: Tangerine orange synthetic yarn.

WING: Dyed coffee brown bucktail.

HACKLE: Dark furnace tied on as a collar in front of wing.

Polly states that a size 8 for this pattern makes the fly slightly smaller than the naturals but it is essential to get a good float and the fish do not really mind...until they taste it!

GOLDEN STONE

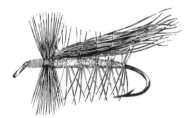

HOOK: Mustad 38941, size 8.

THREAD: Antique gold.

RIBBING: Dyed gold hackle tied Palmer over the body.

BODY: Antique gold synthetic yarn.

WING: Natural light brown bucktail dyed gold.

HACKLE: Dyed gold tied on as a collar in front of wing.

ISONYCHIA BICOLOR

HOOK:	Mustad 94840, size 8.
THREAD:	Tan 1248 Nymo.
WINGS:	Natural black hackle tips tied upright and divided.
TAIL:	Dyed brown cock ringneck pheasant body plumage fibers (Church Window).
RIBBING:	Yellow 2780 Nymo thread. Wrap six turns.
BODY:	Burgundy wine synthetic yarn.
UNDER HACKLE:	Trim a web free yellow saddle hackle down to 3/16″ on each side and wrap two turns behind and two turns in front of wings.
HACKLE:	Deep purplish dun gray.

LITTLE BROWN STONE

HOOK:	Mustad 38941, sizes 12-14.
THREAD:	Brown 1523 Nymo.
TAIL:	Dark brown ringneck pheasant body plumage fibers.
RIBBING:	Brown 1523 Nymo thread. Wrap six turns.
BODY:	Seal brown synthetic yarn.
WING:	One dark grizzly hackle tip tied flat over the body and extending to the bend of the hook.
HACKLE:	Dark grizzly tied on as a collar in front of the wing.

LITTLE YELLOW STONE

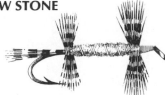

HOOK:	Mustad 38941, sizes 10-12.
THREAD:	Yellow 2780 Nymo.
TAIL:	Dyed pale yellow grizzly hackle fibers.

REAR HACKLE:	Dyed pale yellow grizzly.
RIBBING:	Yellow 2780 Nymo thread.
BODY:	Chartreuse synthetic yarn.
FRONT HACKLE:	Dyed pale yellow grizzly.

NOTES: The rear hackle should be shorter than the front hackle with the barbles only extending slightly past the point of the hook. Proper body color can be obtained by dying yellow synthetic yarn with no. 31 light green Rit dye.

MEADOW HOPPER

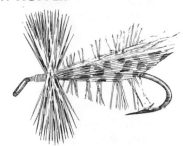

HOOK:	Mustad 38941, sizes 8-14.
THREAD:	Brown.
RIBBING:	Light ginger tied Palmer over the body. Trim off on each side and trim taper down to almost zero at the front of the fly.
BODY:	Pale yellow synthetic yarn.
WINGS:	Light brown mottled turkey quill sections dyed pale yellow and tied in at each side.
OVERWING:	Small bunch of yellow bucktail.
HACKLE:	Cream, dark ginger and light grizzly mixed.

Although I favor the Letort Hopper over all hopper patterns, many feel just as strongly about Polly's Meadow Hopper.

YELLOW DRAKE

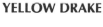
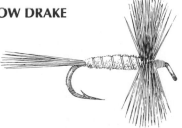

HOOK:	Mustad 94840, sizes 10-12.
THREAD:	Maize 2785 Nymo.
TAIL:	Light dun gray hackle fibers.
RIBBING:	Maize 2785 Nymo thread.
BODY:	Pale cream synthetic yarn.
HACKLE:	Light dun gray.

NYMPHS

BIG YELLOW MAY

HOOK:	Mustad 38941, sizes 6-8.
THREAD:	Yellow 2780 Nymo.
TAIL:	Barred lemon wood duck fibers.
SHELLBACK:	Dyed lemon wood duck barred teal flank feather.
RIBBING:	Yellow tying thread. Rib over the shellback.
BODY:	Yellow synthetic yarn.
LEGS:	Dyed lemon wood duck barred teal fibers tied in at the throat.
WINGCASE:	A small bunch of dyed lemon wood duck barred teal fibers tied in over the body and extending ½ the length of the body.

NOTES: Select a dyed lemon wood duck barred teal flank feather which is light cast for the shellback. Feathers for the wingcase and legs should be dark cast and have a distinct heavy barring.

BLACK DRAKE

HOOK:	Mustad 38941, size 10.
THREAD:	Gray 9041 Nymo.
TAIL:	Speckled guinea fibers tied short.
BODY:	Dubbed beaver belly fur with guard hairs left in.
LEGS:	Speckled guinea fibers tied in at each side and slanting downward.
WINGCASE:	Small bunch of natural black ostrich.

BLACK MIDGE PUPA

HOOK:	Mustad 7957B, size 12.
THREAD:	Gray 9041 Nymo.
HEAD:	Black ostrich tied in at rear of hook.
LEGS:	A small collar of pale grizzly hackle tied in front of the head.
BODY:	Dubbed muskrat fur. Dub so there is a heavy taper at the back.

This nymph is tied reverse on the hook.

BLONDE BURLAP

HOOK:	Mustad 7957B, sizes 4-12.
THREAD:	Tan.
TAIL:	Honey dun hackle fibers tied short.
BODY:	Bleached burlap jute strand tied with a good full taper. Pick out and make fuzzy after the body is wrapped.
HACKLE:	Soft honey dun tied on as a collar and tied back.

NOTES: Polly bleaches his burlap for his pattern using 20 volume hydrogen peroxide. He places it in a jar with the burlap and leaves the burlap in until it is the same color as it was when it was dry.

BROWN NONDESCRIPT

HOOK:	Mustad 38941, sizes 8-12.
THREAD:	Brown 1523 Nymo.
TAIL:	Dyed brown barred mallard fibers.
RIBBING:	Heavy yellow thread.
LEGS:	Stroke the hackle barbles of a dark furnace saddle hackle down towards the butt. Then trim off barbles on each side starting at zero at the tip and wider at the butt. The widest portion should be about ½".
BODY:	Dark brown synthetic yarn.

NOTES: The trimmed saddle hackle is tied in by the tip at the rear of the body using the yarn body material. One full turn of yarn is first wrapped, then the tip is tied in. The yarn is wrapped forward and then the saddle hackle. Ribbing is wrapped in between the turns of saddle hackle.

This pattern was originated by Jim "Red" Chase of Toppenish, Washington. He gave it to Polly to try. Polly modified it, putting on dark brown tuft of marabou for the tail, and it has proven to be a real producer.

CASUAL DRESS

HOOK:	Mustad 38941, sizes 4-10.
THREAD:	Gray 9041 Nymo.
TAIL:	Bunch of muskrat fur taken from the back and tied in short. Leave guard hairs in the fur.
BODY:	Dubbed muskrat fur. Leave guard hairs in and pick out and make very shaggy.
COLLAR:	Tie in a collar of muskrat belly fur.
HEAD:	Black ostrich.

DARK CADDIS EMERGENT

HOOK:	Mustad 3906B, size 8.
THREAD:	Black.
RIBBING:	Orange 1560 Nymo.
BODY:	Light burnt orange synthetic yarn.
HACKLE:	Furnace hackle tied on as a collar and tied back. Clip off hackle barbles on both the top and bottom. Hackle legs should be long enough to reach the rear of the body.
HEAD:	Black ostrich.

DARK STONE

HOOK:	Mustad 38941, sizes 2-6.
THREAD:	Tan.
TAIL:	Two fibers of dyed dark brown ringneck pheasant quill.
BODY:	Dubbed cream badger fur. Paint the back of the body with a dark brown enamel. Apply color down to the middle of the sides. Work the enamel well into the fur so the fuzzy effect is not destroyed.
LEGS:	Dyed dark brown ringneck pheasant quill fibers tied in at throat.

WINGCASE:	Bunch of blackish-brown ostrich tied in at head and extending over ⅓ of the body.

FLEDERMOUSE

HOOK:	Mustad 38941, sizes 2-12.
THREAD:	Turf Tan 1148 Nymo.
BODY:	Dubbed muskrat and dyed dark brown rabbit fur mixed in equal parts.
COLLAR:	Muskrat and dyed dark brown rabbit tied on as a collar and extending back around the body ⅓.
WINGCASE:	Dyed dark brown barred teal fibers tied in at head and extending over ⅓ of the body.

This is one of the better producing patterns that Polly ties. I have had people tell me that they have used this fly successfully in a number of heavily fished waters throughout the world.

FRESHWATER SHRIMP

HOOK:	Eagle Claw 1197, size 8.
THREAD:	Tan.
TAIL:	Pale ginger marabou tied well down on the bend of the hook.
BODY:	Dubbed bleached beaver fur. Color should be tannish cream.
LEGS:	Soft ginger hackle tied Palmer over the body. Clip off hackle barbles on top and sides.

NOTES: Depending on the time of year and the area you are fishing, you may find that a small amount of olive rabbit fur blended into your beaver fur will be of help. As the season progresses and the algae commences to proliferate the shrimp will take on a pale olive cast.

GOLDEN STONE

HOOK:	Mustad 38941, sizes 4-6.
THREAD:	Antique gold.
TAIL:	Two small bunches of dyed dark gold barred teal fibers tied in a short V.

RIBBING: Heavy antique gold thread.

SHELLBACK: Dyed dark gold barred teal feather tied over the back with ribbing.

BODY: Gold synthetic yarn.

LEGS: Dyed dark gold barred teal fibers tied in at throat.

WINGCASE: Dyed dark gold barred teal fibers tied in at head and extending over ⅓ of the body.

NOTES: You may find it difficult to obtain thread for the ribbing. I suggest flat monofilament dyed dark gold. It works great.

GREEN DAMSEL

HOOK: Mustad 38941, size 10.

THREAD: Olive.

TAIL: Olive marabou. After tailing material is tied in pinch off fibers so they are short.

BODY: Dubbed pale olive rabbit fur.

LEGS: Dyed pale olive barred teal.

WINGCASE: Olive marabou tied in at head and extending ⅓ over the body. Wingcase should be at least one shade darker than the tail.

GREEN ROCK WORM

HOOK: Eagle Claw 1197B, size 8.

THREAD: Black.

BODY: Caddis green synthetic yarn.

LEGS: Dyed green speckled guinea fibers tied in at throat.

HEAD: Black ostrich.

HARE'S EAR

HOOK: Mustad 3906B, sizes 8-16.

THREAD: Black.

BODY: Dubbed muskrat and medium brown rabbit fur mixed in equal parts.

COLLAR: Muskrat belly fur tied on as a collar and extending around the body ⅓. Pull out guard hairs.

WINGCASE: Small bunch of dyed brown speckled guinea fibers tied in at head and extending back over the body ⅓.

ISONYCHIA BICOLOR

HOOK: Mustad 38941, sizes 8-10.

THREAD: Henna 1224 Nymo.

TAIL: Dyed dark brown ringneck pheasant body feather fibers.

RIBBING: Yellow 2780 Nymo.

BODY: Fiery brown synthetic yarn.

LEGS: Dyed dark brown ringneck pheasant body feather fibers tied in at throat.

WINGCASE: Dyed seal brown Brahama hen hackle tip tied in at head and extending back over the body ⅓.

ISONYCHIA VELMA

HOOK: Mustad 38941, sizes 6-8.

THREAD: Henna 1224 Nymo.

TAIL: Three fibers of dyed purple ringneck pheasant center tail feather.

RIBBING: Gold wire. Wrap eight turns.

BODY: Deep purplish brown synthetic yarn.

LEGS: Medium brown ringneck pheasant body plumage fibers tied in at throat.

GILLS: Purplish brown marabou tied in over the body and extending ⅔ the length of the body.

WINGCASE: Dyed purplish brown ringneck pheasant body feather, Church Window, tied in over the gills and extending ⅓ the length of the body.

This nymph is native only to the West Coast and is best fished from mid-June to the end of August.

LIGHT CADDIS

HOOK: Eagle Claw 1197B, size 8

THREAD: Black.

BODY: Dubbed cream fox or badger fur.

LEGS: Barred lemon wood duck fibers tied in at throat.

HEAD: Black ostrich.

LIGHT CADDIS EMERGENT

HOOK: Mustad 3906B, sizes 8-10.

THREAD: Black.

BODY: Pale yellow synthetic yarn.

LEGS: Light ginger variant hackle tied on as a collar and tied back. Clip off hackle barbles on both top and bottom. Legs should be long enough to reach the rear of the body.

HEAD: Black ostrich.

LITTLE BROWN STONE

HOOK: Mustad 38941, sizes 10-12.

THREAD: Brown 1523 Nymo.

TAIL: Dyed dark brown ringneck pheasant neck feather fibers tied in at each side and extending to the center of the body.

WINGCASE: Purplish ringneck pheasant neck feather tied in at head and extending ⅓ over the body.

LITTLE YELLOW STONE

HOOK: Mustad 38941, size 10.

THREAD: Light yellow.

TAIL: Small bunch of dyed chartreuse barred mallard fibers tied short.

BODY: Dubbed dyed chartreuse rabbit fur.

LEGS: Dyed chartreuse barred mallard fibers tied in at throat.

WINGCASE: Bunch of dyed chartreuse barred mallard fibers tied in at head and extending ⅓ over the body.

The Little Yellow Stone is also referred to as the Willow Fly and it emerges from June through the middle of August. I have had more success with this pattern by blending in a small amount of yellow synthetic fur with the rabbit to give the body a little more yellow.

MOSQUITO LARVA

HOOK: Mustad 9672, size 14.

THREAD: Gray 9041 Nymo.

TAIL: Small bunch of finely speckled guinea fibers tied short.

RIBBING: Gray 9041 Nymo thread.

BODY: Gray synthetic yarn.

LEGS: Small bunch of finely speckled guinea fibers tied in at throat and extending to the center of the belly.

NOTES: Body should have a full cigar taper to it. After tying the head with a nice full taper place a small dot of black head cement on each side of the head for eyes.

MUSKRAT

HOOK: Mustad 38941, sizes 6-16.

THREAD: Black.

BODY: Dubbed muskrat fur.

LEGS: Speckled guinea fibers tied in at throat.

HEAD: Black ostrich.

NEAR ENOUGH

HOOK: Mustad 38941, sizes 8-14.

THREAD: Sand 2042 Nymo.

TAIL: Dyed tannish gray barred mallard fibers.

BODY: Dubbed gray fox fur with guard hairs removed.

LEGS: Dyed tannish gray barred mallard fibers tied in at each side and slanting slightly downwards.

WINGCASE: Bend the butts of barred mallard fibers back over the body after tying in legs and use for wingcase. Trim to ⅓ the length of the body.

NOTES: The tannish gray color for the barred mallard is obtained by using 1 part no. 14 gray Rit dye and 2 parts no. 16 tan Rit dye.

This is one of Polly's newest creations and it fills the need for a universal May Fly nymph to simulate a variety of species.

RED MIDGE PUPA

HOOK: Mustad 94840, sizes 12-14.

THREAD: Red 0538 Nymo.

HEAD: Dark gray ostrich tied in at rear of hook.

LEGS: A small collar of pale grizzly hackle tied in front of head.

RIBBING: Red 0538 Nymo thread.

BODY: Crimson red synthetic yarn wrapped so there is a fat taper at rear.

This nymph is tied reversed on the hook.

TAN MIDGE PUPA

HOOK: Mustad 94840, sizes 12-14.

THREAD: Cork 2063 Nymo.

LEGS: A small collar of pale grizzly hackle tied in front of head.

RIBBING: Cork 2063 Nymo thread.

BODY: Fox buff synthetic yarn wrapped so there is a fat taper at rear.

NOTES: When tying the midge pupas the hackle or gills should be tied slightly back and extend no further than the point of the hook. Select grizzly hackle which is web free.

This nymph is tied reversed on the hook.

YELLOW DRAKE

HOOK: Mustad 9672, size 10.

THREAD: Light yellow.

TAIL: Small bunch of barred lemon wood duck fibers.

BODY: Dubbed cream badger fur.

LEGS: Barred lemon wood duck fibers tied in at each side and slanting slightly downwards.

WINGCASE: Bend the butts of the barred lemon wood duck fibers back over the body after tying in the legs and use for wingcase. Trim to ⅓ the length of the body.

WET FLIES

COPPER COLONEL

HOOK: Mustad 38941, sizes 4-6.

THREAD: Black.

BODY: Oval copper tinsel wrapped over an orange floss underbody.

HACKLE: Soft dark furnace.

WING: Coffee brown bucktail tied rather sparse.

HEAD: Fluorescent orange lacquer band is applied across the top at the base of the wing. (Optional)

This fly is tied to simulate the Dark Stone. It is often very effective during a late run off when the water is high and dirty yet the hatch is on. Oval copper tinsel is hard to find. I have had success in finding a limited amount of copper mylar piping on some of the notions counters which works real well. If all else fails simply take a copper scouring pad apart.

DARK STONE

HOOK: Mustad 38941, sizes 4-6.

THREAD: Black.

TAIL: Dark brown mottled turkey tail feather fibers tied short.

RIBBING: Gray button hole twist thread.

BODY: Tangerine orange synthetic yarn.

HACKLE: Soft dark furnace.

WING: Coffee brown bucktail tied rather sparse.

HEAD: Fluorescent orange lacquer band is applied across the top at the base of the wing. (Optional)

GOLDEN STONE

HOOK: Mustad 38941, sizes 4-6.

THREAD: Antique gold.

RIBBING: Antique gold button hole twist thread.

BODY: Antique gold synthetic yarn.

HACKLE: Dyed gold barred teal fibers tied in at throat.

WING: Natural light brown bucktail dyed gold.

LITTLE YELLOW STONE FEMALE

HOOK: Mustad 38941, sizes 10-12.

THREAD: Yellow 2780 Nymo.

TAIL: Dyed pale yellow grizzly hackle fibers.

EGG SAC: Large bunch of crimson red hackle fiber tied in above the tail and clipped down to about 1/16".

RIBBING: Yellow 2780 Nymo thread.

BODY: Chartreuse synthetic yarn.

HACKLE: Dyed pale yellow grizzly.

WING: Two dyed pale yellow grizzly hackle tips tied flat over the body and extending to the bend of the hook.

STREAMERS AND STEELHEAD FLIES

BLACK LEECH STREAMER

HOOK: Mustad 79580, sizes 4-8.

THREAD: Black.

TAIL: Crimson red hackle fibers tied short.

BODY: Peacock herl. Wrap an underbody of olive yarn to give the peacock a fuller effect. Reverse wrap the body with fine silver wire.

HACKLE: Black tied on as a collar then tied back and down.

WINGS: Four black saddle hackles tied in on edge over the body. The two center hackles should be tied with the concave side out to give the wing more effect.

MINNOW STREAMER

HOOK: Mustad 9672, sizes 6-10.

THREAD: Brown.

TAIL: Cock ringneck pheasant center tail fibers.

RIBBING: Flat silver tinsel.

BODY: Magenta floss.

WING: A bunch of cock ringneck pheasant center tail fibers.

NOTES: Ribbing on this pattern is only wrapped over the front half of the body. Ribbing should be tied in at the center of the body before the floss is wrapped.

POLAR CHUB

HOOK: Mustad 38941, sizes 2-6.

THREAD: Olive.

TAIL: White polar bear hair.

BODY: Oval silver tinsel. Wrap an underbody of white floss to give the body a good full taper.

WINGS: Under wing of white polar bear hair. Middle wing of golden olive polar bear hair. Top wing of dyed olive dark brown bear hair.

CHEEKS: Jungle Cock or suitable substitute.

NOTE: This pattern is also good when tied with silver bead chain eyes. When doing so the cheeks are left off.

POLLY'S PRIDE

HOOK:	Eagle Claw 1197N, sizes 1-6.
THREAD:	Black.
TAIL:	Fluorescent red hackle fibers.
RIBBING:	Flat silver tinsel.
BODY:	Fluorescent red yarn.
HACKLE:	Soft fluorescent red tied on as a collar and tied back and down.
WING:	White marabou.
TOPPING:	Six strands of black ostrich.

Polly first started tying this pattern in 1936 and because of its nationwide popularity it has become his trade mark through these many years.

SILVER ADMIRAL

HOOK:	Eagle Claw 1197N, sizes 1-6.
THREAD:	White.
TAIL:	Hot pink hackle fibers.
RIBBING:	Flat silver tinsel.
BODY:	Hot pink yarn.
HACKLE:	Hot pink tied on as a collar and tied back and down.
WING:	White polar bear hair.

This is a Steelhead pattern which is most useful during dirty water conditions.

SILVER GARLAND MARABOU

HOOK:	Mustad 79580, sizes 2-8.
THREAD:	Olive.
BODY:	Silver tinsel chenille.
WINGS:	Two white marabou plumes with four insect green strands of ostrich tied in at each side.
TOPPING:	Four teal blue ostrich herl strands tied in on top.
CHEEKS:	Jungle Cock or suitable substitute.

This is a very good pattern for use in rivers with a population of Whitefish. Especially effective in the late fall when there is a minimum number of insect hatches.

SILVER SPRUCE

HOOK:	Mustad 9672, sizes 4-10.
THREAD:	Black.
TAIL:	Five strands of peacock sword.
BODY:	Flat silver tinsel. Wrap an underbody of white floss to give the body a slight taper.
WINGS:	Two silver badger hackles.
HACKLE:	Silver badger tied on as a collar.

Polly ties this pattern strictly for Browns and Brookies. He finds that the silver body is much more effective than the peacock on the regular Spruce.

UMPQUA RED BRAT

HOOK:	Eagle Claw .1197B, sizes 2-8.
THREAD:	Black.
TAIL:	Small bunch of barred mallard fibers tied short.
RIBBING:	Flat silver tinsel.
BODY:	Red chenille.
HACKLE:	Barred mallard tied on as a collar and tied back. Hackle should be long enough to reach the bend of the hook.
WING:	Crimson red polar bear hair.

This fly is one of my own personal favorites when fishing in British Columbia.

WHITEFISH

HOOK:	Eagle Claw 1197N, sizes 1-6.
THREAD:	Tan.
TAIL:	Two honey dun hackle tips tied in on edge with concave side in.
BODY:	Oval silver tinsel. Wrap an underbody of white floss to give the body a good full taper.
HACKLE:	Small bunch of hot pink hackle fibers tied in at throat.
CHEEKS:	Jungle Cock or suitable substitute.
WING:	Four honey dun neck hackle tips. Tie with concave sides out. The two inside wings should be tied slightly shorter to give the wings more action in the water.

This pattern has been a most effective fly for winter Steelhead. Also, it has proven its worth as a salt water fly.

APPENDIX

FLY FISHING CLUBS of the UNITED STATES and CANADA

The following is a listing of fly fishing clubs which are affiliated with the Federation of Fly Fishermen. I strongly recommend your participation and support should one be located in your area. They all offer some very fine fellowship plus they can often give you more of an insight into meeting your own fishing conditions. Many of the clubs also have special buying privileges which allows you to purchase fly tying materials and tackle at a discount. Should there not be a club in your area and you would be interested in establishing one, contact the Federation of Fly Fishermen, 519 Main Street, El Segundo, California 90245, for assistance.

ALASKA FLY FISHERS
P.O. Box 1593
Anchorage, Alaska 99510

THE DAME JULIANA BERNERS FLY FYSHYNGE
ASSOCIATION
2906 Will Rogers Place
Anchorage, Alaska 99503

DESERT FLY CASTERS
P.O. Box 1331
Mesa, Arizona 85201

ARIZONA FLYCASTERS CLUB
P.O. Box 691
Phoenix, Arizona 85001

TUCSON FLY FISHING CLUB
P.O. Box 6733
Tucson, Arizona 85716

ARKANSAS FLY FISHERS
7710 Cantrell Road
Little Rock, Arkansas 72207

WHITE RIVER FLY FISHERS CLUB
Lakeside Terrace, Rt. 6
Mountain Home, Arkansas 72653

SALTWATER FLYRODDERS OF AMERICA
INTERNATIONAL
Pacific #1, 290 E. Marathon Road
Altadena, California 91001

SIERRA EAST FLYFISHERS
P.O. Box 1334
Bishop, California 93514

FLYCASTER, INC.
P.O. Box 821
Campbell, California 95008

CHICO FLY FISHING CLUB
P.O. Box 1025
Chico, California 95926

FLY FISHERS OF DAVIS
P.O. Box 525
Davis, California 95616

DOWNEY FLY FISHERS
10999 Little Lake Road
Downey, California 90241

SISKIYOU FLYFISHERS
Box 255
Dunsmuir, California 96025

ROYAL ORDER OF THE STONE FLY
4750 Encino Avenue
Encino, California 91316

FLY FISHERMEN FOR CONSERVATION, INC.
P.O. Box 4441
Fresno, California 93744

FLY FISHERS CLUB OF ORANGE COUNTY,
INC.
P.O. Box 423
Fullerton, California 92632

FRESH AND SALTY FLYFISHERS OF GARDENA
P.O. Box 67
Gardena, California 90248

SAN GABRIEL VALLEY FLYFISHERS
P.O. Box 5423
Hacienda Heights, California 91745

INGLEWOOD FLY FISHERMEN
P.O. Box 426
Inglewood, California 90306

LIVERMORE FLY FISHERMEN
P.O. Box 387
Livermore, California 94550

LONG BEACH WOMENS CASTING CLUB
6165 Cerritos Avenue
Long Beach, California 90814

LONG BEACH CASTING CLUB
P.O. Box 4063
Long Beach, California 90804

AMERICAN MEDICAL FLY FISHING
ASSOCIATION
7130 Morningside Drive
Loomis, California 95650

MASTERS OF THE MAYFLY
13934 Bora Bora Way #209E
Marina Del Rey, California 90291

STANISLAUS FLY FISHERMEN
P.O. Box 3072
Modesto, California 95353

NAPA VALLEY FLY FISHERMEN
P.O. Box 2373
Napa, California 94558

PALM SPRINGS ROD AND GUN CLUB, INC.
P.O. Box 4440
Palm Springs, California 92262

NORTHERN CALIFORNIA FLY FISHERMEN
1859 Salida Way
Paradise, California 95969

PASADENA CASTING CLUB
P.O. Box 6M
Pasadena, California 91102

TRI-CITY FLYFISHERS
P.O. Box 1192
Riverside, California 92502

CALIFORNIA FLY FISHERMEN, UNLIMITED
P.O. Box 2547
Sacramento, California 95812

SALINAS VALLEY FLY FISHERMEN
P.O. Box 1793
Salinas, California 93901

SAN DIEGO FLYFISHERMEN'S CLUB
1650 El Prado
San Diego, California 92101

GOLDEN GATE ANGLING AND CASTING
CLUB
Angler's Lodge, Golden Gate Park
San Francisco, California 94118

OAKLAND CASTING CLUB
14918 Lark Street
San Leandro, California 94578

WILDERNESS FLY FISHERS
P.O. Box 985
Santa Monica, California 90406

NORTHERN CALIFORNIA JAPANESE
AMERICAN FLYCASTERS
949 Exmoor Way
Sunnyvale, California 94087

PALO ALTO FLYFISHERS
665 Endicot Drive
Sunnyvale, California 94087

SIERRA PACIFIC FLYFISHERS
14423 Burbank Blvd.
Van Nuys, California 91401

VENTURA FLYFISHERS
P.O. Box 150
Ventura, California 93001

DIABLO VALLEY FLY FISHERMEN
P.O. Box 4988
Walnut Creek, California 94596

BOULDER FLYCASTERS
P.O. Box 541
Boulder, Colorado 80302

FRONT RANGE FLY FISHERS
4072 South Quebec street
Denver, Colorado 80237

PIKES PEAK FLY FISHERS
1131 Mears Drive
Colorado Springs, Colorado 80915

THE NORTHERN COLORADO FLY FISHERS
P.O. Box 1931
Fort Collins, Colorado 80522

CONNECTICUT SALTWATER FLYRODDERS
ASSOCIATION
7 Hideaway Lane
Norwalk, Connecticut 06850

CONNECTICUT FLY FISHERMEN'S
ASSOCIATION, INC.
P.O. Box 42
Windsor Locks, Connecticut 06096

ATLANTA FLYFISHERS CLUB
P.O. Box 90274
East Point, Georgia 30044

BOISE VALLEY FLY FISHERMEN, INC.
P.O. Box 311
Boise, Idaho 83701

HELLS CANYON FLYCASTERS
3816 15th Street
Lewiston, Idaho 83501

MAGIC VALLEY FLY FISHERMEN
Route #1
Murtaugh, Idaho 83344

NAMPA ROD AND GUN CLUB, INC.
Nampa, Idaho 83651

THE PORTNEUF FLY FISHERS
P.O. Box 8863
Pocatello, Idaho 83209

MINI-CASSIA FLY FISHERMEN
534 6th Street
Rupert, Idaho 83350

UPPER SNAKE RIVER FLY FISHERMEN
575 Targhee
St. Anthony, Idaho 83445

SUN VALLEY FLY FISHERS, INC.
P.O. Box 895
Sun Valley, Idaho 83353

NORTHERN ILLINOIS FLY TYERS
709 S. Highland Ave.
Arlington Heights, Illinois 60085

NORTHERN FLY TYING CLUB
3638 N. Sayre
Chicago, Illinois 60634

ANGLER'S CLUB OF CHICAGO
2011 Glendale
Northbrook, Illinois 60062

INDIANAPOLIS FLY CASTERS
6040 Bryan Drive
Indianapolis, Indiana 46227

POTOMAC VALLEY FLY FISHERMEN
P.O. Box 1064
Frederick, Maryland 21701

MARYLAND FLY ANGLERS, INC.
P.O. Box 3606
Baltimore, Maryland 21214

ANTIETAM FLY ANGLERS
Route 3, Box 171A
Smithsburg, Maryland 21783

GRANT'S KENNABAGO CAMPS, INC.
FLY FISHING CLUB
Oquossoc, Maine 04964

ANDOVER FLY FISHERS
P.O. Box 204
Andover, Mass. 01810

UNITED FLY TYERS, INC.
59 Temple Place, Room 603
Boston, Mass. 02111

GREATER LOWELL FLY FISHERS, INC.
22 Forest Park Road
Dracut, Mass. 01826

BLUE DUN ANGLING AND GUNNING CLUB
27 Murray Hill Road
Meaford, Mass. 02115

BERNARD HILL FLYFISHERS
35 Minges Road West
Battle Creek, Michigan 49017

MICHIGAN FLY FISHING CLUB
P.O. Box 114
Dearborn, Michigan 48121

FREESTONE FLY FISHERS
1466 Lathrop
Saginaw, Michigan 48603

HILLBILLY FLY RODDERS
2622 E. Glenwood
Springfield, Missouri 65804

OZARK FLYFISHERS
6727 Manchester Ave.
St. Louis, Missouri 63139

ROCKY MOUNTAIN RIVER RATS
2215 North Drive
Butte, Montana 59701

SOUTHWESTERN MONTANA FLY FISHERS
West Yellowstone, Montana 59758

LAS VEGAS FLY FISHING CLUB
2105 Mariposa Avenue
Las Vegas, Nevada 89105

JOE JEFFERSON CLUB, INC.
Log Cabin and Saddle River Road
Saddle River, New Jersy 07458

SALTY FLYRODDERS OF NEW YORK, INC.
20-37 21st Street
Astoria, N.Y. 11105

PUTNAM TROUT ASSOCIATION
P.O. Box 10
Carmel, New York 10512

CASTLE CREEK FISHING CLUB
Road #2
Corning, N.Y. 14830

BEAVERKILL FLYFISHERS, INC.
24-16 Bridge Plaza S.
Long Island City, N.Y. 11101

HENRYVILLE CONSERVATION CLUB, INC.
342 Madison Avenue
New York, N.Y. 10017

THEODORE GORDON FLYFISHERS, INC.
24 E. 39th Street
New York, N.Y. 10016

FONTINALIS FLY FISHERMEN
Road #3 Evergreen Lane
Port Jarvis, N.Y. 12771

BEAVERKILL-WILLOWEMOC (BEA-MOC) ROD
AND GUN CLUB
Roscoe, N.Y. 12776

ROCKWELL SPRINGS TROUT CLUB
P.O. Box 305
Castalia, Ohio 44824

MIAMI VALLEY FLY FISHERS, INC.
245 Acorn Drive
Dayton, Ohio 45419

ZANESFIELD ROD AND GUN CLUB, INC.
Zanesfield, Ohio 43360

GREEN COUNTRY FLYFISHERS
P.O. Box 1053
Bartlesville, Oklahoma 74002

PRAIRIE FLY FISHERS
P.O. Box 94033
Oklahoma City, Oklahoma 73109

CAMAS VALLEY FLY FISHERS
P.O. Box 134
Camas Valley, Oregon 97416

McKENZIE FLYFISHERS
P.O. Box 1832
Eugene, Oregon 97401

KLAMATH COUNTRY FLY CASTERS
P.O. Box 324
Klamath Falls, Oregon 97601

ROGUE FLYFISHERS
P.O. Box 1086
Medford, Oregon 97501

ANGLERS CLUB OF PORTLAND
P.O. Box 02112
Portland, Oregon 97202

THE STEAMBOATERS
528 Cottage Street, NE Apt. No. 360
Salem, Oregon 97301

BRODHEADS FOREST AND STREAM
ASSOCIATION
Road 4, Box 198E
East Stroudsburg, Penn. 18301

SUSQUEHANNOCK FLY FISHERS
P.O. Box 385
Lebanon, Penn. 17042

WHITE CLAY FLY FISHERMEN
Route #1
Landenberg, Penn. 19350

RHODY FLY RODDERS
261 Hardig Road
Warwick, Rhode Island 02886

DALLAS FLYFISHERS
P.O. Box 36244
Dallas, Texas 75235

GOLDEN SPREAD FLYFISHERS
P.O. Box 9273
Amarillo, Texas 79105

NORTHERN UTAH FLYFISHERS
P.O. Box 489
Clearfield, Utah 84015

ORDER OF THE ROYAL COACHMAN
142 S. 2nd East
Pleasant Grove, Utah 84062

FLAT ROCK CLUB
236 S. Main Street
Salt Lake City, Utah 84101

WASATCH FLY CASTERS
1521 E. 7380 S.
Salt Lake City, Utah 84121

TWIN HARBORS FLYFISHERS
303 W. 10th Street
Aberdeen, Washington 98520

FIDALGO FLY FISHERMEN
P.O. Box 325
Anacortes, Washington 98221

FOURTH CORNER FLY FISHERS
P.O. Box 1543
Bellingham, Washington 98225

EVERGREEN FLY FISHING CLUB
P.O. Box 221
Everett, Washington 98206

OLYMPIC FLY FISHERS
P.O. Box 148
Edmonds, Washington 98020

ALPINE FLY FISHERS
P.O. Box 3298
Federal Way, Washington 98002

LOWER COLUMBIA FLY FISHERS
P.O. BOX 1495
Longview, Washington 98632

SOUTH-SOUND FLY FISHING CLUB
Box 2792
Olympia, Washington 98507

OLYMPIC PENINSULA FLYFISHERS
Route 2, Box 1988
Port Angeles, Washington 98362

CLEARWATER FLY CASTERS
E. 238 Main Street
Pullman, Washington 99163

NORTHWEST FLY ANGLERS
P.O. Box 4166 Pioneer Square Station
Seattle, Washington 98104

NORTHWEST FLY FISHERMEN
3852 Williams Avenue West
Seattle, Washington 98104

OVERLAKE FLY FISHING CLUB
4310 48th Avenue N.E.
Seattle, Washington 98105

WASHINGTON FLY FISHING CLUB
P.O. Box 80282
Seattle, Washington 98108

WASHINGTON STEELHEAD FLYFISHERS
3018 N.E. 103rd
Seattle, Washington 98125

INLAND EMPIRE FLY FISHING CLUB
P.O. Box 2926
Spokane, Washington 99220

CASCADE FLY FISHING CLUB
19202 Bonney Lake Blvd.
Sumner, Washington 98390

PUGET SOUND FLYFISHERS
P.O. Box 99961
Tacoma, Washington 98499

YAKIMA FLY FISHERS ASSOCIATION
901 S. 1st Street
Yakima, Washington 98901

WADERS OF THE WOLF
7817 Jackson Park Blvd.
Wauwatosa, Wisconsin 53213

WYOMING FLY CASTERS
144 Buck Creek Road
Casper, Wyoming 82601

PLATTE VALLEY FLY CASTERS
P.O. Box 1011
Saratoga, Wyoming 82331

MONTREAL ANGLERS & HUNTERS, INC.
260 Alexis Nihon Blvd., Apt. 210
Montreal, Quebec, Canada 378

IZAAK WALTON FLY FISHERMANS CLUB
4198 Corine Court
Burlington, Ontario, Canada L7L1J1

MANITOBA FLY FISHERS ASSOCIATION
23 Whitehall Blvd.
Winnipeg, Manitoba, Canada R2C0YZ

OSPREY FLYFISHERS OF B.C.
2505 E. 19th Ave.
Vancouver, British Columbia, Canada V5M2S2

TOTEM FLY FISHERS OF B.C.
6435 Neville Street
Burnaby 1, British Columbia, Canada

WEST COOTENAY FLYFISHERS CLUB
3631 Carnation Drive
Trail, British Columbia, Canada

LONELY LOON FLY FISHING CLUB
RR4 Braelock Road
Kelowna, British Columbia, Canada

KAMLOOPS FLYFISHERS
P.O. Box 554
Kamloops, British Columbia, Canada

HOOK AND HACKLE CLUB
Box 6949 Postal Station D.
Calgary, Alberta, Canada

APRIL POINT FLY FISHING CLUB
Box #1
Campbell River, British Columbia, Canada

FLY SHOPS AND SUPPLIERS OF MATERIALS AND TACKLE ITEMS

The following is a partial listing of mail-order dealers. Many of the dealers are highly specialized while others carry almost a complete selection of everything a fly-tyer or fisherman might want.

SIERRA TACKLE
Box 338
Montrose, California 91020

S & M FLY TYING MATERIALS
95 Union Street
Bristol, Connecticut 06010

OJAI FISHERMAN
218 North Encinal Avenue
Ojai, California 93023

HANK SHOTWELL
Box 3761
New Haven, Connecticut 06525

PRICE'S DISCOUNT FEATHERS
P.O. Box 53
Three Rivers, California 93271

JOE'S TACKLE SHOP
186 Main Street
Warehouse Point, Connecticut 06088

BUZ'S FLY AND TACKLE SHOP
805 West Tulare Avenue
Visalia, California 93277

FISHIN' FOOL FLY SHOPPE
760 Main Avenue N.
Twin Falls, ID 83301

CREATIVE SPORTS ENTERPRISES
2333 Boulevard Circle
Walnut Creek, California 94595

TACK-L-TYERS
939 Chicago Ave.
Evanston, IL 60202

HANK ROBERTS
1035 Walnut Street
Boulder, Colorado 80302

BUD WILCOX
Rangeley, Maine 04970

THE FLY-FISHER
315 Columbine Street
Denver, Colorado 80206

RANGELEY REGION SPORTS SHOP
Box 850
Rangeley, Maine 04970

ROBERT J. STONE
20 Brookside Circle
Springfield, Massachusetts 01129

THOMAS AND THOMAS
22 Third Street
Turner Falls, Massachusetts 01376

UNIVERSAL VISE CORP
22 Main St.
Westfield, Massachusetts 01085

UNIVERSAL IMPORTS
P.O. Box 1581
Ann Arbor, Michigan 48106

DAN BAILEY'S FLY SHOP
209 West Park Street
Livingston, Montana 59047

STREAMSIDE ANGLERS
Box 2158
Missoula, Montana 59801

BUD LILLY'S TROUT SHOP
Box 387
West Yellowstone, Montana 59758

BOB JACKLIN'S FLY SHOP
West Yellowstone, MT 59758

DICK SURETTE
FLY FISHING SHOP
Box 686
North Conway, New Hampshire 03860

REED TACKLE
Box 390
Caldwell, New Jersey 07006

OLIVER'S ORVIS SHOP
44 Main St.
Clinton, New Jersey 08809

FLY FISHERMAN'S HEADQUARTERS
169 Route 46 (Mine Hill)
Dover, N.J. 07801

H. L. LEONARD
25 Cottage Street
Midland Park, New Jersey 07432

FLY FISHERMAN'S BOOKCASE AND
TACKLE SERVICE
Route 9A
Croton-on-Hudson, N.Y. 10520

E. B. AND H. A. DARBEE
Livingston Manor, N.Y. 12758

FIRESIDE ANGLER, INC.
P.O. Box 823
Melville, N.Y. 11740

ANGLER'S ROOST
141 East 44th Street
New York, N.Y. 10017

ANGLER'S WORLD
16 E. 53rd Street
New York, N.Y. 10022

HOOK & HACKLE
Box 1003
Plattsburgh, N.Y. 12901

GENE'S TACKLE SHOP
P.O. Box 7701
Rochester, N.Y. 14622

ANGLERS NOOK
Box 76
Shushan, N.Y. 12873

HACKLE AND TACKLE
553 North Salina Street
Syracuse, N.Y. 13208

ANGLER'S MAIL
6497 Pearl Road
Cleveland, Ohio 44130

THE BARBLESS HOOK
23 N.W. 23rd Place
Portland, Oregon 97210

KAUFMAN'S STREAMBORN FLIES
P.O. Box 23032
Portland, Oregon 97223

CASCADE TACKLE COMPANY
2425 Diamond Lake Blvd.
Roseburg, Oregon 97470

BECKIE'S SPORTING GOODS
1336 Orange St.
Berwick, PA 18603

AMERICAN ANGLERS
P.O. Box 521
Bethlehem, Pennsylvania 1801r

ED KOCH'S YELLOW BREECHES FLY SHOPPE
Box 205
Boiling Springs, Pennsylvania 17007

THE FLY-TYER'S SUPPLY SHOP
P.O. Box 153
Downington, Pennsylvania 19335

RAYMOND C. RUMPF AND SON
P.O. Box 176
Ferndale, Pennsylvania 18921

THE ROD AND REEL
P.O. Box 132
Leola, Pennsylvania 17540

JACK'S TACKLE
301 Bridge Street
Phoenixville, Pennsylvania 19460

BEEGLE'S ORVIS SHOP
336 First Street, Aspinwall
Pittsburgh, Pennsylvania 15215

TWIN RIVERS TACKLE SHOP
1206 N. River Drive
Sunbury, PA 17801

E. HILLE
815 Railway St.
Williamsport, PA 17701

HERTER'S INC.
RFD 2, Interstate 90
Mitchell, South Dakota 57301

TERRY HELLEKSON
P.O. Drawer 489
Clearfield, Utah 84015

THE FLY LINE, INC.
2935 Washington Blvd.
Ogden, Utah 84401

THE ORVIS COMPANY, INC.
Manchester, Vermont 05254

SHOFF'S TACKLE SUPPLY
P.O. Box 1227
Kent, Washington 98031

PATRICK'S FLY SHOP
2237 Eastlake Avenue E.
Seattle, Washington 98102

NEAL'S FLY AND TACKLE
5427 Pacific Avenue
Tacoma, Washington 98408

TACKLE-CRAFT
P.O. Box 489
Chippewa Falls, Wisconsin 54729

HIGH COUNTRY FLIES
Box 1022
Jackson, Wyoming 83001

ANGLING SPECIALTIES COMPANY
Box 97
Ancaster, Ontario, Canada L9G 3L3

THE HACKLE HOUSE
P.O. Box 505
Oakville, Ontario, Canada

TOM C. SAVILLE, LTD.
9 Station Road
Beeston, Nottingham, England

E. VENIARD, LTD.
138 Northwood Road
Thornton Heath, England CR48YG

INDEX